Riding the Bull, Beating the Bear

Riding the Bull, Beating the Bear

Market Timing for the Long-Term Investor

Edward M. Yanis

John Wiley & Sons

Acknowledgments

This book is not merely a chapter in my life, but the culmination of a lifetime dream. I owe a tremendous debt of gratitude to all those people who, often in unforeseen ways, made the completion of this book possible. Life is very short, and I am aware that, if one is lucky, the opportunity to thank the people who have had a positive influence on one's life may come only once. For me, this is it. This is a rare chance for me to reflect back on my life and to express my appreciation to those who helped me reach this point.

First, on a professional note, I want to thank my "red-team" reviewers, an eclectic group of friends at Lockheed Martin, who accepted the challenge of being a red-team member. At that stage, *Riding the Bull, Beating the Bear: Market Timing for the Long-Term Investor* was only a group of briefing papers built around the concept of the Y-Process. Paul Palosky, Sal Chowdhury, John Corbett, and Lee Fleisher provided comments on areas that needed additional investigation and evaluation to make the book more appropriate for the average investor.

I would like to thank my editorial team of Bill Waddington, Lee Fleisher, and Mike Oliver for their help and guidance in making this book possible. They had faith in my abilities and me and supported my challenge of the veracity of the securely established, university-taught, "efficient market theory."

In addition, I thank those people who were my Beta Group. To Harrison Frank, Charles Pruzansky, Rita Teicher, and Mona Berman who had faith in the Y-Process and invested their hard-earned money in the market for three years using the Y-Process as their market timing tool. By so doing, they verified the Y-Process's outstanding utility for providing superior financial growth and protection against prolonged declines in stock prices. Your payoff was your financial success and my payoff was your letters of thanks and endorsement.

I also owe a debt of gratitude to Joel Parker, Public Relations, who first encouraged me to write a book and to his wife and partner, Charlotte, who provided me with the three words that established my writing style—"keep it simple."

On a personal level, I must thank my best friend and wife Judith, who edited drafts of the chapters, and shared in the disappointment of book agent responses, as well as the excitement, labor, and tension of this project and still had encouraging words to offer. To Judy, my heartfelt thanks.

Contents

Preface

*R*iding the Bull, Beating the Bear is a book about personal finance, preservation of capital, security selection, market timing, and retiring
wealthy. The cornerstone of this book is a newly developed technology
called the *Y-Process*. Simply stated, the Y-Process is a mathematical model
that forecasts the risk–reward ratio of any equity portfolio. Based on this
forecast, a Y-Process-managed portfolio will alert the investor one week in
advance of whether to buy, sell, or hold his or her stock. In essence, this
is the market-timing aspect of this technology.

The Y-Process has been validated by back testing a stock market
benchmark for the past 71 years. The benchmark selected is the one most
professional money managers use, that is, the S&P 500 Index. The results
of back testing are truly startling. An investor using the Y-Process would
have (1) beat the market 67 out of the last 71 years (including ties), (2)
never had a losing year (there were 17 S&P 500 losing years), and (3) for
the year ending in 2000, had a 40-year annualized return of 20.7 percent
versus 11.8 percent for the S&P 500.

Besides consistently beating the market, another key reason for mastering this powerful technology is that the Y-Process removes emotion
from the decision making required of the investor. The factual data that
support the validity of the process and straightforward formulas allow the
process to be useful to intermediate and experienced investors alike.

Introduction

New Insights into Building Wealth By
Managing Investment Risks

Few financial endeavors have been written about, diagnosed, or have occupied the time of stock market investors with less success than the attempt to "beat the market." For 35 years I have pursued this dream. Most Wall Street professionals claim that no investor can beat the market consistently. This view is supported by modern finance theory and is taught by academia in the nation's leading business schools. It seemed that I was doomed to pursue a dream that could never be realized.

However, in 1986, while doing research on techniques for moderating investment risk, I stumbled across some dramatic statistics. For the 25 years from 1970 through 1994, the Dow Jones Industrial Average (the DJIA Index is the world's most used indicator of U.S. stock market trends) advanced 475 percent, an increase of almost sixfold over 6,318 trading days. When I removed the 75 days contributing to the largest positive cumulative *gains*, I found that the DJIA had a *loss* of 51 percent; the original DJIA index value dropped by half.

The most astonishing part of the data reveals that when the 75 days contributing the largest *negative* amounts are removed, the advance jumps to 5,200 percent, an *increase* of 53-fold over the original amount. Upon further research, I discovered that these conclusions apply equally as well to stock market statistics that date back to the 1930s.

Until recently, it has been difficult to apply financial findings such as these to guide current investments, enhance returns, reduce risk, and anticipate downturns because of the unavailability of high-power personal computers (at an affordable cost) and the modern computer processing technology required to solve these esoteric mathematical problems. The key to the development of *accurate* and *consistent* "precursors" to market downturns has been to apply computer processing to a mathematical solution I call the Y-Process.

THE Y-PROCESS CAN BE USED TO INCREASE RETURNS BY REDUCING RISK

The Y-Process has universal application for all stock portfolios. I empirically tested it against various types of securities, both domestic and international, including stocks, mutual funds, index funds, and index stocks. In *every* test case, the Y-Process provided the desired results: lowered investor risk and enhanced returns.

To test the accuracy and consistency of the Y-Process, I back tested the Standard and Poor's (S&P) 500 Index with and without the Y-Process over the past 71 years. The S&P 500 was chosen because it is generally accepted by Wall Street as the benchmark for the U. S. stock market. The results: Over the past 71 years, an *unmanaged* S&P 500 investment (buying once and holding onto the purchase) resulted in 23 years of negative returns. With a Y-Process-managed S&P 500 index—buying and selling the index using the Y-Process's simple formula—there *wasn't a loss in any of the 71 years*. The significance of these results cannot be overstated.

A second test produced similar outstanding results. It was a comparison of the S&P 500 *cumulative* returns with a single buy-and-hold (unmanaged) investment and with a single buy Y-Process-managed investment. Table I.1 provides the results for each of four decades.

Table I.1   **Cumulative Returns on Investments in the S&P 500**

Years	Single Buy-and-Hold Investment in the S&P 500	Y-Process-Managed Single Investment in the S&P 500
10 years (1988–1998)	5-fold	7-fold
20 years (1978–1998)	13-fold	61-fold
30 years (1968–1998)	13-fold	280-fold
40 years (1958–1998)	31-fold	1,155-fold

For each of the 10-year periods shown, a buy-and-hold strategy is not the best approach to achieve superior returns. Why? If you invested in the S&P 500 20 years ago, applying the Y-Process, you would have gained an outstanding return of 61 times your original investment versus a return of only 13 times using a buy-and-hold strategy. If you had invested 30 years ago using the Y-Process, your net worth would have increased 280 times your original investment versus 13 times using a buy-and-hold strategy. Moreover, in each of the decades illustrated, the Y-Process provided the investor an average 42 percent less risk than the buy-and-hold strategy.

This book defines risk as the percentage of time over the year that an investor is in the stock market. Being riskless is defined as the percent of time the investor is invested in U.S. Treasury bills or bonds. For example, if during the year, you are invested in an equity mutual fund or stocks for 30 weeks and one day, then you are at risk $(30.2/52) * 100$ or 58.1 percent. The complement of this is the percentage of time you are riskless or $100 - 58.1 = 41.9$ percent.

BENEFITS FOR INVESTORS

The Y-Process provides investors a tool to help them achieve their financial goals. This book divulges publicly, for the first time, the mathematical solution of the Y-Process for personal use. Now, investors will be able to follow the Y-Process's derivation and apply it to their own stock portfolio. The Y-Process furnishes investors the ability to reliably and consistently call major market turns, allowing them to take conservative measures in a timely fashion. In essence, investors will now be able to take total control of their portfolio using this unique risk-reduction management tool to (1) beat the market, (2) enhance returns, and (3) incur less risk.

Chapter 9 contains the Y-Process equations. To assist the reader to verify his or her stock or mutual fund Y-Process calculation, I provide some technical assistance at my web site. You can view selected market indexes, funds, and stocks by logging on to the Y-Process web site. At the back of this book is a business reply card that provides 13 weeks free of charge of technical support for the aforementioned selected market indexes, funds, and stocks. This extra help should provide you sufficient confidence that you are performing the calculations correctly.

THIS BOOK IS WRITTEN FOR THREE
LEVELS OF INVESTORS

Part One. Chapters 1, 2, and 3 are written for the *novice* investor. The objective is to introduce those persons making their first venture into the stock market to the language, tools, techniques, and investment knowledge to take charge of their financial future. It walks the investor through important investment principles, concepts, and strategies. Worksheets are provided to help novice investors establish an understanding of their risk tolerance, assist them in determining their financial status and defining their short-, intermediate-, and long-term goals.

Part Two. Chapters 4 through 7 focus on the *intermediate* investor, taking them to the next level of understanding. The objective is to help informed, risk-sensitive investors to become more effective managers of their portfolios, with renewed confidence in making risk–reward decisions.

Part Three. Chapters 8 through 12 are written for the *sophisticated* investor. These chapters describe the conceptual development, testing, and verification of the Y-Process. The objective is to demonstrate how the Y-Process can be used as another important tool in the investor's tool kit, possibly the only tool with a 59 percent risk reduction[1] capability and a 98 percent confidence factor of outperforming the market. Suggestion: For sophisticated investors who are anxious to use the Y-Process, go to Part Three, learn the Y-Process, and apply it to your portfolio now.

TWO NEW DISCLOSURES IN THE WORLD
OF INVESTING

This book discloses for the first time, in Chapter 10, a significant financial revelation, a new efficient market theory *form*. This form will affect the way economics and finance academics teach investment and business courses leading to Master of Business Administration (MBA) degrees, Certified Financial Planner (CFP) certification, and Certified Financial Analyst (CFA) certification.

The second disclosure is a new anomaly to the efficient market theory (also described in Chapter 10). Efficient market theory anomalies are not unique; there are six existing today. The last one was discovered in 1972.

SPECIAL FEATURES

Riding the Bull, Beating the Bear is a serious, down-to-earth, easy-to-read educational commentary on stock market investing. It contains chapter subtitles and paragraph subheads that have visual appeal with the inclusion of worksheets, tables, and graphs. Endnotes are used for references and to clarify some of the detail. A glossary is included that will help the reader to easily locate financial and technical terms used throughout the book.

Riding the Bull, Beating the Bear

PART ONE

The Novice Investor's First Venture into the Stock Market

Part One is written for the *novice* investor. The objective is to introduce those persons making their first venture into the stock market to the language, tools, techniques, and investment knowledge they would need to help them to take charge of their financial future. Chapters 1, 2, and 3 walk the reader through important investment principles, concepts, and strategies. Worksheets are provided to establish risk tolerance; they also assist the reader in determining his or her financial status and defining short-, intermediate-, and long-term goals.

Chapter 1

Accumulating Wealth Begins with Six Simple Tenets

A Financial Checkup Will Prepare You to Take the Steps Required to Establish and Attain Your Financial Expectations

TAKING CONTROL OF YOUR FINANCIAL FUTURE

Building personal wealth and taking control of your financial future starts with six simple tenets. I created a mnemonic for these tenets: "**Go** in the direction of **hi**gh-risk investments and in time you will lose your money and miss great opportunities." This is a "hybrid" anagram that contains six two-letter combinations (in bold print). The reader is challenged to match this anagram to these tenets:

1. *Set specific financial **go**als*. The goals you choose affect your investment choices. There are no right or wrong investment goals. They can be whatever you want them to be. Your goals will be influenced by your age, income, job security, ability to take risks, and financial prospects.
2. *Develop the habit of **in**vesting*. The best chance to acquire measurable wealth lies in developing the habit of stashing away a fixed amount of money on a regular basis and investing that money where it can do the most for you. If you are in a hurry, this book will not help you. Buy a lottery ticket instead. But if you are

patient, this book will show you how to accumulate a six- or seven-figure chunk of money while you still have enough lifetime left to enjoy it. Obtaining wealth this way takes you on a trip that is short on thrills, but it's also short on spills.

3. *Diversify your investments.* No investment performs well all the time; as a rule, when one thing is down, something else tends to be up. One way to protect yourself is to diversify. Common sense tells you not to put all your eggs in one basket. Some investment experts believe that you can actually increase your returns with a sensible diversification strategy.

4. *Invest within your risk tolerance.* Investing requires taking some risks. You can undertake a successful investment strategy by quantifying how much risk you are willing to take. Your hope for investment success depends in part on your ability to reduce those risks without passing up reasonable rewards. And, as you will learn in Part Three, there are ways to lower your risks.

5. *Understand the time value of money.* The time you have to achieve your goals will influence the kinds of investments you might consider. The reason is rooted in a concept called the time value of money and its close cousin, opportunity cost. Becoming a successful investor often lies in being able to identify the winning side of the time-value equation. You will also learn that reasonable rewards, over time, will be enough to generate the wealth you seek.

6. *Understand the meaning of opportunity cost, the first cousin of the time value of money.* When you miss an opportunity for obtaining a realistic rate of return on your investment it is at a cost of meeting your financial goals. The opportunity cost of not receiving money today is the interest (return) you forfeit when the dollars are received in the future rather than today. Stating it another way, opportunity cost is the cost of doing one thing and not another. To be an alert investor or buyer, ask yourself before you make any investment or spending choice: "What else could I do with the money?" There is one other caution if you tend to be a procrastinator. Not investing present dollars always involves a cost; the cost is the loss of an opportunity to earn a realistic return on these dollars. Thus, it is bet-

ter to invest a dollar today than to invest that same dollar in the future or, worse yet, not to invest it at all.

GOAL SETTING

Investment goal setting is an intensely personal affair that will be guided by your own personal style and preferences. Be aware that the clarity with which you can envision your investment goals makes a big difference in whether you can apply the discipline needed to reach them. If you can decide where you want to go and when you want to get there, you can get there. Your success depends on two critical items: First, the time you have to achieve your goals; and, second, where and how much of your money to allocate to various types of investments. Here are two examples:

- *College tuition.* Estimate the amount you will need for your children's college education. Then subtract the amount you believe you will be able to pay from your projected salary at the time they are in college and any loans or scholarships you think you can rely on. Don't let the projections of $200,000 or more for college tuition in 15 years scare you off. Save all you can and expect that both you and your child will be able to earn and borrow more.
- *Retirement.* When you retire, how much will you need to supplement Social Security and pension payments and to give yourself a comfortable lead over inflation? A good rule of thumb is to seek retirement income (including Social Security, pensions, income from investments, etc.) equal to at least 70 percent of your current income. This figure assumes that your medical insurance, for example, Medicare, keeps up with the cost of medical care.

Do not underestimate how much money you will earn on your retirement savings after you retire. Remember, after retirement you will have more time to attend to your investment strategies and by that time you should be an experienced investor using the Y-Process to reduce your risk and enhance your returns. To a large extent, these earnings can still be tax-deferred until you withdraw them. And your tax bracket could well be less, but don't count on it.

Where do you stand now? The first thing you should do is determine the state of your financial health. Worksheets 1.1 and 1.2 lay the necessary groundwork for setting your investment goals and making plans to reach them. These worksheets allow you to establish your financial baseline, and they will assist you in starting your investment program. I suggest

Worksheet 1.1   Personal Balance Sheet

Assets		Liabilities	
Cash on hand	$	Balanced owed on mortgage	$
Savings accounts		Auto loans	
Checking accounts		Student loans	
Certificate of deposit		Home-equity credit line	
Money market funds		Other credit lines	
Savings bonds		Credit card bills due	
Market value of home		Other outstanding bills	
Market value of other real estate		Total Liabilities	
Cash value of life insurance		Current Net Worth (Date:)	$
Surrender value of annuities		(Total Assets – Total Liabilities)	
Vested equity in pension plans			
Vested equity in profit sharing			
Roth, 401(k), or 403(b) plans			
Individual Retirement Accounts			
Keogh plans			
Stocks owned			
Bonds owned			

Worksheet 1.1   (*continued*)

Assets	
REITs owned	
Equity mutual funds: (list separately)	
Bond mutual funds	
Estimated value of other investments:	
Collectibles	
Precious metals	
Antiques	
Household furnishings	
Silverware	
Automobiles and trucks	
Boats, planes, recreational vehicles	
Furs and jewelry	
Loans owed you	
Other assets	
Total Assets	$

that you make copies of the worksheets so that you can use them annually to update the status of your financial health. Worksheet 1.1, Personal Balance Sheet, allows you to determine what type of financial condition you are in. Use this worksheet to calculate current assets, liabilities, and net worth. When you know the source of your current net worth, you can determine the strength and weakness of your financial position.

Worksheet 1.2, Investment Allocation, allows you to determine the status of your investment mix. Complete this worksheet at least once a year so you will know how your investment mix is changing and can take action, if necessary, to bring it back into line with a mix that matches your goals and your risk tolerance.

Worksheet 1.2   Investment Allocation

	Market Value	Percent of Total
Cash		
Savings accounts		
Money market funds		
Treasury bills		
Total Cash	$	
Stocks		
Individual shares		
Mutual funds		
Total Stocks	$	
Bonds		
Individual bonds		
Mutual funds		
Unit trusts		
Total Bonds	$	
Rental real estate	$	
Limited partnerships	$	
Precious metals	$	
Other investments	$	
Collectibles	$	
Total investments	$	100

Most people have several goals at once that can be separated into short-, intermediate-, and long-term goals. Your goals are likely to change, so it is important to reassess them from time to time. For instance, the kinds of growth-oriented investments that might be perfectly appropriate while you are accumulating a retirement nest egg and have a long-term horizon may be inappropriate after you retire and need part of your investments as income to pay the bills. Under these circumstances, the investment universe is so vast—not just stocks, mutual funds, bonds and certificates, but also hybrids too numerous to mention here—that you will never be at a loss for choices. Let's examine each of these three types of goals.

Short-Term Goals

Suppose, for instance, that a cruise to Alaska is one of your goals and that you want to go next summer. Such a short time horizon suggests that the stock market would not be a good place to invest the money you are setting aside for the trip. The market is subject to wide swings, and you would not want to be forced to sell your stocks in a downswing just because the time had come to buy your tickets. Don't put any money you think you might need in the next three to five years into the stock market. Where should you invest your money then? Certificates of deposit (CDs) that mature about the time you will need the cash or a money market fund that allows you to withdraw your cash instantly by writing a check would be a better choice for this goal.

Intermediate-Term Goals

Maybe you would like to buy a larger house within three or five years. With more time, you have more flexibility. Safety is still important but you are in a better position to ride out bad times in the financial markets. For intermediate-term goals such as this, you should consider long-term CDs that pay more interest than the short-term certificates you would buy to help finance your cruise. You could even consider mutual funds that invest in stocks that pay good dividends but do not tend to fluctuate much in price. Such an investment would give you high income (for reinvesting in more fund shares), a chance to ride along if the stock market zooms, and pretty good protection against all but a catastrophic drop in stock prices. (In Part Three, I teach you a strategy to protect yourself against even this type of market meltdown condition.)

Long-Term Goals

Ah, here is the real wealth-building opportunity. Wise investors have always known that those who have risen to great wealth from humble beginnings had a long-term perspective. Interestingly, the truly rich seem to come from one of two categories: first, the hardworking entrepreneur who learns early to reinvest in his or her business; and, second, the serious employee who never seemed to have a penny to spend but moves to a grand home in Arizona or North Carolina five years before the rest of us retire.

A comfortable retirement is probably the most common of all financial goals. A college education for the kids is another common goal. For long-term goals such as these, consider a wide range of possibilities: stocks, corporate and government bonds, and long-term CDs among them. You should also take maximum advantage of tax-sheltered plans, such as individual retirement accounts (IRAs), in which earnings accumulate tax-free and contributions to which may be tax deductible, self-employment plans (SEPs), if applicable, or 401(k) plans offered by your employer, which provide many of the same advantages as IRAs.

With several years and sometimes decades ahead of you, financial assets that are not strictly investments also come into play: home equity, pension plans, and Social Security, for example. The size and accessibility of those assets should influence your goals and choices.

MAKING INVESTING A REGULAR HABIT

As a new investor, your task is to create a plan that suits you and to stick with it. For most people who start with a small amount of money, the best chance to acquire measurable wealth is the same way marathoners train for long-distance races. Marathoners start with a plan to run 26.2 miles. They build their body muscles and endurance by following strict training programs using continuous and rhythmic running styles. As a long-term investor, you should develop a similar type of style. Develop the habit of putting money into an account (where it does the most good for you) on a consistent and regular interval. The rewards can be considerable. Here are some examples.

Suppose you take $5,000 and put it in the bank, where it earns a nice, safe, 5.5 percent rate of interest. Twenty years later you return to the bank to claim your deposit and discover that it has grown to a not very impressive $14,500. This return is no miracle but it does indicate the possibilities of compounding.

Meanwhile, your sister-in-law has developed the habit of investing on a consistent and regular basis. She socks away $5,000 in one-year CDs, at the same bank, with instructions to roll over the proceeds into a new certificate every 12 months. In addition, every month she buys another CD for $100 and issues the same instructions. Over 20 years she earns an average of 8 percent interest. Her nest egg: more than $80,000. Now this example illustrates two important tenets. First, the habit of investing, and, second, the time value of money, sometimes referred to as the miracle of compounding!

Although the $80,000 in the second example is a lot better, it is not going to finance a worry-free retirement. Suppose, as a novice investor, your goal is a lot loftier than that. Suppose you would like to have a nest egg of half a million dollars. You have 20 years to get there and $5,000 with which to start. With time, experience, and learning, you will become a sophisticated investor by investing in alternatives that should boost your return above what you would earn in a bank account. What is a reasonable return to plan on and how much will you have to contribute along the way?

For reasons discussed in Chapter 10, The Y-Process-Managed S&P 500 Consistently Outperforms the Market, I believe an average annual return of greater than 15 percent over the long run is a reasonable expectation for individuals who apply the principles presented in this book. At that rate, with $5,000 to start, you will reach your $500,000 goal if you contribute an additional $320 a month to your investment account.

Less ambitious plans can also work wonders. Starting from zero, putting just $50 a month into an investment that pays a compounded average annual total return of 15 percent for 20 years will get you a nest egg of better than $65,000. Stick to the plan for 30 years and you will have more than $275,000. Double your contribution and you will double the size of your nest egg.

Starting small and gradually increasing your monthly investment amount as your income grows is another possibility. For instance, you can start with no initial investments, put $100 a month into your investment account for 5 years, raise it to $200 a month for the next 5 years, $300 a month for years 11 through 15, and $400 a month for years 16 through 20. At the end of the period you will have nearly $227,000. Boost your monthly amount to $500 for years 21 through 25 and your fund will grow to almost $500,000, assuming you earn an average of 15 percent per year.

How common is an average annual return of 15 percent? For the 10-year period through 1999, no fewer than 45 different mutual funds delivered that much or more. You will find most of them listed in many periodicals including *Mutual Funds* magazine, along with lists of other outstanding funds that can help you achieve your goals. Were the 1990s typical for investors? No, they were not. The Dow Jones Industrial Average (DJIA) quadrupled during the decade—a remarkable performance, though not unique, ending the decade in the neighborhood of 11,500. The DJIA also tripled in the 10-year span from 1942 to 1952, and again from 1953 to 1963. In the decade of the 1990s the DJIA and the Standard & Poor's (S&P) 500 essentially ended the decade in a virtual tie at 317 percent. But helping you achieve mediocre investment results is not the goal of this book. If you follow the Y-Process strategy, you should do better than that.

These examples are oversimplified, of course, because they do not take into account taxes or commissions. But the point is the same and it validates the first simple truth of investing—making investing a regular habit is your best chance to acquire measurable wealth.

DIVERSIFYING YOUR INVESTMENTS

There are at least three good reasons to diversify your investments. First, it is common sense not to put all your eggs in one basket unless you like omelets. Our mothers taught us that. Second, no investment performs well all the time; as a rule, when one thing is down, something else tends to be up. And, third, diversification allows you to sleep peacefully at night.

Spread the Risk

One way to hedge your bets is to select a number of investment vehicles you like and divide your money equally among them. Some investment advisers recommend investing an equal amount in a five-part "fixed-mix" portfolio consisting of cash (money market funds, CDs, Treasury bills), bonds, U.S. stocks, foreign stocks, and real estate. Once a year, adjust the mix to maintain the dollar balance. You do that by taking the gains from the winners and spreading them out among the losers so that your asset distribution stays the same. Other than that, sit back and forget it.

For example, if you had stuck with this fixed-mix approach from 1965 to 1990, and your selection of stocks, bonds, and real estate had matched the average market experience for those investments, your cumulative return would have been a shade under 950 percent. Looked at another way, $1,000 invested in 1965 would have grown to $9,500 by 1990. The same amount invested in U.S. stocks would have grown to about $8,700 measured by the S&P 500 Index. The most spectacular returns during that period came from a portfolio of international stocks, that rocketed a phenomenal 2,477 percent, turning $1,000 into $24,770.

The results work out to an average annual return of 10.2 percent for the diversified portfolio over 25 years. That is not bad, but it is not much better than the historical return generated by the stock market alone.

Another Approach: The 40-40-20 Portfolio

Dividing your portfolio equally among domestic stocks, foreign stocks, bonds, real estate, and cash equivalents is only one approach to diversification. Another formula, which is popular with many successful investors seeking to prosper while controlling their risks, is the 40-40-20 portfolio: 40 percent in stocks, 40 percent in bonds, and 20 percent in cash equivalents. Either mix creates a good diversified portfolio, but thinking about a portfolio in such terms can lure you into a misleading sense of permanence about what is actually a very fluid situation. As stock prices and interest rates go up and down, the proportions in your portfolio will shift without your lifting a finger. In addition, there will be times when you want to shift more money into stocks or bonds or cash, for reasons described in Chapter 2 and Chapter 12. It is more realistic to think in terms of ranges rather than fixed percentages. Use Worksheet 1.1 and Worksheet 1.2 to discover how your investments sort out today. The results will suggest moves you should make to get them more in line with the kind of proportion you would like.

How well did various types of investments perform over the years? Table 1.1 is a snapshot of selected recent years of stocks, bonds, Treasury bills, gold, and real estate investments and the inflation value for those years. The investment figures are total returns, which means they include price changes and assume that all earnings from the investment, if any, are reinvested. They should all be compared to inflation figures for those years because inflation is a source of risk. If prices of goods and services increase, the real purchasing power of your assets and the income generated by them is reduced. Inflation erodes the buying power of your assets and income.

Table 1.1   Comparison of Inflation and Various Investment Types from
1975 through 1999

	1975 (%)	1979 (%)	1985 (%)	1989 (%)	1995 (%)	1999 (%)
Inflation rate	6.9	13.3	3.8	4.6	2.8	2.1
Dow Jones Industrials	44.8	10.6	33.6	32.2	33.5	25.2
Long-Term Treasuries	8.3	–0.5	31.6	18.9	–22.9	5.9
Money Market Index	NA	12.8	7.2	8.1	5.5	4.5
Gold	–24.9	126.6	6.9	–2.0	2.3	0.4
Real Estate Investment	27.3	18.3	0.8	–21.9	7.4	NA

Source: Statistical Abstract of the United States, the national data book for years shown.
Each of the five-year intervals starts on January 1st and ends on December 1st.

Stocks and money market funds managed positive returns in each of the six years. Two highly touted investments—gold and real estate—soared, struggled, or nearly collapsed, depending on the year you are looking at. A different selection of years would have shown a different pattern from the ones shown in Table 1.1.

For instance, even with dividends included, the Dow Jones industrials turned in a dismal performance in 1973, 1974, and 1977. Gold soared in each of those years, while real estate investment trusts fell so sharply in 1973 and 1974 that their survival as an investment vehicle was actually in doubt.

The lesson here is not difficult to find: Invest in whatever you want, but invest in something else, too. There is another message in Table 1.1 as well. In the selected years shown, only the stock market index as represented by the DJIA had only positive years and beat inflation in each year except 1979.

Diversification Using the Modern Portfolio Theory

Notwithstanding this commonsense assessment of diversification across many types of investments as shown in Table 1.1, there are additional ways to help investors sleep more soundly every night. Thanks to Harry M. Markowitz who, known as the father of Modern Portfolio Theory (MPT), brought mathematics up to common sense and revolutionized the world of finance in 1950.[1] The MPT brought the scientific approach to risk by encouraging investors to diversify by investing in assets that perform differently from one another. The MPT downplays the talents of the stock picker and emphasizes the cheflike importance of putting the right ingredients into the mix. The insight Markowitz offered was how to make the most money with the least amount of risk.

With time and additional investment experience, the novice investor will move on to a higher level of investing skill. When you reach the sophisticated level, you will learn how to use the MPT in conjunction with the Y-Process to optimize your stock market returns at reduced risk.

EVALUATING YOUR RISK TOLERANCE

Some finance books on investment define risk as the chance you take that you will earn less from an investment than the rate of inflation or less than the interest available at the time from insured savings certificates or U.S. Treasury-backed obligations.

But if you ask most people what they consider as risk they would say: "Risk is the chance that you will lose all or part of the money you have invested." That is true as far as it goes, but it does not go far enough. A more complete definition of risk acknowledges the availability of investments carrying virtually ironclad guarantees that you will get all your money back plus the interest promised you: savings accounts in federally insured banks, savings and loans, or credit unions, for instance. These are and will remain safe despite the past problems of some institutions and the fund that insures their deposits. Also, with all investments, even government-guaranteed ones, you run the risk that your rate of return will be less than the inflation rate.

In fact, savings accounts, CDs, Treasury bills, savings bonds, and a handful of other government-backed investments establish a useful benchmark for measuring risk.

In all financial ventures, a risk–reward relationship applies, no matter what the investment, the reputation of the investment adviser, or the financial condition of the market. The landscape is littered with forlorn investors who forgot this basic fact: The risk you take should be commensurate with your expected return. Conversely, the bigger the promised reward, the bigger the risk.

Does this mean you should avoid all high-risk investments? No. It means you should only invest as much as you can afford to lose, because there is a good chance you *will* lose it. A prudent risk depends on your goals, your age, your income and other resources, and your current and future financial obligations. A young, single person who expects a pay increase regularly over the years and who has few family responsibilities can afford to take more chances than, say, a couple approaching retirement age. The young person has time to recover from market reversals; the older couple may not. You should also learn to recognize the risks involved in every kind of investment. And above all, stay within your risk zone and comfort level.

Establish Your Risk Zone

It is difficult to pick up a book on investing without running into something called the pyramid of risk, and this book is no exception. The pyramid is built on a broad and solid base of financial security: a home; money salted away in insured savings accounts or certificates; plus insurance policies to cover your health, your car, your home, your life, and your ability to earn an income (that is, disability insurance). As you move up from the pyramid's base, the levels get narrower and narrower, representing the space in your portfolio that is available for investments that involve risk. The greater the risks of an investment, the higher up the pyramid it goes and, thus, the less money you should put into it.

The image itself is more important than some of the specifics, that is, what belongs on each level of the pyramid. Weak real estate markets in some places in recent years have raised the question of whether home ownership still belongs at the base of the pyramid. I believe that it does for security as much as for wealth.

Determine How Much You Should Have in Savings

Your goal should be to have three to six months' living expenses in savings. Bank, savings and loan, or credit union accounts are good places to keep this money, but look for opportunities to earn more than the present 2 or 2.5 percent these institutions tend to pay on their run-of-the-mill deposit accounts. If you cannot do better than that in local institutions, consider a money market fund for at least part of your rainy day money. Such funds are not federally insured, but they are prudent, conservative places to put your money and they pay a higher return.

Once you have built the base of your pyramid, you are ready to move up and become an investor. One level up from savings, insurance, and home ownership is the appropriate place for mutual funds that invest in low-risk, dividend-oriented stocks and top-quality government and corporate bonds. Individual stocks and bonds that you pick yourself are on the same level. Most experts would put investment real estate on the next level up from stocks. At the very top of the pyramid are investments few people should try, such as penny stocks, commodities futures contracts, and most limited partnerships.

Thus, the pyramid, which is broad and solid at the bottom and gets narrower and smaller as you move up, is the perfect image for the sensible deployment of your financial resources. As long as you remember that, you will never stray too far out of your risk zone.

Identify Your Risk Comfort Level

We all have a level at which the loss of a certain amount of money causes us pain or discomfort. If you lose less than this value, you are still in your risk comfort level. If you lose more than this amount, then you have established your loss aversion value. Certainly you should never invest in something that makes you uncomfortable or in something you do not understand or invest in someone's tip without doing your homework. It is well known that too many investors seem perfectly comfortable with entirely too much risk until the market goes into free fall. The signs of too much risk are there if you are honest with yourself. If you are constantly concerned or lose sleep when your investment turns down, these are indicators that you are over your risk comfort level, which is not a good position for you to be in.

Included at the end of this chapter is a risk exam that will tell you what type of investor you are—conservative, active, or venturesome. If you are too venturesome, the remedy is obvious. Scale back and move your investments into less risky ventures and above all do not margin your stocks, that is, do not buy stocks with borrowed money.

Recognize the Risks in Any Investment

Risks in Stocks. A company's stock may decline in price because its business climate is unfavorable, or the company hits the skids for whatever exogenous reason, or the company is not being managed well and the shareholders lose faith. Stock may also decline in price because large numbers of investors decide to move into bonds or cash on a particular day and sell millions of shares of stock of all kinds. This behavior drives the market price down and takes dozens of companies along without bothering to differentiate the good from the bad.

Risks in Bonds. Bond prices tend to move in the opposite direction from interest rates, rising in price when rates fall and vice versa. But individual bond issues can be hurt even if interest rates in general are falling. All it takes is for one of the rating services—Standard & Poor's and Moody's are the major ones—to downgrade its opinion of the company's financial stability. A bond issue that is paying an interest rate noticeably higher than that of other bonds with a similar maturity date is probably forced to pay the high rate to compensate investors for the higher risk inherent in a lower safety rating. That, in a nutshell, is the situation with "junk" bonds: low ratings, high interest, and high risk of default.

Risks Everywhere. Real estate values go up and down in synchronism with supply and demand in *local* markets, regardless of the health of the national economy. Gold and silver, which are supposed to be stores of value in inflationary times, have been decidedly unrewarding in times of tolerable inflation. Even federally insured savings accounts carry risks, not that the government will not cover insured deposits, but that their low interest rate will not be enough to protect the value of your money from the combined effect of inflation and taxes.

APPLYING THE TIME VALUE OF MONEY CONCEPT TO YOUR INVESTMENT STRATEGY

An easy way to remember what the *time value of money* really means is to reverse the phrase to *money's value in time*.

The time value of money concept is crucial in financial planning because the value of money changes with time. The value of a dollar today is not equal to the value of that same dollar tomorrow. Now, if that does not make sense, let me explain why. A dollar today is worth more than a dollar expected at some future time because a dollar today can be invested to earn interest, leading to an increase in your wealth. This concept is probably the source of an old Indian proverb: *A bird in the hand is worth two in the bush.*

Which would you rather have, $1,000 today or $1,000 a year from today? Of course you would choose the option to take the money now— anyone would. You should understand that the value of that $1,000 you have today will erode by a year's worth of inflation and a year's worth of lost interest on the money. To put a dollar figure on it, if inflation is 5 percent and you could earn 7 percent interest in a year, the thrill of being handed $1,000 today is worth about 12 percent, or $120; that's a lot more than the thrill of being handed $1,000 a year from today.

Success with your money often lies in being able to identify the winning side of the time-value equation. The time value of money works against you if you are the one waiting to collect the money, but it works in your favor if you are the one who has to pay. Here is an example to explain the winning side of the time-value equation.

Lump Sum or Annuity?

Let's say you have just won your state's $1 million lottery. You are offered the choice of taking the $1 million paid out over 20 years or $500,000 paid in cash. Which should you take?

The answer depends on many factors. From a strictly financial aspect, it depends mostly on what return you could get on your lump sum *after* taxes are paid to the federal government and some state governments. If you choose the lump sum, you would have less than half of the money left (after taxes) or about $230,000. This sum assumes you are married, filing jointly and that your state tax rate is about 4.5 percent. Assuming what is left of your lump sum can be invested over the next 20 years at 12 percent per year, you will be way ahead of the game. In 20 years, the total cumulative return would be $2.2 million. Even if you invested your $230,000 at 7.75 percent for the next 20 years, you would still exceed the million dollars paid out in the annuity choice. (Remember *money's value in time!*)

It is the time value of money that permits state governments and other sponsors of sweepstakes and lotteries to promise fabulous payouts that actually exceed the amount of money they take in by selling tickets. Consider two lotteries, both of which promise a million dollar prize. One pays it right away and the other, which advertises an "annuity value" of a million dollars, pays you $50,000 a year for 20 years, which is a million dollars, all right, but it doesn't cost the lottery sponsor nearly that much. In fact, the sponsor can purchase an annuity contract from an insurance company that will fulfill its obligation for less than half the eventual payout.

Annuities are contracts that pay a certain sum of money in regular installments over a period of time, often 10 or 20 years, rather than in a lump sum. Stretching out the payments creates a big benefit for the state that owes the money because it collects interest on the unpaid amount while the recipient waits to collect. For instance, if the $50,000 were paid out in annual installments stretched over 20 years, and the state earned 7.25 percent on the unpaid amount, all it would need to meet that schedule of future payments would be about $25,000 today. Thus, your choice of selecting a lump sum in lieu of $50,000 per year would really be no contest. That is, of course, unless you choose to invest your lump sum in a savings account that pays one of the lowest returns of most investments.

For comparison, in the first quarter of 1999, the average taxable money fund yielded 4.4 percent, and half returned more. That easily beat the insured money market accounts at banks and thrifts (2.8 percent) and 60-day CDs (3.1 percent). It even matched five-year CDs, which tied up your money for 60 long months and subjected it to early withdrawal penalties. And it is far above the 1 percent inflation rate of the 1990s.

Paying the Kids' College Bills

Your future biomedical engineer daughter faces education costs exceeding $250,000 when she enters Columbia University or Brown University in 18 years. That is a huge sum, but because you are familiar with the time value of money, you know the smart thing to do is to find a way to pay those bills today, when your dollars are worth more than they will be in 18 years. Assuming a time value for the money at 12 percent per year (meaning you could earn that much on the money between now and the time you have to pay it), the value of the $250,000 you need 18 years from now is a shade under $32,500 today. Salt that away in an investment earning 12 percent a year and you will have the bills covered. If you do not have $32,500, gather as much of it as you can and get the time value of money working for you, easing at least some of the burden when the college bills come due. Or raise your sights a bit. If you could manage to earn 15 percent on the money, you would need just slightly over $20,000 today to have $250,000 by your daughter's freshman year. Chapter 10 describes an investment strategy, using the Y-Process, to achieve such a goal.

UNDERSTANDING OPPORTUNITY COST: FIRST COUSIN OF THE TIME VALUE OF MONEY

An example of opportunity cost illustrates its worthiness as a goal-setting strategy. For example, paying off the mortgage. Ignorance of opportunity cost can cause you to think you are doing something smart when you are not. For instance, you have probably heard praises sung for cutting your mortgage time in half by boosting your monthly mortgage payments. Because you pay off your mortgage sooner than a 30-year loan, you pay less interest and thus save tens of thousands of dollars. But the homeowner with the 15-year mortgage parts with the money sooner than the 30-year buyer. And you just learned that the time value of money suggests some caution may be in order before making extravagant claims of savings. You need to answer the following two questions: What else might you do with the extra money you would be spending on the higher monthly payments required by the 15-year mortgage? How much could that money earn if you invested it in something other than mortgage payments?

Suppose it costs you an extra $200 a month to pay off the loan in 15 years instead of 30 years. That's $200 a month that is not available for something else—investing in a mutual fund, for example. Say the mortgage rate is 7 percent and the mutual fund earns 9 percent. You could benefit from that 2 percent difference by putting the money in the fund instead of paying off the mortgage. Two hundred dollars a month earning 12 percent compounded for 15 years grows to almost $42,000. That is your *opportunity cost* of paying off your mortgage early. Before you crow about how much you have saved by prepaying your 30-year mortgage, you should subtract your opportunity cost from your savings.

There is one more important aspect that you should consider in your opportunity-cost equation. The Internal Revenue Service allows you to deduct mortgage interest from your federal taxes. And, depending on your tax bracket, for every $100 you deduct, the IRS hands you back $15 to $39.

GETTING STARTED

Unless you have already accumulated a pile of riches, you are likely to find that when you add up the cost of all your desires, the total exceeds the amount you are confident you can accumulate by first paying yourself every month and then investing; especially if you are not yet persuaded that you can achieve investment returns of more than, say, 10 percent a year.

The good news is that you are probably more ready to take an aggressive investing stance than you realize—and with a little bit of discipline using the Y-Process you can probably build that nest egg faster than you expect.

Before you complete the process of negotiating your financial goals with yourself, take the following risk test. It will help you determine what kind of investor you are—and what kind of investor you may want to become.

THE DONOGHUE RISK TEST

1. You buy an investment based on the strategies in this book. But a month later, the entire stock market declines and the value of your investment goes down 15 percent. The fundamental reasons why you bought it still seem sound. Do you:

   a. Sit tight and wait for it to go back up?
   b. Sell it and rid yourself of further sleepless nights?
   c. Buy more—if it looked good at the original price it looks even better now?

2. Which would you rather have done?

   a. Invested in an aggressive growth mutual fund that failed to increase in value over six months
   b. Invested in a money market fund, only to see an aggressive growth fund you had been thinking about rise 50 percent in value in six months

3. Would you feel better if:

   a. You doubled your money in a stock market mutual fund?
   b. Your money market fund investment saved you from losing half your money in a market slide?

4. Which situation would make you feel happiest?

   a. You win $100,000 in a publisher's contest
   b. You inherit $100,000 from a rich relative
   c. You earn $100,000 by risking $2,000 in the options market
   d. Any of the above—you're happy with the $100,000, no matter where it came from.

5. Your apartment building is being converted to condominiums. You can either buy your unit for $80,000 or sell the option for $20,000. The condo's market value is $120,000. You know that if you bought the condo, it might take six months to sell. The monthly carrying cost would be $1,200, and you would have to borrow the down payment for a mortgage. You don't want to live in the building. So what do you do?

   a. Take the $20,000
   b. Buy the unit and then sell it on the open market

6. You inherit your uncle's $100,000 house, free of any mortgage. Although the house is in a fashionable neighborhood and can be expected to appreciate at a faster rate than inflation, it has deteriorated badly. It would net $1,000 monthly if rented as is; it would net $1,500

per month if renovated. The renovations could be financed by a mortgage on the property. You would:

a. Sell the house
b. Rent it as is
c. Make the necessary renovations, then rent it

7. You work for a small but thriving privately held electronics company. The company is raising money by selling stock to its employees. The managers plan to take the company public, but not for four or more years. If you buy the stock, you will not be allowed to sell until the shares are traded publicly. In the meantime, the stock will pay no dividends. But when the company goes public, the shares could trade for 10 or 20 times what you would pay. How much of an investment would you make?

a. None at all
b. One month's salary
c. Three months' salary
d. Six months' salary

8. Your cousin, a biologist who has made large profits investing in the stock market, tells you that unusual gains can be expected in the stocks of certain small companies. He recommends a mutual fund that invests

in them. You know nothing about publicly traded small companies, but you have heard they are risky investments. What do you do?

a. Invest in the mutual fund immediately based on your cousin's recommendation
b. Send for the mutual fund's prospectus, and watch the newspaper for information to help you decide whether your cousin's suggestion is correct
c. Leave your money in a bank or money market mutual fund
d. Call a stockbroker for advice, and buy shares in IBM when the broker tells you IBM is less risky

9. Your long-time friend and neighbor, an experienced petroleum geologist, is assembling a group of investors (of which he is one) to fund an exploratory oil well that could pay back 50 to 100 times its investment if successful. If the well is dry, the entire investment will be worthless. Your friend estimates the chance of success is only 20 percent. What would you invest?

a. Nothing
b. One month's salary
c. Three months' salary
d. Six months' salary

10. You learn that several commercial real estate developers are considering purchase of undeveloped land in a certain location. You are offered an option to buy a choice parcel. The cost is about 2 months' salary and you calculate the potential gain to be 10 months' salary. Do you:

   a. Purchase the option?
   b. Let it slide; it's not for you?

11. You are on a TV game show and can choose one of the following. Which would you take?

   a. $1,000 in cash
   b. A 50 percent chance at winning $4,000
   c. A 20 percent chance at winning $10,000
   d. A 5 percent chance at winning $100,000

12. It is 1992, and inflation is returning. Hard assets such as precious metals, collectibles, and real estate are expected to keep pace with inflation. Your assets are now all in long-term bonds. What would you do?

   a. Hold the bonds
   b. Sell the bonds and put half the proceeds into money funds and the other half into hard assets
   c. Sell the bonds and put all the proceeds into hard assets
   d. Sell the bonds, put all the money into hard assets, and borrow additional money to buy more

Scoring

Now it is time to see what kind of investor you are. Total your score using the point system below for each answer you gave.

Your score

_____	1.	a-3	b-1	c-4	
_____	2.	a-3	b-1		
_____	3.	a-2	b-1		
_____	4.	a-2	b-1	c-4	d-1
_____	5.	a-1	b-2		
_____	6.	a-1	b-2	c-3	
_____	7.	a-1	b-2	c-4	d-6
_____	8.	a-5	b-3	c-1	d-1
_____	9.	a-1	b-3	c-6	d-9
_____	10.	a-3	b-1		
_____	11.	a-1	b-3	c-5	d-9
_____	12.	a-1	b-2	c-4	d-6
_____	Total				

If you scored below 18, you are a *prudent investor* who tends to take calculated risks but only with solid investments that you believe to be undervalued. Stick with sober, conservative investments until you develop the confidence or desire to adopt more aggressive strategies. But when interest rates are falling and a bull market in stocks seems to be starting, do not eliminate the possibility of investing part of your funds in growth mutual funds.

If you scored between 18 and 32, you are an *active investor* who tends to seek a more balanced approach to risk and return. As an active investor you are willing to take calculated risks to achieve gains. You will consider various investment strategies, and in the long run you will achieve greater gains.

If you scored 33 and over, you are an *aggressive investor*. You tend to take bigger risks in anticipation of bigger returns. Remember that the search for more return carries *greater risks*. If, however, you know you will not hit home runs all the time and are willing to strike out once in a while, you might as well get up to the plate and swing for the fences. As you advance in your investing skill level and you read Part Three, you will learn how to use the Y-Process to enhance your returns while minimizing your risk.

Source: From W. E. Donoghue, *The Donoghue Strategies* (New York: Bantam Books, 1981), p. 41.

Chapter 2

Investment Choices for the Prudent Investor

Bonds Can Be Safe, but Only If You Don't Need the Money

STOCK VERSUS BONDS

For the novice investor, when I write about stock, I am referring to an investment that gives you an ownership certificate of a corporation, that is, a stock certificate. A bond is any debt security, such as an IOU or a corporate promissory note. The bottom line then is that stocks (or equities) mean *ownership* and bonds mean *debt*.

Bonds come in a variety of maturities. The long bond is the U.S. government's 30-year bond. Its yield is the one often cited by the media when interest rates are being discussed. Treasury notes have shorter terms, maturing in 2, 5, or 10 years. Treasury bills (T-bills) mature in 13, 26, or 52 weeks. The minimum purchase amount for all of these bills is $1,000.

The prudent investor should use Yanis's first principle of investing: *Preservation of capital with realistic returns.* Modern, sophisticated investors who are willing to develop a well thought-out, sound strategy for managing their investments qualify as the only truly prudent investors. The key to developing such a strategy is to adopt *preservation of capital with realistic returns* as your first principle of investing.

Does the preservation of capital mean to invest only in bonds? No. For the average investor, preservation of capital means retaining your principal—the dollar value of your original investment plus any growth. However, preservation of capital is much more complex. Many investors believe that risk-free government bonds provide a conservative preservation approach. You learn in this chapter that investing in bonds has severe limitations. There are better ways to preserve your capital.

What does "realistic returns" mean? Realistic returns are dividends, interest, and capital gains on your investments, which then can accumulate wealth. The stock market has the potential to maximize your wealth. No other investment available to intelligent novice investors with average resources, a willingness to take risks, and a limited amount of time to spend on active management delivers as well as stocks over the long term: not real estate, gold, or bonds, and certainly not savings accounts.

For the novice investor, it is important to note that as long-term investments, *stocks outperform bonds*. According to University of Pennsylvania Professor J. Siegel's book, *Stocks for the Long Run*,[1] from 1802 to 1997 the stock market offered an average nominal annual return of 8.4 percent per year compared with 4.8 percent for long-term government bonds. From 1926 to 1997, stocks outperformed bonds 10.6 percent to 5.2 percent. From 1966 to 1997, the difference was 11.5 percent versus 7.9 percent. Money that you are investing for decades will grow more quickly in the stock market than it will in bonds.

What Are the Real Returns of Stocks and Bonds?

Much can be learned by reviewing the history of risk–reward relationships in both the stock and bond markets. Probably the best study of comparative investment results ever undertaken was performed by Roger Ibbotson, who evaluated records back to 1930. These results are summarized in Table 2.1. Ibbotson calculated the compound annual returns (including reinvested dividends and interest) of the Standard & Poor's (S&P) 500 Index (a proxy for the stock market) and long-term government bonds.

Study Table 2.1 and match the returns of stocks and bonds against each other and against the inflation rate. Ibbotson has two columns for each period studied. The first column contains nominal returns for stocks versus bonds. The second column contains a comparison of inflation-adjusted returns for stocks versus bonds. In every period shown over the 70 years evaluated, stocks outperformed bonds except for the rapid inflationary period (1970–1979) where stocks and bonds tied and underperformed the inflation rate. This result leads us to a very important topic for investors: Inflation must be taken into account when making investment decisions.

INFLATION CAN BE HAZARDOUS TO YOUR FINANCIAL WEALTH

Inflation erodes the purchasing power of the dollar. However, the real loss that an investor experiences is best understood by a historic comparison of stocks and bonds. Research on returns and inflation over an extended period of time has shown that the nominal return on common stocks has exceeded the rate of inflation by about 5 percent. But this is not the whole story. Table 2.1 shows the long-term results from 1930 through 1998, a period that includes the two biggest stock market crashes[2] in history, plus the Great Depression. When nominal returns are adjusted for inflation[3] as they are in Table 2.1, inflation-adjusted returns (sometimes called "real" returns) highlight the unrelenting impact of inflation on an investor's purchasing power.

Some interesting conclusions can be drawn from Table 2.1. The first conclusion is that long-term bonds may let you sleep well at night but at a price—in this case lost performance. Next, in all cases presented, returns from stocks outperform the returns from bonds, except during rapid inflationary times. During expanding inflationary periods, returns of both stocks and bonds drop and *both* underperform the inflation rate. Therefore the inflation-adjusted values for the S&P 500 and long-term government bonds are negative numbers.

Just the opposite happens during disinflationary times. Both bonds and stocks prosper during disinflationary periods, as experienced by the inflation-adjusted results of the decade of the eighties. Finally, the disinflationary rates of the nineties and to date (not shown) is driving returns back toward the mean of the last 70 years—the long-term inflation rate is 3 percent while nominal and inflation-adjusted returns of stock are in high double-digits.

Table 2.1 Comparison of Nominal and Real Returns for Stocks and Bonds over Various Periods

Investment Types/Inflation	Long-Term Returns 1930–1998		Postwar Returns 1946–1998		Rapid-Inflation Returns 1970–1979		Disinflation Returns 1980–1989	
	Nominal (%)	Inflation-adjusted (%)	Nominal (%)	Inflation-adjusted (%)	Nominal (%)	Inflation-adjusted (%)	Nominal (%)	Inflation-adjusted (%)
S&P 500 Index	10.4	7.08	12.3	7.77	5.4	-1.86	17.3	11.61
Long-term government bonds	5	1.8	5.2	0.96	5.5	-1.77	12.6	7.14
Inflation rate	3.1		4.2		7.4		5.1	

Note: Data modified from R. Ibbotson's 1996 *Yearbook* to update long-term returns to 1998.

STOCKS ARE THE LONG-TERM WINNERS

Historically, stocks have kept investors far ahead of bonds, money market investments, or inflation. Why? The potential riskiness of the stock market in the short run is the corollary to why, in the long run, the market is the best place to invest. Companies sell stock when they need to raise capital but are unsure of the returns their investments will generate. To persuade investors to buy, companies must offer a promise of reward substantially greater than the rewards those investors could achieve by holding bonds or money market securities. In diversified portfolios, such as the 500 companies of the S&P 500, stock investments that succeed have more than compensated for those that have failed.

If an investor bought $1,000 of long-term government bonds in 1930 and reinvested all of the interest, at the end of 1998, such an investment would have accumulated a risk-adjusted value of just over $1,855. If an investor bought the S&P 500 for $1,000 in 1930 and reinvested all dividends, at the end of 1998, the risk-adjusted investment would be worth nearly $153,000. That is a dramatic difference. And, an investor can expect to do even better than this example if investments are managed wisely—for example, by using the Y-Process investment strategy presented in Part Three of this book.

WHAT YOU NEED TO KNOW ABOUT BONDS

Bonds are IOUs issued by corporations, state and city governments and their agencies, and the federal government and its agencies. When you buy a bond, you become a creditor of the corporation or agency; it owes you the amount shown on the face of the bond, plus interest. You get a fixed amount of interest on a regular schedule —every six months in most cases—until the bond matures after a specified number of years, at which time you are paid the bond's face value. If the issuer goes broke, bondholders have first claim, ahead of stockholders.

THE RISK OF RISK-FREE BONDS

Buying a bond fund to hold indefinitely is a high-risk approach that an intelligent investor would never consider. The only higher-risk approach is to invest your money *only* in bonds. Investors in the millions thought they were making a safe decision investing in long-term bond funds in the past. Many of them lost money.

However, bonds do belong in your investment plan for good reasons, but possibly not for the reasons most investors think. Some examples:

- Economic forces that depress stock prices in the early stages of a recession tend to boost bond prices.
- Bonds can generate impressive profits from capital gains when the original bonds are bought at a discount and suddenly the prime rate is reduced significantly. The result is an immediate jump in the value of the bonds.
- Bonds can provide a predictable stream of relatively high income that can be used for living expenses or for funding other parts of your investment plan.
- Certain types of bonds offer valuable tax advantages and unique opportunities to invest a modest amount with a reasonable prospect of collecting a large amount years later.

Note that the word *safety* does not appear in any of the examples. Many investors think bonds are among the safest investments, but such a notion can be costly. Bonds entail several kinds of risks.

Interest rate changes create one of the chief risks you face as an investor in bonds. The single most important thing to remember about the relationship between the market value of the bonds you hold and changes in current interest rates is: *As interest rates rise, bond prices fall; as interest rates fall, bond prices rise. The further away the bond's maturity or call date, the more volatile its price tends to be.*

Interest rate rises are not the only potential risk for bond investors. Another risk is the chance that the organization that issued the bonds will be unable to pay them off. Assessing the credit worthiness of companies and government agencies issuing bonds is a job for the pros. The best known are Standard & Poor's and Moody. Standard & Poor's assigns investment grades to companies from AAA, AA, A to BBB. For these grades the risk of default is low. Grades below BBB are considered either speculative (BB or B) or in real danger of default (various levels of C and a D indicate that the issue is close to or actually in default). You can consider any issue rated speculative or lower to be a "junk" bond, although brokers and mutual funds usually call them "high-yield" issues.

RELATIONSHIP BETWEEN PRICE AND YIELD

When a new bond is issued, the interest rate it pays is called the *coupon rate*, which is the fixed annual payment expressed as a percentage of the face value. An 8 percent coupon bond pays $80 a year interest on each $1,000 of face value, a 9 percent coupon bond pays $90 and so on. That is what the issuer will pay—no more, no less—for the life of the bond. But it may or may not be the yield you can earn from that issue; understanding why is the key to unlocking the real potential of investing in bonds.

Take a bond offering with a coupon interest rate of 9 percent, meaning that it pays $90 a year for every $1,000 of face value. What happens if interest rates rise to 10 percent after the bond is issued? New bonds will have to pay a 10 percent coupon rate or no one will buy them. By the same token, you could sell your 9 percent bond only if you offered it at a price that produced a 10 percent yield for the buyer. So the price at which you could sell would be whatever $90 represents 10 percent of, which is $900. Thus, you lose $100 if you sell. Even if you do not sell, you suffer a paper loss because your bond is now worth $100 less than you paid for it. Selling a bond for less than you paid for it is called selling at a *discount*.

But what if interest rates were to decline? Say rates drop to 8 percent while you are holding your 9 percent bond. New bonds would be paying only 8 percent and you could sell your old bond for the value of what $90 represents 8 percent of. Because $90 is 8 percent of $1,125, selling your 9 percent bond when interest rates are at 8 percent would produce a $125 capital gain. That $125 gain is called a *premium*. Actual prices are also affected by the time remaining before the bond matures and by the likelihood of the issue being "called," that is, when a company elects to redeem the bond prior to its maturity date.

TREASURIES: THE SAFEST BONDS OF ALL

One way to eliminate the default risk entirely is to stick with IOUs from the U.S. Treasury. Because the federal government backs them, there is virtually no chance that you will miss getting a payment of interest or principal or that the federal government's credit rating will be lowered. Buying Treasuries does not eliminate the market risk, however; once issued, their value fluctuates with interest rates, just as does the value of corporate bonds. But the risk of default is nil.

Treasuries have other attractive features as well. Interest (but not capital gains) is exempt from state and local income taxes. Because the market for them is so vast, they are easy to buy and easy to sell. Commissions tend to be modest. In fact, you can buy Treasuries direct at regularly scheduled auctions (you do not have to attend) and eliminate commission charges entirely.

All these advantages do come at a price though. Treasuries tend to yield a little less than corporate bonds with comparable maturity, even AAA-rated corporate bonds. But for the peace of mind they provide, that is a small price to pay. Table 2.2 provides a brief overview of the characteristics of the five most prominent types of bonds. This overview of the world of bonds is a handy reference for the future.

RISK-REDUCING STEPS YOU SHOULD TAKE AS A BOND INVESTOR

Bond investors should consider certain aspects of the purchase prior to the purchase, such as the ideal time to buy, potential volatility, and diversification using maturity dates, safety ratings, and types of bonds. This set of rules will serve as a handy reference for bond buyers:

- *Do not buy bonds when interest rates are low or rising.* Put your cash in a money market fund or in certificates of deposit maturing in three to nine months. The ideal time to buy bonds is when interest rates have stabilized at a relatively high level or when they seem about to head down.
- *Reduce the potential volatility of your bond holdings.* Stick to short- and intermediate-term issues with maturities of three to five years. They fluctuate less in price than longer-term issues and they do not require you to tie up your money for 10 or more years in exchange for a relatively small additional yield.
- *Diversify your bond holdings by acquiring bonds with different maturity dates.* A mix of issues maturing in one, three, and five years will

Table 2.2 Classes and Characteristics of Bonds

Type of Bond	Par Value	Maturity Period	Trading Details	Rated	Tax Status	Call Provisions
Corporate bonds[a]	$1K	Short term: 1–5 years Intermediate: 5–10 years	By brokers on any exchange or OTC	Yes	Taxable	Callable
Municipal bonds[b]	$5K and up	From 1 month to 40 years	By brokers or OTC; often, investment bankers under-write whole issues and resell to dealers and brokers	Yes	Exempt from federal taxes; exempt from state and local taxes under special conditions	Sometimes callable
T-bonds and T-notes[c]	$1K, $5K, $10K, $100K, and $1M	Bonds over 10 years Notes 2–10 years	New issues by auction at any Federal Reserve Bank Outstanding issues by brokers or OTC	Not rated Risk-free	Exempt from state and local taxes	Usually not callable
T-bills[d]	$10K (also issued in amounts up to $1M)	3 months, 6 months, 1 year	New issues by auction at any FRB Outstanding issues by brokers or OTC	Not rated Risk-free	Exempt from state and local taxes	Not callable
Agency bonds,[e] e.g., bonds of mortgage associations; Ginnie Mae, Fannie Mae, and Freddie Mac	$1K to $25K and higher	30 days to 20 years	By brokers or OTC; directly through banks	Some issues are rated by some services	Taxable, but federal agency bonds are exempt from state and local taxes	Not callable

Note: A call provision is an option, written into the security's provisions, whereby the issuer may redeem the bond prior to its maturity date.

[a]These bonds are readily available to investors as companies use them rather than bank loans to finance expansion and other activities.

[b]More than one million municipal bonds have been issued by states, cities, and other local governments to pay for construction and other projects.

[c]These long-term debt issues of the federal government are a major source of government funding to keep operations running and to pay interest on the national debt.

[d]Treasury bills are the largest component of the money market—the market for short-term debt securities. The government uses them to raise money for immediate spending at lower rates than bonds or notes.

[e]Federal and state agencies also issue bonds to raise money for their operations and projects.

protect you from getting hurt by interest rate movements you cannot control. (Mutual funds, which are discussed in Chapter 3, are an excellent way to achieve diversity in your bond investments.)

- *Do not buy any bond with a safety rating lower than A.* Watch for news that may affect the rating while you own the bond.
- *Invest for maximum safety of principal.* Stick with bonds issued by the U.S. Treasury Department.

BALANCING RISK AND REWARDS

Many seasoned investors in the decade of the nineties, in the years where double-digit gains in the stock market were commonplace, may have been seduced into putting all their cash into stocks. For these people and many others, the current dilemma is whether to stay invested in the market or boost their fixed-income holdings. Just what investment mix makes sense is a matter of sharp debate, even among investment professionals.

Investment authorities insist that you should always have fixed-income assets (bonds) in your portfolio for funds that are needed in the next several years. Many pension funds, for instance, have traditionally balanced risk and return with a mix of 60 percent stocks and 40 percent bonds.

Chapter 3

Mutual Funds: The Ideal Investment for Beginners

Start with Just One No-Load Index Fund
If That's All You Can Afford

WHAT MUTUAL FUNDS HAVE TO OFFER

Mutual funds are among the most flexible and potentially advantageous investments. They are especially suited for the beginning investor. The mutual fund industry has grown exponentially since the first fund was formed in 1924. At this writing there are over 8,000 funds (more than there is stock on the New York Stock Exchange) investing greater than $4 trillion on behalf of stockholders. Some funds have no minimum investment requirement. You can buy $25 worth of shares if you want. A typical minimum is $1,000 to open an account, with minimum additional investments of $50 or $100. This makes mutual funds ideal vehicles for long-term accumulation programs through dollar cost averaging.

Funds come in various types, sizes, and shapes, with different strategies and objectives. This chapter focuses on just two types of funds: (1) Money Market Funds and (2) Index Funds. For the novice investor, it will take a year or so of investing and following your funds in the financial section of your local newspaper before you are ready to move on to the next level of investing.

Before we get into the specifics, an overview of the concepts, advantages, and limitations of mutual funds is in order. A mutual fund is simply an investment company that sells shares of its stock to the public, and invests the proceeds in an investment mix of stocks and bonds of other companies. Mutual fund stockholders share in the income, profits, and losses of their funds' investments. At the end of every business day, the typical fund calculates the total market value of all of its investments and deducts its liabilities to determine the value of each outstanding share.

AUTOMATIC DIVERSIFICATION

The single greatest advantage of a mutual fund is that it is a portfolio of many securities. Owning shares of a mutual fund gives you a small ownership interest in all the stocks, bonds, and other investments in the fund's portfolio. Whether your aim is to own a cross section of growth stocks or high-tech stocks, you can find a fund or funds to suit you. Because they provide instant diversification, well-selected mutual funds are a better choice than individual stocks (or bonds) for investors with modest amounts of money to place at risk.

A FAMILY OF FUNDS

Most mutual fund companies offer investors a family of individual funds. A family may include stock, bond, and money funds, as well as international stock and bond funds. The company's managers pride themselves on offering many types of individual funds and hire experts who make the investment decisions for each fund. Because they provide expert portfolio management, investing in a fund is a better choice than investing in a portfolio of individual stocks, especially for beginning investors who are still unsure of their own stock-picking prowess.

SELECTION FLEXIBILITY

Investors may find it convenient to invest only in a single mutual fund family, using the company's resources as their core account and broker. But most of the major investment companies act as a one-stop resource for investing in other popular mutual fund companies. A toll-free call is all it takes to buy, sell, or exchange shares in thousands of different funds. For example, Fidelity Investments, the largest mutual fund company in the world, has close to 200 individual mutual funds in its family. Some investors may want to add other choices, from other fund families, into their portfolio.

In addition, you can easily switch your money from one member of the family to another, usually with a phone call, providing a convenient way for you to move your money from, say, a stock fund to a money market fund.

EASE OF PURCHASE AND SALE

You can buy funds through a broker or through the mail. You can sell them the same way or with an 800-number phone call. By law, a fund must buy back its shares when you want to sell them. The price at which fund shares are bought and sold is based on the fund's *net asset value*, which is the market value of the fund's holdings, minus management expenses, divided by the number of shares outstanding. The price you pay or receive will be based on the net asset value calculated at the close of trading on the day you place your order. Many mutual funds impose a sales charge or load on investors that buy new shares. A major difference between load and no-load funds is that you buy and sell no-load funds at their net asset value plus a commission, but sell them back to the fund at their net asset value. Later in this chapter I cover the many types of mutual fund costs.

SMALL MINIMUMS AND FRACTIONAL PURCHASES

Some funds have no minimum investment requirements. You can buy $25 worth if you want. More typically, funds have a minimum of $1,000 to open an account, with minimum additional investments of $50 or $100. As noted earlier, this makes funds ideal vehicles for long-term accumulation programs through dollar cost averaging.

One nice advantage of funds is that their price per share doesn't affect how much you can invest, since funds sell fractional shares, which is not done with normal stock purchases. So if you want to invest $1,000 and the fund is $17.56 a share, you get 56.948 shares. If the price is $2.96 a share, you get 2,960 shares. However, the price per share of a fund should never be a consideration in your investment decision. A $4-a-share fund can increase or drop in percentage just as far and as fast as a $400-a-share fund.

AUTOMATIC REINVESTMENT OF EARNINGS

You can request that dividends paid by stocks in the fund's portfolio and the interest from bonds and capital gains earned from selling securities be reinvested automatically in more shares. Reinvested earnings is a critical element in any long-term investment plan.

If you would like to receive regular income from your shares, funds will set up automatic payment plans for you. If dividends and interest earned are not enough to cover the payments to you, the fund will sell shares to cover them.

SHAREHOLDER SERVICES

Most funds have set up well-staffed telephone systems to handle inquiries about everything from current account balances to requests for descriptive brochures and order forms. Funds love individual retirement accounts or 401(k) accounts because they know such accounts are likely to stay there for some years. Funds have simplified the custodial paperwork to the point that it is virtually painless for the investor.

Another advantage of owning mutual funds is that the mutual fund companies do most of the paperwork for their stockholders. Capital gains and losses on the purchase and sale of securities, as well as dividend and interest earnings, are neatly totaled for each stockholder at the end of the year for their tax purposes. Funds also do all of the day-to-day paperwork chores, including handling of stock certificates, brokerage tickets, statements, transfer agents, and so forth. All an investor has to do is send his or her money to a fund and the mutual fund company does the rest.

MUTUAL FUND COSTS—LOADS, FEES, AND EXPENSES

Investing in mutual funds may be the road to riches but there is no free lunch. Investors owning a stock mutual fund subject themselves to a variety of costs, fees, and charges as well as taxes on any profit and capital gains. Be an informed investor and be aware of all costs of fund ownership.

SALES CHARGES

Many mutual funds impose a sales charge or load on investors who buy new shares. Suppose that the load published by a fund is 8.5 percent. Suppose the fund has a 10 percent total return the first year you own it. What is the sales fee and what is the return? A load of 8.5 percent means that $850 of a $10,000 investment is kept by the broker, so only $9,150 of your money was placed in the fund. The sales fee equals 9.3 percent[1] of the amount actually invested by you, but you still earned 10 percent on the amount invested, or $915, not 10 percent on $10,000. Sadly, most funds quote their sales charges as a percentage of the cost of shares purchased plus the commission. Such a deceptive practice makes commission rates appear to be slightly lower than they really are.

Taking fees into account is important when calculating your gain, but in comparing funds, keep in mind that a fund's total return is a fund's total return, period. A sales fee, if any, does not mean that the return on your investment is lower, it means that less of your money is invested initially. Sales charges are usually reduced for larger transactions.

Many mutual funds, including virtually all money market mutual funds, are no-load and charge no sales loads at all. I recommend that if you are using a check-cashing capability that you use money market funds as a holding account where you can draw money out of the fund.

REDEMPTION AND REINVESTMENT FEES

When investors sell (redeem) shares of a fund, they may incur another charge, a redemption fee. Most funds do not have redemption fees, but some charge up to 5.3 percent of the amount of money initially invested. Back-end loads are sales charges deducted at the end of the transaction rather than at the beginning. However, the charges usually scale down with the passing of time. For example, a fund might charge a 5 percent redemption fee on the sale of shares sold within one year of purchase, whereas shares sold in their second year would incur a 4 percent fee, and so on down to a 1 percent fee in the fifth year, and nothing thereafter.

Other funds levy a small redemption fee on the full sale value of shares sold within a specified period, say, within the first six months or one year after purchase. Such redemption fees are usually imposed to discourage investors from frequent trading.

Nearly all funds permit investors to automatically reinvest all capital gains and income distributions in new shares with no sales charge.

RULE 12b-1 FEES

When you buy a fund from a broker, you pay a sales charge or commission, typically for the advice they offer. Commissions have been around for as long as mutual funds. But in 1980, the Securities and Exchange Commission (SEC) wrote Rule 12b-1, authorizing fund companies to add a new annual charge for marketing and distribution, which might include advertising costs or an annual payout to the broker who sold you the fund. Fees, and other fund expenses, are deducted each and every year from the fund's assets.

In July 1992, the National Association of Securities Dealers capped the Rule 12b-1 Fee at 0.75 percent to recover the sales commission but then added another 0.25 percent as a broker's service fee. These fees are nothing more than a different type of hidden load. Whether such charges are said to be pursuant to a distribution plan or an administration services agreement, they end up enriching salesmen and fund sponsors, not investors.

TRANSACTION COSTS

As a fund buys and sells securities, it incurs brokerage commissions. Transaction costs are normally much lower for mutual funds than for individual investors because funds buy and sell in large quantities. Nevertheless, all trading costs are ultimately borne by shareholders. The more actively a fund turns over (trades) its portfolio, the more transaction costs it will incur.

PORTFOLIO MANAGEMENT FEES

Every mutual fund contracts with an investment adviser to make investment decisions. Shareholders must bear the cost of the fee paid to the manager, which usually ranges from 0.25 percent to 1.25 percent of fund assets per annum. Generally, the larger the fund, the lower the percentage fee. Annual management fees in excess of 0.75 percent should generally be considered excessive.

OPERATING EXPENSES

Mutual funds incur various day-to-day operating costs, including rent, telephone expense, employee salaries, prospectus and annual report printing, and so forth. As these expenses are incurred, they are paid from fund assets, and therefore reduce stockholders' returns. Typical fund operating expenses range from 0.10 percent to 1.25 percent per year. Added to management fees, total operating expenses exceed 2 percent per annum for some funds. Total annual expenses average 1.45 percent for all equity funds, 1.05 percent for all taxable bond funds, and 0.85 percent for all tax-free bond funds.

The message is clear. If you must buy a load fund, or one that charges a commission, get one with a front-end load and no Rule 12b-1 fee. You are better off with a straightforward, up-front haircut on your investment than little nibbles over the years. Note: Most investors would incur far lower costs themselves if they bypassed mutual funds and purchased index stock directly. We cover this topic in Part Two. There are other costs (on both load and no-load funds) to know about: These costs are collected by the fund sponsors by lowering the value of the stock when it is calculated on a daily basis.

LOAD VERSUS NO-LOAD FUNDS

Two primary reasons for choosing a load fund are that you need investment advice or you have located a special money manager who is available only in a load fund.

If you have an interest in investing in funds, there are many sources available to help in selecting your own funds. There is much information available from Morningstar Mutual Funds, a Chicago, Illinois, mutual fund analysis firm, which started operations in 1984. The availability of information and heightened consumer interest has shifted the balance from broker-sold funds toward funds that are sold direct to the investor.

Fidelity is a good example of the blurring of the line between load and no-load groups. It sells funds a number of ways: directly to the public without a sales charge, directly to the public with a sales charge, through registered representatives, and through its own fee-based advisory service.

DO YOU GET WHAT YOU PAY FOR?

The notion that you "get what you pay for" does not apply to mutual funds. There is no assurance that funds with loads have anything extra to offer an investor. Numerous studies bolster that insight. One study by Morningstar proves the point. Morningstar divided its mutual fund universe into two groups in mid-1995 to study the difference between load and no-load funds. It found that load funds had a higher annual expense ratio—1.62 percent, on average, compared with 1.11 percent for no-load funds. It also found that no-load funds are a bit less aggressive, on average, in investment style. As for performance, the no-load funds outperformed in the short run when the load-fund performance was adjusted to account for loads.

Another 23-year performance study of no-load funds by the *Buyer's Guide* provides definitive proof that no-load funds reward their shareholders with superior returns. And that superiority exists *before* adjusting for sales charges. In other words, the performance gap widens further in favor of no-load funds when sales loads are charged against the performance of the load funds. Put another way, sales charges do not buy superior performance, they just buy a salesman.

Table 3.1 displays the performance of all U.S. growth funds over five separate intervals from 1971 through 1993. All Funds in the table (col-

Table 3.1   **Growth Funds' Annual Rates of Return from 1971 through 1993**

Years	No-Load Funds Only (%)	All Funds (Load and No-Load) (%)
1971–1975	−0.4	−1.0
1976–1980	24.0	16.9
1981–1985	11.2	11.2
1986–1990	10.5	10.2
1991–1993	23.1	21.1
All 23 Years	12.5	10.6

umn 2) included both load and no-load growth funds. In each period shown, no-load funds performed as well, or better, than all funds combined. Over the entire 23 years, no-loads provided an average annual return of 12.5 percent, the equivalent of an initial $10,000 investment growing to $150,000. Meanwhile, all growth funds returned only 10.6 percent per year, the equivalent of an initial $10,000 investment increasing to $101,400.

WHAT IS THE FUND'S EXPENSE RATIO?

The expense ratio shows how the costs of running the fund eat up much of your potential earnings. The fund must deduct expenses (except for sales fees) before calculating its total return, and hence the total return is a much more important number. If you are going to invest in an index fund that invests in a stock market index, for example, the Dow Jones Industrial Average (DJIA) or the Standard & Poor's (S&P) 500, pay close attention to its expense ratio. Since an index fund is designed to track an actual stock index, a high expense ratio will tend to load the fund down and drop its return below the actual stock index's return.

MONEY MARKET FUNDS

The standard of excellence in the consumer money market is a well-run money market mutual fund (money fund, for short). Nearly every mutual fund family and every stockbroker offers a money fund.

ADVANTAGES AND LIMITATIONS

Money funds have been around since 1970 and have an unblemished track record for safety, liquidity, and competitive yields. The earnings on their portfolios determine their returns. Perhaps the best part of the deal is that managers obtain high yields while taking only 0.47 percent, on average, of the funds' assets per year in management fees. And if you are in a mutual fund family, when you sell a stock fund the assets can be moved into a safe haven money fund.

Money funds are not insured as are bank or fund money market deposit accounts, but no money fund has ever failed or is ever likely to fail. So why give up 1 percent or more in interest to invest in a bank money market account? As an extra added attraction, money funds offer benefits that bank money market deposit accounts do not. Many offer unlimited free checking privileges, and most offer free wiring of money to a bank account and convenient access to other investments in a mutual fund family. There is one limitation that may be considered a drawback; most money funds require that a minimum check value of $500 be written.

You do not know exactly how much you will earn with a money fund. But, if interest rates are rising you will probably earn more than a bank certificate of deposit (CD) would offer, and if they are falling, you will be elsewhere making a killing in your stock fund. And credit risk should never be an issue in the money market. The money market is a very exclusive club. Consumers should always deal exclusively with risk-free (federally guaranteed) or regulated money market institutions. Securities and Exchange Commission mutual fund regulations make mutual funds essentially as safe as banks. All investments by money funds must be kept in a bank trust department. No money fund manager has access to the investments, so no one can run off to an offshore island with the money. The SEC also regulates money funds' investment practices. No money fund has ever invested in anything that did not pay off as agreed at maturity.

TAX-FREE MONEY MARKET FUNDS

Tax-free money market funds are an exciting development of the 1980s. These funds operate much like taxable money market funds, but they invest in short-term money market instruments issued by municipalities, state governments, and government authorities. The interest payments are exempt from federal income tax.

You can decide whether a tax-free money market fund makes sense for you by converting a tax-free money fund's yield to its taxable equivalent. You do this by multiplying the tax-free fund's yield by a factor derived from your tax bracket and then you can compare it with a taxable alternative. For instance, if you are in the 28 percent federal tax bracket and the investment you are considering is not exempt from your state's taxes, the conversion multiplier is 1.389. If you are in the 31 percent federal tax bracket, the conversion multiplier is 1.449. To determine these conversion multipliers, divide one by your appropriate tax bracket, either 1.28 or 1.31.

In several states with high state income taxes, such as New York, California, and Massachusetts, double tax-free money funds have been offered. These funds invest in in-state tax-exempt instruments, so their income is exempt from state taxes as well. Triple tax-free money funds are available to New York City residents. These invest in New York City tax-exempt issues and are triple exempt from state, local, and federal taxes.

INDEX FUNDS: BUYING THE BENCHMARK

Most investments promise to beat the averages, to help you do better than the next guy. Indexing uses a very different approach. An index fund simply buys a large number (or all) of the securities listed in an index—seeking to duplicate that index's performance. The first index fund ever developed was by the Vanguard Group. Vanguard developed the *500 Portfolio* that seeks to track the performance of the S&P 500 Index, which emphasizes stocks of large U.S. companies. By its nature, indexing emphasizes broad diversification, minimal trading activity, and razor-thin costs. As a result, index fund investors benefit from a reduction of certain investment risks, the possibility of lower taxable distributions, and the ability to keep a higher percentage of investment returns.

Back in 1975, when the Vanguard Group started developing its first index fund, indexing was in its infancy. Paul Samuelson, the Nobel-laureate economist, started a lively intellectual debate about what he saw as the obvious advantages of indexing. Samuelson argued that although all stock pickers and mutual fund managers try to beat the market average, few succeed. In fact, on average, it has been determined that the performance of 75 percent of all mutual funds lag behind the market average every year.

There are good reasons why mutual funds lag behind the S&P 500 Index. The costs of trading, administration, and other fees mean that fund managers must beat the market index by about 2 percent, if they are to come out even after expenses. For example, Vanguard has done a good job of tracking the average. From August 1976 through August 1987, the fund earned a 407.7 percent rate of return, compared to 435.0 percent for the S&P 500 Index.

REDUCED INVESTOR COST AND RISK

A traditional mutual fund buys and sells securities based on the fund manager's judgments about which stocks are likely to provide the greatest return to investors. This traditional *active* approach typically gives fund managers latitude in managing the fund's holdings. As a result, investors in these funds are often not entirely sure how their money is being invested at a given moment. Also, the fund's performance, which is dependent on the adviser's strategies and tactics, comes at a significant yearly cost: typically 1 percent to 2 percent or more of assets invested.

An index fund holds roughly the same securities in the same relative amounts all the time, so there is no need for a manager. Instead, these funds are "passively managed," which means that the securities are bought and held. They are rarely traded. Some active mutual fund managers move out of the market and into cash when they think the market is weak. But an index fund is always fully invested in the securities of the index it tracks.

Indexing's *passive* approach is more objective and predictable, and available for as little as one-sixth the yearly cost. As its name implies, index investing relies on indexes that combine groups of stocks to measure the performance of the total market or a specific market segment.

The idea behind indexing was to minimize trading, eliminate management fees, and reduce the other costs of doing business by simply putting together a basket of the same stocks that make up the total market index. An investor buying into this mutual fund would get performance that matched the market at a very low cost.

BUYING THE MARKET

The goal of an index fund is to track the performance of the stock market. When the total market advances, a good index fund follows. When the market declines, so does the fund. The fund gets its name because it follows a broad index of the market. Rather than using a portfolio manager to pick stocks that he or she thinks will outperform the market, an index fund uses investors' money to purchase a group of stocks that are weighted in the same way as a broad market index. For example, a typical stock index fund contains the same stocks as the S&P 500 Index, a broad gauge of the market. Table 3.2 provides a partial list of the mutual fund industry that tracks the S&P 500 Index funds.

The concept of indexing caught on more slowly with individual investors than with institutional investors, although the Vanguard fund did its job of tracking the market and cutting expenses. When Vanguard brought out the fund, the expense ratio was 45 basis points, (0.45 percent) of assets under management. By 1988, it had dropped to 26 basis points followed by another drop in 1997 to 19 basis points. That compares to an average equity fund expense ratio of 110 basis points or 1.1 percent. To put it another way, on an investment of $10,000, the annual management fee would be $19 for the Vanguard fund compared to $110 for the average stock fund. In 1986, Vanguard took the idea of indexing one step further. It introduced the Extended Market Portfolio, which buys stocks in the Wilshire 4500 index (a broadly diversified index of stocks of medium-size and small U.S. companies). This is an index of all stocks traded, except for

Table 3.2 **Partial List of Index Funds That Track the S&P 500 Index (June 2001)**

Fund Name	Expense Ratio (%)	Fund Name	Expense Ratio (%)
Aon S&P 500	0.29	Munder Index 500 A	0.39
BT Index Funds 500	0.25	One Group Eq Index A	0.60
BullPro Fund	1.33	Schwab S&P 500	0.35
California Inv Tr S&P 500	0.20	Schwab S&P 500 Select	0.19
DFA U.S. Large	0.15	Scudder S&P 500	0.40
Dreyfus BASIC S&P 500	0.20	SEI S&P 500 A	0.25
Dreyfus S&P 500	0.50	SSgA S&P 500	0.17
Fidelity Spartan Market	0.19	Strong Index 500	0.45
First American Eq Index	0.60	T. Rowe Price Equity Idx	0.40
Galaxy II Large Co.	0.40	Transamerica Premier	0.25
INVESCO S&P 500 I	0.55	USAA S&P 500 Index	0.18
Kent Index Equity	0.68	Vanguard Index 500	0.18
Northern Funds Stock Ind	0.55	Victory Stock Index	0.57

the S&P 500. Now an investor can buy the entire market by putting together a combination of the two indexes. John C. Bogle, the CEO of Vanguard, said "We think we'll move from the idea of index matching to
market matching. If you buy 70 percent of the S&P and 30 percent of the
Extended Market Portfolio, then you'll match the overall market."[2]

INSTITUTIONAL INVESTORS AND INDEXING

The really influential investors are the institutional investors who invest
billions of dollars for pension funds, insurance companies, and mutual
funds. Because they invest in such large quantities, they pay less in fees,
commissions, and expenses than individual investors do, similar to the
wholesale and retail business in any product area. For example, a restau-
rateur buys his meat in the wholesale market. There he pays far less per
pound for a porterhouse steak because of the quantity he buys than you
pay in the retail market when you visit your local butcher.

Because of their low cost and their ability to track the market, index
funds have long appealed to institutional investors. Costs to these big
money managers are extremely low, much less than an individual investor
pays. For example, a typical fee for an actively managed institutional fund
is 40 basis points. But for an index fund, that fee is 8 basis points, or 0.08
percent of assets under management.

Individual investors must pay more for index funds than institutions
do (see Table 3.2). And many mutual fund companies have been reluctant
to offer index funds to the public at all.

ADVANTAGES AND DISADVANTAGES

Obviously, you are better off simply "owning the market" with an index
fund than investing in a mutual fund that underperforms the market. An
index fund will *never* outperform the market, but neither should it underperform by much. First, a good index fund will closely track the movement
of the index it follows, falling slightly shy of the market's performance because of administrative fees. Second, because index funds are not actively
managed or traded, there is no management fee. Finally, an index fund
saves you from the chore of picking a money manager and monitoring his
or her performance. If you believe that the stock market is a good bet over

time but you do not want to bother with these details, an index fund is a good choice for you.

Even if you are a conservative investor, an index fund can work for a portion of your money. Your investment is almost certain to grow much more quickly than it would in any guaranteed bank account. Your biggest risk is that you might need the money at a time when the market is in the doldrums. For that reason, it is always prudent to put only a part of your portfolio in stocks. If you want to buy an index fund, first check the performance of the index that the fund purports to mimic. Next, check to see how close the fund has come to tracking the index; also check the expense ratio. As you can see in Table 3.2, the expense ratio can vary from 15 to 133 basis points. A true index fund should have low costs and it should demonstrate good success in following the index.

PART TWO

Assisting the Intermediate Investor to Become a More Effective Manager at Wealth Building

Part Two is written for the intermediate investor. A majority of intermediate investors are long-term, buy-and-hold investors with diversified portfolios who are pursuing their journey of wealth building to support a comfortable retirement. The objective of Part Two is to help informed, risk-sensitive intermediate investors become more effective managers of their portfolios, giving them renewed confidence in making risk–reward decisions. After you complete Part Two, you will be prepared to go on to Part Three and learn about more sophisticated investment strategies.

Chapter 4

The Psychology of Investing

*Learn to Sort Out the Psychological Factors That
Affect Your Investment Decisions*

Even today, after the 1990s decade of stunning gains in the stock market, there are investors who hate themselves; they are full of remorse over their bad investment decisions and missed opportunities. In fact, that characterization probably describes most investors, since even small failures seem to stand out more than the successes. Despite all our emphasis on hard, cold, clear-headed analysis, emotion often governs investing decisions. People make financial mistakes for many reasons. No matter how smart we think we are, we all make mistakes about money that cost us thousands of dollars every year—often without our even being aware of them. The culprits: a series of mental blind spots and knee-jerk reactions that befog financial judgments. We listen to poor advice. We succumb to euphoria, fear, anxiety, overconfidence, and any number of other human failures.

This chapter is not about the stock in trade of self-appointed experts who blather on about the "psychology of money making," and charge high fees for all too obvious advice. Rather, it focuses on more common and insidious mental errors that just about every investor makes often, partly because investors are not aware of them. These mistakes are inbred; they are the universal byproduct of the shortcuts that are built into our machinery to enable us to cope with the intricacies of life.

Researchers have spent years sorting out the psychological factors that affect us when we enter the stock market. "They are like optical illusions," says psychologist Amos Tversky of Stanford University, who, along with Daniel Kahneman of University of California, Berkeley, helped pioneer a study nearly three decades ago on fallacies in decision making. "Fortunately we can learn to recognize and compensate for many of the most common errors."[1] Understanding how urges work can help investors keep damaging emotions under control. Some of the more common mistakes attributable to psychological factors are presented here.

OVERCONFIDENCE

Many of us have bountiful optimism and abundant self-confidence. In many ways, there are useful traits. Self-confident, optimistic people tend to be happier, more motivated, and more likely to persevere. When we turn these characteristics to investing, however, optimism and self-confidence can become our downfall. Innate overconfidence makes us too quick to assume that what we know is accurate and complete—particularly when our information is sketchy. In the financial world, we are not interacting with people; we are interacting with prices. Prices do not care how we feel on any particular day. In general, overconfidence is a negative characteristic when buying and selling stocks and bonds.

Studies suggest that investors err in fairly consistent ways. We react too much to short-term performance. We overestimate the chances of success with long-shot investments, such as initial public offerings and risky technology stocks. We see patterns in stock market returns where there are none. We sell stock market winners too quickly and hang on to losers too long. Finally, the more we trade the more poor decisions we are likely to make. Then we pay further through trading costs and lost opportunities.

Advice to Avoid Overconfidence. To overcome this mental lapse, one investment adviser suggests writing down everything that you know that might affect the outcome for each investment and purchase. Next, list what you do not know that might be important. Ponder both lists before making your decision. Note that, no matter how long your list is of the things you do not know, the true list is probably much longer.

FEAR OF LOSS

Research has shown that most investors are averse to risk, preferring a sure thing to an alternative that is less certain but potentially more profitable. Studies have shown that people hate to lose a dollar more than they like to win a dollar. Most people prefer not to take risks that could reduce their profits, even if the risk offers the chance of making more. But investors will take big risks to try to avoid a loss, even if the risk may deepen their loss.

Tversky and Kahneman's study of this phenomenon asked people to choose between two alternatives:[2]

1. Imagine that someone has just handed you $1,000. Now you *must* choose between these two options:
   Option A: You win $500 more for sure.
   Option B: You take an even chance of doubling that $1,000 or winning nothing more.
2. Imagine that someone has just handed you $2,000. You must choose between the two options:
   Option A: You lose $500 for sure.
   Option B: You take an even chance of losing $1,000 or losing nothing.

Tversky and Kahneman found that in the first of these two situations, about 72 percent of the people chose option A—the sure gain. By contrast, in the second situation, only about 64 percent chose option A—the sure loss. That is odd, since the consequences are identical. In both situations, the sure thing—whether a gain or loss—leaves you with $1,500. Likewise, each gamble offers an even chance of ending up with $1,000 or $2,000.

Why the inconsistent answers? Among other things, our willingness to take a risk depends on how we view our current situation. *We tend to accept risk more readily when we see it as a chance to avoid a certain loss.* Therefore, we choose the second question's gamble to avoid the sure $500 loss. We are more conservative, however, when we consider opportunities to add to our financial gains; as a result, when we answer the first question, we take the sure $500 and refuse to gamble for the additional $1,000.

Advice to Alleviate Fear of Loss. Not everyone has the stomach to be in the stock market. If you are susceptible to selling everything in a panic, you ought to avoid stocks and stock mutual funds.

There is always something to worry about. Avoid weekend thinking and ignore the latest dire predictions of newscasters. No one can consistently predict interest rates, the future direction of the economy, or the stock market. Dismiss all such forecasts and concentrate on what is actually happening to the companies and mutual funds in which you have invested. Sell a stock because the company's fundamentals deteriorate, not because the sky is falling. Don't assume that past investment results are meaningful, especially when you are considering short-term numbers.

When choosing a mutual fund, for example, consider other factors, such as how volatile the fund has been over the past one, three, and five years. Look at the big picture—consider an individual investment as part of your total portfolio. Most importantly, be sure you can afford to sustain the loss if the fund's value declines.

DEEP REGRET OVER ERRORS

Research has also shown that most people have a strong aversion to feelings of regret. Investors often try to avoid such feelings by holding on to poor investments when the logical and rational course of action is to unload them. Moreover, most people feel regret more deeply when that regret involves an *unwise action* they have taken rather than when it is simply related to a *missed opportunity.*

One study of this phenomenon asked people what they would choose in the following two situations:[3]

Situation A: You win $150 dinner with your spouse at a local restaurant next Saturday night. Then a friend invites the two of you, and another guest, to his home for dinner the same evening. The other guest is the candidate for governor whom you very much want to meet. Choose between the two dinners.

Situation B: You have paid $150 in advance to have dinner with your spouse (or significant other) at a local restaurant. The $150 is not refundable. Now you get the same invitation from your friend. Choose between the two dinners.

Most people find it hard to skip dinner at the restaurant in the second situation because they have already paid for it. But the $150 should not affect their thinking since they can't get their money back. Instead, they should decide which dinner would give them more pleasure and choose that one. *Future costs are what matter*. But often people cannot forget the money they have spent in the past.

That pervasive problem offers a further explanation for our tendency to support lost causes. An example should reinforce this concept. Joseph Nestor, an engineer at General Electric, took a call from his stockbroker who persuaded him to invest $21,000 in HIP Reuters, a Health Maintenance Organization that trades on the American Stock Exchange. The stock fell from $10.50 to $2.50, but then Joseph shelled out another $7,500 for additional shares, hoping to recoup his loss. "The broker said it was a good idea." Joseph says. "I had to make up the difference somehow." Joseph continued to hold the shares, despite having absorbed a total loss of about $18,500 on his investment of $28,500.[4]

Advice to Avoid Deep Regret over Errors. Don't look back and don't expect all of your decisions to be perfect. Generally, investors would make better decisions if they had no memory. Don't think about what you paid for a stock; instead consider whether you would buy it at today's price.

OVERLOOKING OPPORTUNITY COST

Researchers have found that most investors put an inflated value on things they own—a phenomenon known as the *endowment effect*. As a result, they demand too high a price when they go to sell. By holding out, they often fail to sell when selling makes sense. The ideal selling opportunity may be missed; investors may lose the opportunity to move their money into something more profitable. This mistake is known as *opportunity cost*.

Take the case of Jack and Jill Jacoby. In 1997 they received an offer of $180,000 almost immediately after putting their Voorhees, New Jersey, home on the market. But they turned it down because a friend who lived nearby had recently sold his house for $220,000. "Our home wasn't quite as nice as his," says Jack, a psychiatrist, "But we felt that if he had gotten $220,000 and we lived on the same block then we should hold out." Result? It took two years to find another buyer at $145,000—$35,000 less than the original offer.

The opportunity cost to Jack and Jill was not only the $35,000. They neglected to consider two additional costs. First, the two years of cost on the money they borrowed from a savings and loan at an 8.5 percent interest rate for the new home they purchased, while their existing home was sitting there waiting for a buyer. The money they borrowed could have been reduced by the original offer of $180,000. Second, the two years of taxes they had to pay on their empty home while waiting for the sale to occur. These additional costs total $40,600. In all, the opportunity cost to Jack and Jill was $75,600.

Researchers have found that most people perceive continuous events in discrete or binary form as up or down, black or white, successful or not. Therefore, they place special and even irrational importance on obtaining certain thresholds. Assume you bought a stock at $20. After two years it is still at $20, and you decide it has little upside potential. Most people would sell. If the stock were $19 most investors infected with this endowment effect phenomenon would refuse to sell. Even if it meant leaving capital in an unpromising asset, they would hang on for years in the hope of "getting out even." Sound familiar?

Advice to Avoid Overlooking Opportunity Cost. Before you spend, invest, or turn down an offer to purchase your home, consider at least half a dozen other uses for the money. If you can do some fast, back-of-the-envelope calculations, determine the opportunity cost for rejecting a bid on your home or, for that matter, for hanging on to a poor performing mutual fund or stock. When an investment performs poorly or is going nowhere, don't hang on too long if there is a potential for investing in some other asset that has a higher probability of enhancing your returns. On the other hand, if an investment posts gains, review the potential for additional profits before you decide to sell. The secret is to understand your own motives when you make a decision.

INABILITY TO STICK WITH AN INVESTMENT STYLE AND STRATEGY

In every trading session, the stock market offers its opinion. Often investors are left scratching their heads, wondering whether they should listen. This reaction is, of course, especially true when your stocks and/or stock mutual funds are getting clobbered. It is hard not to have doubts when you are losing money. When the broad stock market or a particular sector tumbles, some investors will extrapolate that short-term trend and expect prices to keep on falling. They are the ones who are most likely to jump. Other investors sit tight, but maybe not for long. Sticking with your strategy isn't always easy. The question is, how do you battle those doubts? Stick with your investment plan? When should you cave?

The key word most Wall Street professionals use is *confidence*. *Buy and hold and pray* is a tough discipline. Certified Financial Planners advise that you should have a strong sense of where you are going (goals/objectives) and how you are going to get there (strategic plan). Often, that doesn't happen. Most people just get into the market and start mucking around.

There is a downside to confidence. The greater your expectations, the more likely you are to be disappointed. The skimpier your investment knowledge, the easier it is to get rattled. The more unfamiliar an investment, the greater the temptation to cut and run when the market declines. Unfamiliarity is one good reason it is so difficult for normal investors to invest in foreign stocks, especially emerging markets, whereas, it is relatively easy to own familiar investments such as the Dow Jones blue-chip stocks. When circumstances are unfamiliar and values fall, investors perceive high risk. *You have to manage your own expectations.* But, unswerving confidence should only extend so far. It can be helpful in fending off doubts about the amount that you have in stocks and the way that your investments are diversified. But when it comes to individual stocks and mutual funds, confidence should not be confused with blind devotion or marrying your stocks "until death do you part."

Advice for Helping You to Stick with Your Investment Style and Strategy. Before you start dabbling in stocks and mutual funds, go back to basics, that is, settle on your asset allocation. Establish your target mix of stocks, mutual funds, bonds, and cash investments, for example, Treasury bills and money market funds. Next, decide how to diversify your stock market investments among large-, medium-, and small-capitalization funds. Thereafter, you should not be swayed by the market's gyrations. This assumes your asset allocation and diversification make sense given your time horizon and stomach for risk.

As discussed earlier, one reason people may stay with a loser is because they do not like to accept the loss. The danger for them comes when the market starts moving up again. As these investors begin to recoup their losses, they often breathe a sigh of relief *and then bail out*, thus canceling the chance for future profits.

How do you keep yourself invested for the long haul? Write down your stock–bond–cash combination and your stock-diversification mix. Make a note of the reasons you adopted this strategy and what sort of long-run returns and short-term losses you expect. When stocks next dive, take a moment to read what you wrote in quieter times. Without that reminder, an understanding of why you got into this scenario in the first place vanishes and investing becomes a short-term game.

With individual stocks, conviction is even more difficult, because mistakes are so much more common. You should not, however, judge your stocks by day-to-day share price movements. Instead, write down your three top reasons for owning a stock, such as a target earnings growth rate, reliable dividend increases, or price–earnings ratio. If any of those things change, it is an investment breaker, regardless of the stock price. If you just look at stock price changes, you may make decisions that have nothing to do with your original conviction.

You don't want the performance of the market to make you think you made a mistake. If you are in small-cap funds and you underperform the large-cap indexes, you should not use that as a reason to sell. Underperformance relative to comparable funds is more worrisome. But even then, I would not become concerned unless a fund lagged behind its peers for a year to a year and a half. I would become concerned if there was a change of fund manager or the fund's assets grew or shrank rapidly.

LISTENING TO JUST ONE ADVISER

Listening to just one adviser, especially to his or her short-term advice, is a major mistake. People on Wall Street are paid to have opinions. More than a few professionals will say the U.S. stock market is headed for big trouble at any given point in any given year. Let's say you believe this advice to the point of selling all your stocks. Will the expert you followed then tell you when to get back into the market? Will that expert make up for any gains you forgo should the market rise rather than fall while you are on the sidelines?

Advice for Those Who Listen to Just One Adviser. If you are mulling an all-or-nothing market-timing decision based on somebody else's forecast, remember that in November 1995, almost no one on Wall Street predicted that the Asian economy would blow up in 1997, that gold prices would drop to 14-year lows in 1999, or that the Dow would break through 10,000 in March of 1999, a 100 percent gain in just three and a third years.

NOT DIVERSIFYING

Perhaps the surest path to ruinous investment losses is to keep your assets concentrated in relatively few securities or classes of securities. Has your employer's stock been a stellar performer over the last few years? Great! But if that stock now accounts for half of your financial assets (in your retirement plan, for example), how would you feel if the price were to collapse.

Advice for Those Who Do Not Diversify. Effective diversification means using common sense to structure a portfolio of stocks and other financial assets (at a minimum, a cash cushion, and perhaps bonds) that makes sense for your risk tolerance. Warren Buffet, the noted value investor, once said about diversification, "that it's good for people who don't know what they're doing." If you are that confident in your investment savvy, go back to the beginning and read the first mistake: overconfidence.

MARRYING YOUR STOCKS

Loss of objectivity often leads to loss of money. It is healthy to respect well-run companies and to want them to succeed, especially when you own their stocks. But the closer you are to an investment, the less likely you are to see the big picture. And if the big picture is changing to the disadvantage of your company, you may not realize it until it is far too late.

Advice for Those Marry Who Their Stocks. Fast-growing, popular growth companies don't necessarily stay that way forever. You have to be able to recognize when a company's prospects no longer justify the affection you may feel for the stock. Just think of the two blue-chip stocks that were once blue-chip market leaders: The B & O Canal Barge Co. and the U.S. Buggy Whip Company. (Note: These companies are examples that I created to make a point. I'm sure that research would uncover defunct companies that would have the same effect.)

BUYING STOCK BECAUSE IT IS CHEAP

Master mutual fund manager and investor Peter Lynch once put together a list of the "10 most dangerous things people say about stock prices." One of them was, "The stock price is $3. What can I lose?" The answer, Lynch noted, is that you can lose 100 percent of your investment if the company ends up in bankruptcy. His point was that low-priced stocks often get that way for good reason; the company that issued the stock is poorly run and/or has bad business prospects.[5]

Advice for Those Who Buy Stock Because It Is Cheap. You can outperform the Wall Street experts by investing in companies or industries you already know. Never invest in a company without understanding its finances. The biggest losses in stocks come from companies with poor balance sheets.

You have to know what you own and why you own it. "This stock is hot and bound to go up!" doesn't cut it. If you can't find companies that are attractive, put your money in Treasury bills until you discover some.

This advice is good for those who do not yet use the Y-Process. When you learn about the Y-Process in Part Three, you will be able to modify this advice appropriately.

NOT PAYING ATTENTION TO COSTS

Maybe you have heard that line about the broker proudly showing off his new yacht to a friend. "And where are your customers' yachts?" the friend asks. Simply put, as an investor, you should get what you pay for. If you are paying high commissions for financial advice or investment transactions facilitated by an adviser, you should be earning a realistic return on the portfolio that adviser has constructed. If you are not, and you have had at least a year's experience to judge, it is probably time to find a new adviser. As for your mutual funds, have you ever looked at the management fees you pay?

Advice for Those Who Don't Pay Attention to Costs. If your fund's expense ratio is well above average, you should be getting well above average returns. Think of it this way: Every percentage point in expenses that your fund manager takes is a percentage point off your return—a loss to you.

NOT WORRYING ABOUT TAXES

The Internal Revenue Service (IRS) just loves it when you decide, for no good reason, to sell an investment at a gain in a taxable account. The IRS takes its cut every time. The federal government reduced long-term capital gains tax rates in 1997. Hold an investment for 12 months now, and any gain you realize when you sell will be taxed at a maximum of 20 percent, down from the maximum possible 39.6 percent for capital gains before the law was changed.

Advice for Those Who Don't Worry about Taxes. Twenty percent is 20 percent of your money. If your capital gain is $1,000, that means the IRS gets $200. Many states then take their own little piece of your action. Of course, when it is time to sell an investment, it is time to sell. But you should have a fundamental or strategic reason for selling. If you are not sure whether to sell, maybe the IRS's outstretched hand will help convince you to err on the side of holding on and allowing the magic of compounding investment returns to work for you.

HEEDING COLD CALLS

It is amazing that this process continues, but it does: Broker Smith, whom you do not know, gets your phone number and calls. "How would you like a stock tip?" he asks. That's when you should give Broker Smith a tip: "You've got the wrong party!" Anyone who tries to sell you anything over the phone, with no knowledge of your financial situation or your risk tolerance, is a discredit to the professional investment business.

Advice for Those Who Heed Cold Calls. If a broker or other financial adviser wants to meet you in person and talk about your total investment picture, it may be worth your time. But if you ever buy a security from someone you don't know and who doesn't know you, you deserve the losses you are likely to suffer. Unfortunately, the elderly are the most vulnerable. If you have a parent who is vulnerable to slick sales people, keep a close eye on their vulnerability and suggest that they check with you before they buy or sell stock or mutual funds.

GETTING CAUGHT UP IN WALL STREET'S HYPE

Newspapers, financial commentators, and TV's financial broadcasters sell the hype about the market's breakthrough of Dow Jones's whole round numbers. The big one was on March 29, 1999, when the Dow broke 10,000. This just panders to the multizerophiliacs,[6] and sells more copy and advertisement fee increases.

On the day after the Dow broke 10,000, the morning newspapers declared, in their largest bold font, "Dow hits 10,000 and stays there." Multicolored charts and tables displaying "The march to 10,000" enhanced this phenomenon.

The risk to you as an investor getting caught up in this hype is that it could be *hazardous to your wealth*. Such hype provides an excuse to neglect your careful, insightful strategic planning. Instead of preplanned, decisive steps, investors jump on the "can't lose bandwagon," making risky and imprudent snap decisions. Then one morning they wake up and find that the party is over.

Advice for Those Who Get Caught Up in Wall Street's Hype. Before you do anything zany, consider "milestones" in their percentage equivalents. When the market breaks through 20,000, that will represent a 100 percent change from its 10,000 milestone. But, in the interim the Dow has to pass through other milestones: 11,000, 12,000, 17,000, 18,000, 19,000. In terms of percentages, this series represents a magnitude growth in descending order: 10 percent, 9.1 percent, 6.3 percent, 5.9 percent, and 5.6 percent, respectively. The reason? Future gains have a smaller percentage impact due to the Dow's higher levels.

Putting this numbers game in perspective, as recently as October 20, 1987, the Dow had a one-day gain of 5.9 percent. Percentagewise that is equivalent to the Dow going from 17,000 to 18,000 in one day. Can it happen? It's possible.

Chapter 5

Benchmarking: Going Beyond the S&P 500 Index

For the Knowledgeable Investor, Benchmarking Is Critical to Measuring Success and Evaluating Prospective Investments

FINDING THE RIGHT BENCHMARK TO INTERPRET RETURNS

Benchmarks are useful measurements for comparing performances of *individual* mutual funds with indexes that reflect similar investment categories. However, investors should be careful about comparing their total investment portfolio's performance with a single benchmark. A diversified portfolio should consist of a mix of funds with different styles and objectives. Under such circumstances, benchmarks become an effective way to measure the specific rates of return of the individual funds within the investor's portfolio.

If investors want to determine whether their respective investment returns are ahead or behind from one year to the next, they need to realize that it may depend on their dividend reinvestment policy. For example, from 1973 through 1998, *before* dividends were reinvested, the Wilshire 5000, which tracks the entire U.S. market, sported the best *cumulative* annual returns with 1,213 percent. This rate compares with 1,160 percent for the Standard & Poor's (S&P) 500 and 979 percent for the Dow Jones Industrial Average (Dow). However, if the dividends for these three indexes were reinvested, the average annual return for those 25 years would have been 13.6 percent for both the Dow and the S&P 500 and 13.4 percent for the Wilshire 5000.

Investors also need to be aware that all indexes are not created alike. The Dow is a price-weighted index of 30 stocks, meaning that changes in the value of high-priced stocks affect the value of the Dow more than do changes in low-priced stocks. The S&P 500 is weighted according to *market capitalization*—shares outstanding times the price of each stock.

This mathematical difference provides some strange outcomes. Since Disney's market capitalization is about eight times that of Union Carbide's, Disney's weight in the S&P 500 is eight times that of Union Carbide's. In the Dow, however, Union Carbide has roughly twice the weight of Disney because the price of Union Carbide's stock is twice that of Disney's. This inconsistency makes the Dow a questionable index. Some financial historians argue that the reason for the Dow's price weighting was that the Dow was created in 1896, when capitalization weighting would have been too cumbersome for Charles Dow to calculate by hand.

WHICH BENCHMARK BEST MEASURES STOCK MARKET PERFORMANCE?

Table 5.1 indicates how the top three stock market benchmarks compare on an annualized basis through 1998.

Table 5.1   **Comparison of Three Stock Market Benchmarks on a Total Annual Return Basis**

Index	One Year (1998) (%)	3 Years (Annualized) (%)	5 Years (Annualized) (%)	10 Years (Annualized) (%)
DJIA	18.1	23.8	22.3	18.8
S&P 500	28.7	28.3	24.1	19.2
Wilshire 5000	23.4	24.4	21.8	18.1

Note: Annual return with dividends reinvested.
Source: The Wall Street Journal, January 4, 1999 (Lipper Inc.).

DUELING BENCHMARKS

Six of one, half-dozen of the other is what many market watchers have customarily thought when comparing benchmark indexes, until recently, when the Dow and the S&P 500 broke from their historical lockstep. The Dow probably has the highest name recognition of any market indicator; it has been around since the nineteenth century. Its movement tops most daily news stories on the stock market. But the S&P 500 is probably more reliable as a market indicator because of its size: 500 blue-chip companies that include the 30 Dow companies. It is the principal barometer used by most Wall Street professionals and more knowledgeable amateurs, because it reflects a broader swath of the market.

There have been esoteric debates about which gauge is the best to measure the market, but it probably does not matter which one is used. The Dow and S&P 500 performed about the same, that is, they customarily tracked one another. From 1990 through 1996, the Dow had average annual returns of 16.2 percent, versus 14.3 percent for the S&P 500. But, in the last five years, there has been a role reversal between the Dow and the S&P 500, where the S&P 500 outperforms the Dow. This is illustrated by reviewing the results of Table 5.1. While the S&P 500 returned 28.7 percent in 1998, with dividends reinvested, the Dow gained just 18.1 percent, an unusually large difference. That performance difference occurred after the previous year, when the S&P 500 returned 33.4 percent and the Dow returned 24.9 percent.

In hindsight, it is easy to determine what happened. In 1998, technology stocks soared, with Microsoft up 114.6 percent and Lucent Technologies skyrocketing to 175.9 percent. Stocks such as these are heavy hitters in a capitalization-weighted index influenced by companies with the highest value. For example, Microsoft is the largest company in the index, accounting for 4 percent of the value of the S&P 500. So Microsoft's stunning gains had far more effect than if it were just 1 of 500 companies counted equally. It should be noted that Microsoft is also in the Dow.

Is it possible to profit from a performance difference among the three indexes? In 1998, the largest 50 companies in the S&P 500 accounted for 85 percent of its gains; the top 10 alone accounted for 42 percent. So a big upward swing by those heavyweights pushed the whole index up dramatically, even though hundreds of other stocks did not do well. Indeed, 42 percent of S&P 500 stocks fell in price in 1998.

As illustrated in Table 5.1, the Wilshire 5000 underperformed the S&P 500 by five percentage points in 1998—a 23.4 percent total return versus the S&P 500's 28.8 percent return, although the Wilshire's return was a record return in its 25-year history. By contrast, the Wilshire 5000's return beat the S&P 500's return from 1975 through 1981, outperforming the S&P 500 by a full seven percentage points in 1979. Over the 25 years through 1998, the two indexes have delivered virtually identical 16.1 percent average annual returns.

How can an investor profit from performance differences between these two indexes? Obviously, by investing in the index that you expect will perform best. Is there a way to predict which index will outperform which? As William Shakespeare said, "There's the rub." In other words, there is no way of predicting the future based on past performance. That is why the Securities and Exchange Commission requires the following statement to be included in all fund prospectuses: "Past performance is no indication of future results."

COMPARING FUND PERFORMANCE WITH THE PREDOMINANT MARKET INDEXES

Because of the relatively rigid construction of market indexes and the differences between their performance and mutual fund portfolios, most professionals favor comparing fund performance to broad mutual fund peer groups. Thus, the S&P 500 is still the most widely used benchmark for measuring mutual fund performance.

Notwithstanding that most professionals prefer the S&P 500, it is not an appropriate benchmark for the vast majority of funds. It is relevant only for comparing returns of mutual funds that invest in large capitalization[1] domestic stocks. To help the reader match up the right market index with his or her particular fund's style, Table 5.2 summarizes the most popular indexes in use today.

Table 5.2 **Benchmarking the Benchmarks**

Dow Jones Industrial Average (DJIA or Dow)	30 large industrial companies	Owing to its narrow definition, the DJIA is appropriate only for comparing funds indexed directly to it.
Dow Jones Transportation Average (DJTA)	20 stocks in the broadly defined transportation industry (airlines, trucking, rail, etc.)	Transportation sector funds
Dow Jones Utility Average (DJUA)	15 electric and gas utilities	Utility stock funds
Dow Jones Composite Average	65 stocks in the three basic Dow averages	None
Standard & Poor's 500 Index (S&P 500)	500 large industrial and utility companies	Large-cap-oriented stock funds
Standard & Poor's 400 Mid-Cap Index (S&P 400)	400 of the largest stocks, excluding the 500 stocks in the S&P 500	Mid-cap funds
Standard & Poor's 600 Small-Cap Index (S&P 600)	600 of the largest stocks after excluding the 900 stocks in the S&P 500 and S&P 400	Mid-cap and small-cap funds
Russell 1000 Index	The 1,000 largest-capitalization stocks in the U.S.	Large-cap and mid-cap funds
Russell 2000 Index	The 2,000 largest stocks excluding the Russell 1000 Index	Mid-cap and small-cap funds
Russell 3000 Index	All 3,000 stocks in the Russell 1000 and 2000 indexes	Total stock market funds

Table 5.2 **(continued)**

Value Line Average (VLA)	An equally weighted index of 1,900 stocks followed by the Value Line Investment Survey	Mid-cap and small-cap funds
Wilshire 5000 Index	All NYSE, AMEX, and NASDAQ stocks	Total stock market funds
NASDAQ Composite Index	All of the several thousand stocks on the NASDAQ exchange	Over-the-counter funds
NASDAQ 100 Index	100 of the largest stocks on NASDAQ, heavily weighted toward technology	Too narrowly defined for benchmarking
Morgan Stanley Capital International Europe Index (MSCI Europe)	All European stock markets	Diversified European funds
Morgan Stanley Capital International Select Emerging Markets Free Index (MSCI Emerging Markets)	Many developing country markets	Diversified emerging markets
Morgan Stanley Capital International Austral-Asia, Far East Index (MSCI AFEI)	All major stock markets outside the United States	Diversified international funds excluding emerging markets
Dow Jones World Stock Index	2,900 stocks in 34 countries, including 730 U.S. stocks	Diversified international and global funds

Be alert when comparing returns of popular market indexes with fund returns. When measuring the performance of an investment in a mutual fund, it is important to consider the fund's distributions. Whenever a fund makes a distribution, its net asset value is reduced by precisely the amount of the distribution. Because the fund also fluctuates in value due to market changes on the day the distribution is deducted, the actual price change is usually different than the amount of the distribution. Ultimately, funds distribute nearly all profits and losses to investors, so a fund's net asset value could be unchanged over a period of time in which investors nevertheless made a considerable amount of money from the distributions.

Nearly all of the popularly published equity indexes have one significant failing: The index's return is based on its price. This means that for an equitable apples-to-apples comparison, the investor must subtract from the fund's total return its income payout, that is, dividends paid to the investor over the year.

CLASSIFYING FUNDS

Although some funds almost defy classification, rating agencies, such as Morningstar, Lipper, Value Line, and *Mutual Funds* magazine, classify funds into one or more peer groups. The *Wall Street Journal*, for example, publishes indexes of aggregate fund performance for 10 equity fund groups and 11 bond fund sectors based on data supplied by Lipper Inc. All small-cap funds, for example, are grouped together, forming an index, not of small stocks, but of the small-cap funds.

Most investment advisers suggest using several sources, including Morningstar, The *Wall Street Journal*, and even a fund's returns, and the longevity of the portfolio manager.

There is a lot of misinformation in labeling mutual fund investment categories and styles. Some funds are difficult to classify because managers invest across categories. Other funds change their stripes as managers come and go, or as their sponsors strive to acquire and maintain marketable products. It is important to study the mutual fund's prospectus thoroughly to understand management goals. Then, it is important for you to compare the fund investor's objectives to determine if the fund's strategy is reflected in the fund's portfolio. You should understand the differences between funds within the same peer group to make effective investment decisions.

Distinguishing between active and passive investing is an important criteria when choosing the best benchmark. When you consider a passively managed fund (i.e., an index fund), broad-based market benchmarks can be appropriate. For actively managed investments, considering security selection, timing of purchases and sales, and possibly market timing, you need to pay more attention to the fund's peer group. It is important to determine whether the peer group's funds have similar investment objectives and asset holdings.

BENCHMARKING YOUR MUTUAL FUND

A rising tide lifts all boats, but not all mutual funds, as demonstrated in Tables 5.3 and 5.4. An examination of the spread between the best and worst performing mutual fund categories for 1998 and 2000 shows a substantial difference. Table 5.3 provides a comparison of benchmarks for mutual fund investors on a total return basis for 1, 3, 5, and 10 years. It is worthwhile to compare the total annual return of the Dow and the S&P 500 in Table 5.1 with Table 5.3. What a difference two years can make in the stock market. Notice how very difficult it is to outperform the S&P 500 during these years.

Table 5.3 **Benchmarks for Mutual Fund Investors on a Total Return Basis**

Investment Objective	Year 2000 (%)	3 Years (Annualized) (%)	5 Years (Annualized) (%)	10 Years (Annualized) (%)
Dow (w/div[a])	−4.85	12.66	18.11	17.83
S&P 500 (w/div)	−9.1	12.26	18.33	17.46
Small-Co. Index Fund[b]	−2.67	5.29	11.43	16.19
European Region	−6.19	12.58	15.58	12.33
Emerging Markets	−30.59	−5.34	−2.42	1.59
Real Estate	25.62	.36	10.08	11.33
Avg. U.S. Stock Fund	−1.67	11.90	15.37	15.95
Avg. U.S. Bond Fund	5.82	3.90	5.14	7.59

[a]Dividends reinvested.
[b]Vanguard tracks Russell 2000.
Source: Based on data from *The Wall Street Journal,* January 8, 2001.

This leads us to an alternate strategy that you should consider. If managed funds could not outperform the S&P 500 over the periods illustrated in Table 5.3, you should consider replacing your actively managed fund. How? By managing your own fund. The simplest way to do this is to purchase the S&P 500 stock index and manage it using the Y-Process. Part Three of this book contains the technique and investment strategy for doing this. Table 5.4 illustrates how different equity fund indexes compare. Each year you should stay tuned to the equity index that best matches your fund. If your fund does not match or exceed its Lipper Fund Index benchmark return, then you should consider switching to another fund in the fund family or transferring into another mutual fund family.

Other things being equal, and assuming a fund's portfolio matches up well with a particular market index and produces average performance in its class, you should expect it to slightly underperform the index. Underperformance occurs because fund returns are reduced by management fees,

Table 5.4   **Comparison of Lipper Fund Indexes for 1998**

Equity Indexes	Change (%)
Capital Appreciation	19.99
Growth Fund	25.65
Small Capitalization Fund	−0.85
Growth & Income Fund	13.58
Equity & Income Fund	11.78
Science and Technology Fund	46.77
International Fund	12.66
Balanced Fund	−12.80
Emerging Markets Fund	−26.87

Bond Indexes	
Corporate A-Rated Debt	7.27
U.S. Government	7.82
Intermediate Investment Grade	7.85
Short-Term Investment Grade	5.70
General Municipal Debt	5.61
High Yield Municipal Debt	5.50
Global Income	6.34

Rule 12b-1 fees, and operating costs. Furthermore, to facilitate share-holder redemptions and day-to-day portfolio transactions, funds typically hold a small portion of their portfolios in cash on which they earn only money market interest rates. Of course, better-performing funds in a particular category should beat their respective market benchmarks; any fund that consistently underperforms its benchmark by more than one or two percentage points, annualized, should be put on a "watch list" or sold.

USING A WATCH LIST WHEN A PORTFOLIO DECLINES

Deciding whether a mutual fund is worth holding is sometimes a difficult puzzle. You can't get a clear picture until the pieces come together. A watch list is a useful tool in providing alerts when a portfolio declines.

Investors should always pay attention to all their funds, but funds on a watch list require heightened attention. A watch list is a "yellow alert" status indication on a defensive scale in which increased risk developments spur the "red alert" of a sale. Seven events that should put your fund on the watch list are:

1. *Performance starts to lag.* Events that affect a fund eventually hit the bottom line, so lackluster returns raise the yellow flag. In Part Three, you will learn the mechanics of the Y-Process that immediately signal you when the fund crosses the at-risk trip-wire.
2. *The fund manager leaves.* Check into why the manager left. Check the new manager's objectives and goals. Once you are satisfied with the fund's management goals and its performance comparison with its peer group, remove it from your watch list.
3. *The fund changes its stripes.* Any time a small-cap fund becomes popular, assets tend to surge and the fund will outperform its peer group. In such an event, the fund is likely to drift toward buying medium- or large-cap companies. If a fund becomes too large, put it on the watch list to see whether it continues to do the job you bought it for in the first place.
4. *The fund closes to new investors.* This action protects investors by keeping a fund true to its investment objectives. But sometimes it

happens too late, after the fund has passed its optimum size. Cutting off new investors will not make the fund small and nimble again. If a fund closes, and you observe deterioration in performance, you have a potential reason for selling.

5. *Portfolio characteristics change.* Whenever a fund does something out of character, for example, hiking expense ratios or marketing fees or doubling its turnover rate, proceed with caution. If this warning sign is coupled with other negative signals consider selling.

6. *You receive a proxy statement seeking to change the fund.* Funds need investors' permission to change their objective, the types of securities they buy, and other stated goals. If an underperforming fund is asking to widen its investment scope, it may be a sign that the manger feels boxed in and is looking for a way out. If that happens you may want a way out, too.

7. *Your objectives change.* Much of your satisfaction with a fund comes from its meeting your own needs, goals, and comfort levels. The same fund that has been appropriate for you during the last 10 years may not be a good fit in the future. If your investment focus changes, make sure your funds fit in with your new agenda.

Chapter 6

Why Indexing Makes Sense

When Determining Whether You Should Be in a
Traditional Mutual Fund or a Passive Index Fund,
There Is No Right Answer

HOW INDEXING WORKS

Today, there are thousands of mutual funds from which to choose. If you are attracted to a disciplined and predictable investment method, there are many mutual fund companies who offer an unparalleled choice of U.S. stock index funds to meet a wide variety of investment objectives.

All of the U.S. stock index funds track a specific market index and each allows you to implement a well-defined strategy and style for your own investments at a fraction of the cost of the typical mutual fund. Although each has its own precise and consistent objective, they all share a common strategy; they seek to match the investment performance of a specific index or market benchmark.

A traditional mutual fund buys and sells securities based on the fund manager's judgments about which stocks are likely to provide the greatest return to investors. An index fund simply buys a large number (or all) of the securities listed in an index, seeking to duplicate that index's performance.

The traditional actively managed approach typically gives a fund manager latitude in managing the fund's holdings. As a result, investors in these funds are often not entirely sure how their money is being invested at a given moment. Also, the fund's performance, which is dependent on the adviser's strategies and tactics, comes at a significant yearly cost: typically 1 to 2 percent or more of assets invested.

Indexing's passively managed approach is more objective and predictable and available for as little as one-sixth the annual cost of actively managed funds. As its name implies, index investing relies on indexes that combine groups of stocks to measure the performance of an overall market or specific market segment.

By its nature, indexing emphasizes broad diversification, minimal trading activity, and razor-thin costs. As a result, index investors benefit from a reduction of certain investment risks, the possibility of lower taxable distributions, and the ability to keep a higher percentage of investment returns.

DOMINANCE OF ACTIVELY MANAGED FUNDS

In August 1962, the University of Pennsylvania's prestigious Wharton School prepared an exhaustive study of mutual funds. The study's conclusion indicated that performance records varied considerably but, *on average*, they conformed to the market as a whole.

However, more recently, in June 1999, researchers at the discount brokerage firm Charles Schwab & Co. concluded in a comprehensive analysis that just 17 percent of actively managed *large-cap* funds beat the unmanaged Standard & Poor's (S&P) 500 Index over the 10 years through 1998. The index's 10-year annualized return delivered an astonishing 19.21 percent. Whereas, according to Chicago's Morningstar, Inc., all actively managed diversified U.S. stock funds returned 15.6 percent a year over the same 10-year period. Managers of U.S. stock funds did not just lag behind the market, they were essentially humiliated.

Results of both studies suggest that mutual funds have potentially advantageous attributes that make them worthy elements of an investment portfolio. Key advantages are diversification, liquidity, and professional management. However, management is indeed *professional* only if it generates realistic returns on an investment portfolio relative to the risks assumed. Unfortunately, over those same 10 years, these professional managers were little better than were amateur investors. Somewhat less than one in four of all active fund managers actually earned their salary and bonus.

Choosing the Right Mutual Fund

Throughout the 1990s the market underwent a fundamental change. Because of access to the Internet and other new technologies, investors have taken greater control of their portfolios. There are unprecedented information and investment choices available. The major issue with mutual funds is how you determine which is the right one for you. The elements of your financial portfolio should be a mirror of your investment nature, the one thing that has not changed. However, with so many financial choices it may be trickier than ever to match style with substance. If you are going to choose a fund, I suggest you choose a no-load fund. Next, you should choose a fund that matches your style. Whether you are an aggressive, active, or prudent investor, there are investment strategies that you should consider to achieve realistic returns while preserving your capital when buying mutual funds or stock index funds. If you are unsure of which style of investor you are, take the risk test at the end of Chapter 1.

The Stock Index Fund Craze

Although the overwhelming majority of fund assets are actively managed, exchange traded funds have become more popular through the 1990s because so many fund managers failed to beat the market's S&P 500 benchmark. The 10-year annualized return of the S&P 500 Index-based funds through 1998 were nearly as astonishing as the index they track. Most index funds are lean operations that, on average, have an expense ratio of just 0.54 percent of assets, compared with 1.45 percent for the average fund with a stock-picking manager and research assistants.

The indexing craze has been helped by the growing frustration that many fund owners feel as the tax-reporting season approaches. Actively managed funds can wallop investors with large capital-gains tax bills, especially if high turnover is part of a manager's operating style. Customarily, index fund managers buy or sell only as investors come and go or to adjust for changes in the index itself, so their capital-gains distributions are relatively low. For investors, this distinction means that it is wise to include actively managed funds in their tax-sheltered retirement portfolios.

EXCHANGE-TRADED FUNDS

Although index funds provide you a disciplined and predictable method of meeting your investment objectives, with the reduction of certain investment risks and at a small percentage of the cost of a conventional mutual fund, there is another approach to buying the market. This new approach buys a selected market index through a recent development called exchange-traded funds (ETFs). More inclusive than ETFs are exchange-traded portfolios (ETPs). ETPs were created by the *Wall Street Journal* in April 2001 to include exchange-traded funds and HOLDERs, a Merrill Lynch trust whose structure includes a fixed basket of stocks.

Simply put, ETFs and HOLDERs are baskets of stocks, grouped so that they can be traded like shares of common stock. ETFs provide dividends as do ordinary stock. And, like stock, ETFs can be held for either the short or long term. How a particular ETF tracks the market is determined by its composition, the percentage weight of each component, and the method of calculating the index. For example, one of the oldest ETFs is the SPDR,[1] pronounced "spider." Eight spiders are traded on the American Stock Exchange (AMEX), each with its own trading symbol. The first and oldest is the SPY spider, which represents the S&P 500 index. Since the spiders are capitalization-weighted, any change in price of any one of the S&P 500's stock components influences the SPY spider ETF in proportion to the relative market value of that firm's outstanding shares. The market value of the S&P 500 firms is equal to about 75 percent of the value of all stocks listed on the New York Stock Exchange.

S&P 400 MID-CAP ETF

The S&P 400 mid-cap exchange-traded fund represents the "middle" of the market. Like the S&P 500, the S&P 400 is traded on the AMEX as a SPDR under the trading symbol MDY (pronounced middy). Like the

SPYs, MDYs are not static. Standard & Poor's adds and deletes stocks as conditions change, but a given stock would never be included in both the SPY and the MDY.

NASDAQ 100 INDEX

In March of 1999, the NASDAQ 100 Index was introduced and is traded on the AMEX under the trading symbol QQQ, sometimes called *cubes* by industry mavens. This ETF is heavily weighted by high-tech companies and is rebalanced annually so that the index reflects 100 of the largest and most active domestic, nonfinancial common stocks listed by its parent, the NASDAQ Composite Index. The cubes are a capitalization-weighted index and normally have an 85 to 95 percent correlation to their parent index. However, in the heady days of 1999, when the NASDAQ Composite Index increased its seven-plus-year lead over the Dow, soaring 85 percent, a record gain for a U.S. stock index, the cubes outperformed its parent by 16 percent.

EXPANDED CHOICES OF ETFS

Barclays Global Investors, the world's second largest investment institution, was quick to recognize a new trend in equities; specifically, people who wanted the ability to trade a diversified basket of stocks at any point in the trading day. They created ETFs for the broad market indexes. Want the Dow Jones Industrial Average (DJIA)? Buy the Diamonds (DIA). Want the S&P 500 large-capitalization stocks? Purchase the Spiders (SPY).

Then Barclays expanded the investment choices. They asked: What if investors could choose baskets of stocks by investment style, such as value or growth? What if they could choose to invest by company size, small, medium, or large? And, what if they could select segments of the economy, for example, biotechnology, health care, financial services, computers, or energy?

Thus, iShares (see "International ETFs") were born with some 50 alternatives for the investing public. Broad market investors, looking for ETFs of small-cap growth exposure, could consider IWM—the Russell 2000 Growth Index Fund. Similarly, investors might want large-cap value from the Russell 1000 Value Index Fund (IWD).

AN INDEX FUND THAT MATCHES THE ENTIRE U.S. MARKET

For the broadest possible diversification in a U.S. stock ETF, consider buying a portfolio that tracks the Wilshire 5000 stock index. Vanguard's fund, which debuted in 1992, is by far the largest of a group of funds designed to track the performance of the entire stock market as measured by the Wilshire 5000 stock index. Other companies that offer a total stock market index fund include Fidelity, Charles Schwab, T. Rowe Price, and Wilshire Associates.

Like the market itself, these funds are dominated by large-cap stocks, but they allow an investor to get exposure to the approximately 25 percent of the market not in the S&P 500. Wilshire 5000 is a great way for you to start investing in ETFs and get broad market exposure while making only one minimum investment. It is the real-world application of "modern portfolio theory" (which you will learn about in Chapter 7).

How Does an Index Fund Buy the Stocks of the Entire U.S. Market?

A casual investor might think these index funds own every stock in the Wilshire 5000. They do not. Instead, index funds use computer programs to select a representative sample of the stocks that have the same exposure to risk factors and produce the same return as the entire index.

More than 7,000 U.S. companies are now in the Wilshire 5000 index, whose name is based on the size of the U.S. equity market in 1974, when the index was created. These index funds invest in a selection of stocks that resemble the total market in terms of industry weightings, average market capitalization, price–earnings ratio, book value, dividend yield, and other characteristics. In comparison, an S&P 500 Index fund does hold all the stocks in the S&P 500 in about the same proportion as in the index itself. This technique is called *replication*. Complete replication of the target is the ideal, but sometimes that is not practical and sometimes it just does not make sense. While replication creates a proportional copy of an index, sampling recreates the index's fundamental profile with far fewer stocks. It still takes five hundred million calculations at the end of each trading day to keep Vanguard's Total Stock Market Index fund on track.

While replication creates a proportional copy of an index, sampling recreates the index's fundamental profile with far fewer stocks. The number of stocks held in these funds varies from around 1,100 in T. Rowe Price's Total Equity Market to more than 3,100 in Vanguard's Total Stock Market. Of these 3,100 stocks, the top 1,000 represent 90 percent of the total market. The rest of the portfolio, which represents 6,500 or so stocks in the index, is selected by computer program.

INTERNATIONAL ETFs

Since 1990, combined U.S. and international indexed mutual fund assets have increased more than 3,000 percent. Investing only in the U.S. market, an investor misses the opportunities achievable from 60 percent of the world's equity market. iShares are a Morgan Stanley Capital International fund series that tracks a global international portfolio. iShares are designed to give U.S. investors exposure to specific international equity markets through a diversified portfolio of stock for each foreign country selected.

The iShares series index funds contain many of the largest foreign markets and their major local market stock exchange-traded stock, such as Germany's DAX and Japan's Nikkei 225. Chapter 12 provides more detail concerning the existing iShares, 20 countries, their local market indexes, and the symbols used to trade these iShares on the American Stock Exchange. By investing in any of these foreign countries, iShares would provide investment results that correspond to the price and yield performance of their publicly traded securities in the aggregate as compiled by Morgan Stanley Capital International Index. The intermediate investor should be advised that these investments are purchased through a simple stock trade and are free from the complexities, but not the risks, of foreign investing.

ADVANTAGES OF INVESTING IN ETFs

Although many investors have similar objectives (or goals), very few are exactly alike. Certain ETFs, also known as index stocks, which are traded on the American Stock Exchange, provide each investor the opportunity to select the index that best matches his or her investment style and meets his or her investment objectives. Exchange-traded funds can be used for asset allocation, for following index stock momentum trends, or for balancing your portfolio with convenience and efficiency and they are affordable. Because ETFs are easy to trade, they provide the investor with an ideal vehicle for portfolio management. In Part Three, you learn how to assess and manage ETFs' risk using the Y-Process.

- *Tracking and trading portfolios throughout the day.* Unlike mutual funds, the ETF investor does not have to wait until the end of the trading day to purchase or sell ETF shares. This real-time trading feature on the AMEX provides the investor with the power to react swiftly to market changes. In addition, the investor is able to obtain up to the minute share prices electronically from his or her broker or financial adviser or via the Internet.
- *Diversification.* Buying shares of different ETFs is one way to add important diversification and to reduce risk in your stock portfolio. With ETFs, the investor can hedge his or her portfolio against the potential decline of different market segments under varying economic conditions. Diversifying across several ETF types may help the investor to further reduce risk and reallocate assets.
- *Index tracking.* Unlike actively managed equity funds that attempt to outperform the market, each ETF portfolio seeks to provide investment results that correspond to the price and yield performance of its related market index.
- *Lower costs.* Exchange-traded funds are designed for investors who seek a relatively low-cost passive approach to investing with lower operating expenses and management fees. Typically, an ETF portfolio has net expenses of approximately 0.2 percent of its net asset value. There are no sales loads on ETF stock, but ordinary brokerage commissions do apply.
- *Tax efficiency.* Because ETFs are designed to closely track their respective underlying indexes, they are less likely than actively managed portfolios to trade securities, which can result in high capital-gain distributions. The average ETF's portfolio has a turnover rate of 4 percent per year. Indeed, ETFs generally will only sell securities to reflect changes in the composition of the index.

Additionally, since ETF shares are sold through exchange trading, they generally do not require the sale of stocks and the generation of capital gains that is required by mutual funds in effecting cash redemption.

- *Quarterly dividends.* As with stock, ETF portfolios may pay investors quarterly cash dividends representing dividends accumulated on the stocks held by the respective underlying index, less fees and expenses of the ETF shares. There also may be opportunities for dividend reinvestment.
- *Margin eligibility.* Exchange-traded funds can be bought on margin, generally subject to the same terms that apply to common stocks.
- *Short selling on a downtick.* A key feature for active/aggressive investors is that ETF shares can be sold short at any time during trading hours. Selling a stock short, however, must be done on a downtick, that is, the sale of the stock must take place at a price that is lower than the price of the previous (regular) transaction.
- *Convenience.* Exchange-traded funds offer investors the convenience of investing in portfolios of stocks included in domestic indexes, foreign indexes, and sector stock indexes. The composition of these indexes is readily available from your broker, your financial adviser, or electronically from the AMEX web site, www.amex.com, to determine how your money is invested and how your investment is performing.

SELECT STOCK PORTFOLIOS

Some financial advisers recommend the increasingly popular *select* funds, also known as *niche* or *sector* funds, which would make a nice fit with index funds. Typically, they hold 35 or fewer stocks and may invest more than 10 percent of fund assets in a single name. Select funds invest to deliver significantly higher returns. Proven stock pickers have recently delivered market-beating results with select funds. Chapters 11 and 12 in Part Three provide additional data for advanced investors on understanding the advantages and limitations of including select funds as part of their portfolios.

With time, new investment vehicles, such as select stock portfolios, will proliferate the marketplace to feed investors' insatiable appetites for new and innovative products. With so many financial choices, it will become easier than ever to match each investor's style with substance.

PART THREE

Teaching Sophisticated Investors the Judicious Use of the Y-Process

Part Three of this book is written for the sophisticated investor. As an experienced investor, you probably have developed the habit of investing in stocks regularly, have determined your tolerance for risk, and, as a result, have developed a personalized, diversified portfolio. You have met your short-term goals and possibly your interim goals as well. Now, you are in the real wealth-building part of your journey: obtaining financial security to support a comfortable retirement. There is a problem gnawing at you, though; a fear of encountering a bear on your journey that will maul your goal. In Part Three you learn about a unique *active management strategy* that instructs you on how to assess risk and make trading decisions using the Y-Process. Part Three also teaches you how to use the Y-Process to preserve capital during market downturns and when to reenter the market after the worst is over to enhance total returns.

The Y-Process synthesizes the precursors of change in the market's trend, that is, whether a bull market or bear market is in progress. Its greatest value for the investor is its ability to detect the transition from bull to bear, or from bear to bull, very close to major crucial turning points.

The Y-Process was developed using statistical mathematical analysis of 71 years of Standard & Poor's 500 Index data. The Y-Process signals the investor when to enter the market and when to sell the market. Statistics over the past 71 years indicate that, on average, there have been seven turning points per year. However, this does not mean that Y-Process calls *every* turn with total accuracy. Examination of historic "transition data" indicates that there have been anomalies, that is, occurrences of false alarms and whipsaws. Even with these anomalies, statistically over each year, the Y-Process works very well as evidenced by the fact that in the past 71 years, it has *never* had a losing year.

Chapter 7

Beating the Bear

*Learn About the New Bear Market Hierarchy
and Traits That Affect Investor's Judgment
During the Bear's Rampage*

Chapter 7 is the first in a series of six chapters that teach you about a risk-management investment strategy based on the Y-Process. This strategy will guide you in your portfolio selection and management so that you will enhance your returns, reduce risk, anticipate market downturns, and call market turns. The book provides evidence of a market timing/trading strategy that works for stock portfolios and mutual funds. This investment strategy gets you out of the market in time to avoid most of a bear market, and gets you back into the market to take advantage of most of the recovery. The consequences of this timing strategy are (1) to reduce the severity of the drop of your stock portfolio, (2) to put you in T-bills while you are waiting to return to the recovering market, and (3) to shorten the recovery time to your portfolio's value before the bear attacked.

DEFINING A BEAR MARKET

A stock market index normally goes through three phases before being officially declared a bear market, which is a loss of 20 percent or more from its previous high. Phase one is a *routine decline*, a decline of 5 percent or greater; phase two is a *moderate correction*, a decline of 10 percent or greater; and phase three is a *severe correction*, a decline of 15 percent or greater. Rare circumstances cause the market to slice right through these phases; that is, some cataclysmic occurrence that causes the bottom to fall out of the market. Customarily, the uncertainty is associated with a calamitous event that causes a free fall; for example, the assassination of a president, or a terrorist's bombing of a federal building. The recovery from such events is usually rapid. Normal bear markets typically start with a routine decline, and the chance of a routine decline turning into a bear market has been only 9 percent, whereas approximately 25 percent of moderate corrections become bear markets and almost 60 percent of severe corrections typically become bear markets.

ARE CURRENT BEAR MARKET BAROMETERS OBSOLETE?

Historically, Wall Street stockbrokers defined a bear market as when the Dow Jones Industrial Average (DJIA) dropped by 20 percent or more from its previous peak. This paradigm dates back to the beginning of the twentieth century when brokers used ticker tape to transmit stock prices. However, the market has grown from a few hundred companies to well over 7,800, as it is today, so there is a problem with this historical definition. I believe that a bear market in stocks should represent more than just the 30 blue-chip companies of the DJIA.

If asked, most financial analysts, brokers, and money managers would agree that the benchmark for the U.S. stock market is the Standard & Poor's (S&P) 500 Index, which is a much broader based index than the DJIA. Thirty of the S&P 500 companies are included in the DJIA 30. Unfortunately, most Wall Street brokers and analysts have not broken the paradigm of using the DJIA as the benchmark for determining when a bear market occurs. I believe that the S&P 500, which represent the 500 largest corporations headquartered in this country, better reflects the broader stock market's impact on most stock portfolios.

I favor changing the official definition of a bear market as a downturn in the S&P 500 of greater than 20 percent from its previous peak. During the March/April 2001 downturn, the financial newspapers and TV analysts applied the term *bear market* not only to the DJIA but also to the S&P 500 and the NASDAQ Composite Index, the heavily ladened technology index.

Should a Bear Market Be More Than Just a Number?

There is a problem with using a number for the definition of a bear market. For example, in 1998 the sell-off in stocks from mid-July through August was steep and violent, and the question was raised whether this sell-off truly marked the end of the bull market that had begun almost eight years earlier. The answer was not simple. On the last day of August, the DJIA's closing low was down 19.3 percent from its high. Although the DJIA fell through the 20 percent level briefly the following day, it never did stay down below 20 percent. That intraday low turned out to be its lowest point. The good news in August of 1998 was that much of the decline had already happened and conditions for a severe, multiyear wealth-destroying decline turned out to be just a scare.

How would you feel if the market fell 20.5 percent and then returned to where it started in a matter of weeks? To most investors it would not feel much like a bear market. Bears come in different varieties, likewise, bear markets come in different varieties. The 33.5 percent drop in the bear market of 1987 took only four months to its nadir, but dragged on for about two years before recovering most of its losses. At the beginning of the following decade, the bear market of 1990 was a much tamer bear—its downturn hit the minus 20 percent mark and took the same time to its trough as in 1987—four months. The 1990 bear market made a new high only four months after its trough, hence, its stagnation time was one-third as long as 1987, which had the effect of muzzling the bear.

Far more damaging are bear markets such as 1929 and 1973, which brought on years of stagnation. These types of extended bear markets typically occur because something fundamental goes wrong in the global economy.

THE BEAR'S BITE

You may be part of the investment community that had invested hundreds of billions of dollars in stock or stock mutual funds before the stock market decline of April 2001. Prior to that time, the only serious market downturn most young investors experienced occurred a decade earlier—

the bear market of 1990. What made the bear's bite of 2001 particularly damaging was that so many investors based future expectations on previous successful experiences, a decade of sustained growth. Between July 16, 1990 and October 11, 1990, the S&P 500 Index declined about 20 percent, an unpleasant downtrend but not a severe bear market. Compared to some of the grizzlys of the past, 1990 was a teddy bear market, a short-lived and relatively mild downturn. Since 1900 there have been 30 bear markets; since 1933, 13 bear markets have come and gone; and since 1960, eight bears have attacked.

REALITY CHECK OF BEAR MARKETS

To get a reality check of bear markets, a review of stock market history is certainly useful. The technical term *regression to the mean* is used by statisticians to describe a middle point between extreme values; in other words, new values tend to revert to the "expected value." Applying the regression to the mean concept, let's examine what dangers may lie in the bullish expectations of the twenty-first century.

Table 7.1 contains a summary of stock market declines since 1900, the severity of those declines, and how long they lasted. Statistically, the table illustrates that a bear is likely to strike every three years, although in recent history[1] bears have occurred closer to every five years. On average, typical bears take a bite of approximately 35 percent out of the market (in recent history about 31 percent).

MOOD SWINGS OF INVESTOR SENTIMENT

Chances are, a prolonged downturn will maul the stock market several times during your quest to save for retirement. Are you prepared for these events, or will bears impact your retirement plans? The last event someone saving for retirement wants to encounter is a bear market. Most investors dread their wealth being ravaged in a long-lasting decline similar to the bears that savaged portfolios in the 1930s and 1970s. Would you be able to anticipate or recognize a bear if you encountered one? Not a cuddly bear but an honest-to-goodness *Kodiak grizzly* stock market bear?

In the decade of the 1990s, the relative toothlessness of recent bear markets had helped make bullishness practically a cult among investors.

Table 7.1   **Comparison of Twentieth Century Market Losses**

Market Loss Attributes	Decline (5% or more)	Moderate Correction (10% or more)	Severe Correction (15% to more)	Bear Market (20% or more)
Number of times since 1900	319	107	51	30
How often to expect this	About three times a year	About once a year	About once every 2 years	About once every 3 years
Average loss before decline ends	11%	19%	27%	35%
Average length	40 days	109 days	217 days	364 days
Chance of decline turning into a bear market	9%	27%	58%	100%

Note: Averages are means. Days are calendar days, including weekends.
Source: Based on data from Ned Davis Research, Inc., *The Wall Street Journal Statistics*, as modified by the author for the severe correction of July through October 1998 and September 2000 through mid-April 2001.

Investors were lulled by more than a decade of extraordinary 19 percent average annual returns in the market. Most young investors expected that stocks would *always* outperform other investments, as evidenced by the returns of the 1990s. In a bull market's rosy glow, investors increasingly forget normal measures of value, for example, dividend yields did not appear to matter much in those days. People believed that Alan Greenspan[2] and the Federal Reserve Board would prevent investors from getting into trouble. Ask a typical 1990s' investor what he or she would do in the event of a drop in the stock market and most would exclaim, "it's a buying opportunity!"

A strong psychological shift is required for an investor to switch from a bullish to a bearish[3] sentiment. Such a shift in feeling comes when stock prices go down, and down further, and stay down. When that happens, expectations that a given stock will return over time is lowered considerably. There is a transformation in the investor's perception. Fear sets in; people start moving away from stocks into other types of assets, such as bonds. A severe grizzly market elicits such thoughts as "This is the beginning of the end." The longer the recovery time, the greater the chances that fear will turn into terror. Each investor has his or her own pain threshold. Mutual fund statistics[4] demonstrate that there is a high correlation between a severe market downturn and the number of buy-and-hold investors who move out of stocks and into bonds, money market funds, or the equivalent. This is exactly what happened during the bear market of the NASDAQ Composite Index starting in September of 2000.

Investor psychology can change quickly and change to feed negative market volatility. A real Kodiak grizzly bear market reflects not only a fundamental change in investor psychology, but also a change in economic and broad-based market deterioration. I believe that bear markets should be rated by not only the *depth* of their decline, but also by the *time* for the market to recover to its previous peak. Table 7.2 contains a list of the twentieth century's major bear markets and the recovery times from the market's low to the market's previous peak. The worst recovery time occurred in the crash of 1929, which took until November 1954, more than 25 years, before the faithful buy-and-hold investor's stock value returned to its previous peak.

A NEW BEAR MARKET HIERARCHY

For those who are too young to remember, the bottom fell out of the DJIA, a free fall of 48 percent from 381.2 on September 3, 1929, to 198.7 on November 13, 1929. Then, the DJIA rallied back 48 percent to 294.1 by April 17, 1930, only to melt down a stunning 86 percent over the next two years, finally bottoming out at 41.2 on July 8, 1932.

From the view of investor psychology, bearish sentiment must make a significant foothold. That foothold is a function of the *severity* of the bear's bite (percent of decline to the bottom) and *retracement* (the time it takes to return to the last peak). Tables 7.2 and 7.3 provide analyses of the twentieth century's major bear markets for the S&P 500 and NASDAQ markets. The tables provide the severity of each bear market and its retracement

Table 7.2   Twentieth Century S&P 500 Bear Markets

Date of Peak	S&P 500 Decline (%)	Months to Trough	Years to Return to Previous Peak
Sep. 1, 2000	−25.52	7	TBD[a]
Apr. 3, 1998	−22.5	3	0.39
July 16, 1990	−19.9	4	0.68
Aug. 25, 1987	−33.5	4	1.9
Nov. 28, 1980	−27.1	21	0.96
Sept. 21, 1976	−19.4	18	2.9
Jan. 11, 1973	−48.2	22	7.5
Dec. 3, 1968	−36.1	18	2.8
Feb. 9, 1966	−22.2	8	1.3
Dec. 12, 1961	−28.0	6	2.7
May 29, 1946	−28.1	20	4.0
Sep. 3, 1929 (Great crash)	−47.9[b]	2	25.2

[a]To be determined.
[b]DJIA value. Eventually, the Dow fell 89 percent by July 8, 1932.
Source: Based on data from Ned Davis Research, Inc., *The Wall Street Journal Statistics*, November 12, 1998 (updated by author).

Tables 7.2 and 7.3 contain S&P 500 and NASDAQ bear markets that clawed the buy-and-hold investors, took a major bite out of their retirement plans, and cost them significant profits. In the end, for buy-and-hold investors, the real pain of a bear's bite is how long it takes to recover from that bite. As a simple example of the catastrophic impact that a Kodiak grizzly bear market can have on your retirement plans, I present the following case: If your portfolio dropped 50 percent, it would have to *double*—a 100 percent increase—to make it back to the previous peak value. This doubling takes time just to *recapture* lost capital. During this time potential capital gains are lost, and such a loss is an example of the cliche "time is money," the time it takes to recover what you had already made is called opportunity cost. For Kodiak grizzlys, recovery could take many years. Because of this recovery cycle, investors should be *bear-shy*; that is, out of the market during severe corrections and ensconced in T-bills or the equivalent, for example, money markets funds. In the chapters that

Table 7.3 NASDAQ Bear Markets

Date of Peak	NASDAQ Decline (%)	Months to Trough	Years to Return to Previous Peak
Mar. 14, 2001	−61.9	7	TBD[a]
Oct. 8, 1998	−33.1	4	1.01
Oct. 12, 1990	−33.2	4	0.39
Oct. 28, 1987	−36.8	21	1.48
Jul. 25, 1984	−30.3	18	0.51
Aug. 13, 1982	−25.3	22	0.16
Mar. 27, 1980	−24.9	18	0.30
Nov. 14, 1978	−20.7	8	0.70
Oct. 3, 1974	−51.9	6	0.66

[a]To be determined.
Source: Yanis Financial Services, Inc., June 14, 2001.

follow, I explain how an investor can recognize the approach of all types of bears using the Y-Process.

Since the great crash of 1929[5] the stock market has sustained rather mild bears in comparison. A review of the S&P 500 bear markets since 1960 indicates that we have had eight bears. On average, they lasted 11 months, and each cost the investor about 30 percent. As bad as that seems, it pales in comparison with the most severe bear in post-World War II history: 1973–1974. On January 11, 1973, the S&P 500 closed at an all-time high of 120.24. After a grinding downturn that persisted for almost two years it finally bottomed on December 6, 1974, at 65.01. The worst was yet to come. It took an additional seven and one-half years for the S&P 500 to recover to its previous peak. For comparison, in December 1998, a similar 48.2 percent loss from the market's peak (approximately 1,200) would have sent the S&P 500 Index spiraling down to about 620. Putting this in terms of the popular DJIA, which peaked near 9,300, the Dow would have dropped like a rock down a well to 4,817.

For the benefit of the reader I use the following criteria to determine types of bear markets:

- *Bear Market.* A market that declines 20 percent or more *and* lasts for one year or less.

- *Grizzly Bear Market.* A market that plunges 25 percent or more *and* lasts for one to three years before returning to its prior peak.
- *Kodiak Grizzly Bear Market.* A Kodiac grizzly bear market is one that melts down a gut-wrenching, wealth-ravaging 30 percent or more *and* lasts for three or more years before returning to its prior peak.

THE ANGUISH AND COST OF FOLLOWING A BEAR DOWN A BLACK HOLE

I believe that the investment strategy of buy-and-hold is flawed. Most buy-and-hold investors start with good intentions, but after suffering through a severe decline, they customarily panic and sell. Sick over their losses, some never return, while others wait months or years before coming back into the market. As a result, they miss the entire postbear advance. The buy-and-hold-forever investors employ the slogan, "Stay cool—each time the market takes a dive it recovers *and* goes on to new highs." This statement is true, but buy-and-hold-forever investors don't do very well during recoveries. Instead of earning new profits, they are making up past losses. A case in point: in the 1973–1974 bear market, it would have taken a 96 percent gain to recover lost capital, plus the lost opportunity costs. On average, such a recovery would have taken about 7.6 years at 9 percent compounded annually.

SIX TRAITS THAT CAN AFFECT YOUR INVESTMENT JUDGMENT DURING A BEAR MARKET

In addition to investment risk there is a factor I call "investor risk." Investors cannot control the market. The market will continue to soar or sink, surprising us constantly. However, if we use good judgment and control our emotions during bear markets by simply displaying greater discipline, we can avoid foolish mistakes (personal traits) and prevent all types of grief and anxiety while we save money. The six most prevalent traits that many investors have and my advice for handling each in terms of lessons learned are:

1. *Trading too often.* For many, investing is not just a process about making money. It becomes a hobby. Trading stock can become an expensive hobby. If you are enthused about investing, you will probably make a greater effort to save regularly and invest intelligently. But the enthusiasm, coupled with excessive self-confidence, often derived from successful trades, may prompt you to trade too much. Investors enjoy the thrill and sense of involvement that comes with buying and selling stocks or funds. But every time you trade, you have to make two tricky judgments: (1) possibly selling a stock that has generated lackluster returns, and (2) replacing a poor performer with a potentially better performer.

Moreover, the new stock's performance needs to be sufficiently better to compensate for trading costs and expenses not limited to brokerage commissions. When we buy and later sell a stock, we also lose a small amount to the bid–asked spread, the gap between the price at which shares can currently be sold and the slightly higher price at which they can be bought.

Also, trading can generate tax bills when profitable positions held in a taxable account are sold. The Internal Revenue Service will take as much as a 20 percent capital gains tax for securities held for one year, and 18 percent on securities held more than five years for those in higher brackets. For those in the 15 percent bracket, the take is 8 percent.

Lesson Learned: Investing in the stock market as a game, a hobby, or for thrills can become expensive. The market is where you invest your hard-earned money, to grow, it is hoped, and to meet your goals and objectives, for example, college for your kids, a new home, or funding for retirement. To accomplish these goals an investor should have an investment plan with entry and exit thresholds. If you want to play, go to the beach or take up golf.

2. *Believing that after the pain comes the gain.* After stumbling badly in a treacherous Kodiak Grizzly bear market, many investors expect to recoup their losses within a year. That belief, unfortunately, could turn out to be the investor's next mistake. The critical issue is that in the stock market good years do not necessarily follow bad years. The process is unpredictable; one year's performance doesn't tell us anything about the next 12 months.

If you are looking for a quick snap back, history is not very reassuring. True, the S&P 500 Index bounced back smartly from its 1981 and 1990 annual losses. But, after the declines of 1969 and 1977, the market produced only modest single-digit gains. And, of course, 1973's drubbing was merely a warm-up to 1974's thrashing.

Lesson Learned: While the stock market may revert to the mean periodically, it is a longer-term phenomenon. Evidence of mean reversion, which is based on two data points, is tentative at best. Stocks went up in the 1920s and fell in the 1930s. They went up in the 1950s and 1960s and came down in the 1970s. If anything, the evidence of mean reversion suggests that lean years would follow the strong gain of the 1980s and 1990s.

3. *Sticking with a loser.* Whereas some investors will leave a sinking ship, most will stick with a losing stock. Typically, this decision is not based on a sense of conviction; rather investors are trying to avoid facing a bad decision.

Lesson Learned: Having suffered through a declining market, investors do not want to make matters worse. In times of uncertainty, a majority of investors don't do anything. We tend to regret errors of omission less than errors of commission. The brave investor may put more money into the stock market. But this approach may be throwing good money after bad. What is needed is a sound strategy that establishes thresholds for entering and exiting the market for each stock in the portfolio. A sound strategy will be discussed further at the end of this chapter.

4. *Taking needless risks.* You can invest too conservatively and, at the same time, take unnecessary risks. An investor may have too little in equity (stocks, funds, and indexes). Some investors focus on just one or two companies or on a single segment of the market.

Lesson Learned: If you are going to take the risks of investing in stocks, you should make every effort to assure that you will achieve the associated reward. One effective strategy is to diversify by owning a broad mix of large, small, and possibly foreign stocks/funds. Your portfolio should include both value and growth stocks. Value and growth stocks are not incompatible. With a large mix and broad diversification, you have a better chance of gainful participation in the market.

The rationale is that investment strategies rotate. Growth was king in the 1990s, so much so that many investors had written the obituary for value investing. In 2000, many great value investors hung up their spurs. For those who remained, though, revenge was sweet as value came roaring back, beating growth hands down for the year.

5. *Listening to market prognosticators.* How many times have you heard a television financial reporter talk about the DJIA being down "xyz" points because "there were more sellers than buyers." This statement sounds sensible on the surface for a short term, but for the long term, it is inane. If there were constantly more sellers than buyers, the stock market would eventually close.

Another flawed market prognostication is, "It won't be over until investors capitulate." Supposedly, the climax of the bear market will come in a frenzy of selling, when many investors give up hope and sell everything. Only then, so the argument goes, can a new bull market begin. There is a similar problem with this scenario, it doesn't make sense. The fact is, we all cannot panic and sell. We also need somebody to buy.

Lesson Learned: These prognosticators sound so confident and so convincing, but the truth is they don't have a clue. Forget the confident predictions of the media and Internet bulletin-board pundits. These predictions are, at best, nothing more than informed and, sometimes, uninformed guesses. Put too much faith in them and you could repeat the major blunder of the late 1990s, when investors thought technology stocks and their high price–earnings level were fairly valued.

6. *Believing comments from brokers and financial planners.* Wall Street is the only business in America where it is considered perfectly acceptable to proclaim that your customers and potential clients are "too dumb to invest on their own."

Lesson Learned: Most investors do not hire brokers or financial planners because they believe they are too dumb to invest on their own. Rather, many investors hire advisers because they prefer not to expend time and effort associated with managing their own money. The 1990s saw the rise of do-it-yourself investors, who make their own investment decisions using no-load mutual funds and discount brokers. Full-service brokers and planners are developing plans to reclaim lost clients. It is possible that more investors would turn to brokers and financial planners, if such advisers spent more time helping investors and less time disparaging the typical investor.

The Y-Process can help your decision making during bear markets. In Chapter 9, you will learn how the Y-Process has universal application to assist investors to overcome many of the traits that affect their investment decision making during bear markets. The Y-Process, with its capability to develop accurate and consistent precursors to market downturns, assists investors to take better control of their investing. By following Y-Process rules, investors will not only have the discipline to avoid foolish mistakes, but they will also consistently outperform the market with a probability of 94 percent.

Chapter 8

Schools of Strategic Investing

*Three Schools of Stock Market Investing Are at
Odds with Each Other because Each Believes
Only Its Persuasion Is the True Way to Attain
Investors' Nirvana*

ELEMENTS OF SUCCESSFUL INVESTING

Many people invest in stocks or mutual funds because they want their money to grow conservatively and intelligently and because they are confident in their own judgment. If you consider yourself one of these people, and you should, this chapter contains suggestions that will assist you in becoming a more proficient and successful investor. For example, one of the most difficult tasks for most investors is to build, manage, and measure the effectiveness of a stock market portfolio, a portfolio designed to meet their objectives and goals and to stay within their risk tolerance. If you have reached this level of competence, then you have mastered the science of strategic market investing.

Strategic market investing is creating, managing, and measuring the effectiveness of your stock portfolio. To be an accomplished strategic investor you must know the answers to four essential questions:

1. Which securities should I select?
2. When should I buy them?
3. When should I sell them?
4. How well did my portfolio perform?

Historically, three different investment approaches or schools are used by sophisticated investors to answer the four questions of strategic market investing: (1) fundamental analysis, (2) technical analysis, and (3) efficient markets. Each school approaches the questions of security selection and market timing differently. The answer to the question of how well your portfolio has performed is a function of the risk that you are prepared to take to obtain your desired return.

Whether you are a savvy stock market investor or an investor who would like to improve your investing skills, you should determine which school you subscribe to. In some cases, you may decide that you have multiple diplomas. After reading this chapter you may have second thoughts, and you may want to switch affiliations to better meet your financial goals, objectives, and risk tolerance.

AN ASIDE: HOW WELL HAVE PROFESSIONAL MONEY MANAGERS PERFORMED OVER THE YEARS?

Let's take a page out of how professional money managers measure their performance. Professional managers of equity (stock) portfolios who use either technical analysis or fundamental analysis have a common goal to stock selection. They try to outperform the market, that is, they try to achieve increases in a portfolio's value that exceed those of the market as a whole. For professionals who do not *actively* manage their portfolios, they usually buy market indexes or the market benchmark. Here, two primary representative stock indexes or benchmarks measure market swings. The benchmark most widely followed by the general public is the Dow Jones Industrial Average (DJIA) of 30 blue-chip stocks. But most professionals use the Standard & Poor's (S&P) 500 Index as their benchmark to measure their management skills. By most measures, a manager who can beat the S&P 500 Index has had a successful year.

Mutual fund managers, independent investment advisers, bank trust departments, and other professional investors follow hundreds of companies, employ staffs of analysts and economists, and use elaborate computerized trading techniques to beat the S&P 500 performance. Most of them fail. Over the years, on average, greater than 85 percent of all mutual fund managers fail to beat the performance of the "plain vanilla" S&P 500 Index each year, and they are not the same managers every year. For example, according to Lipper Analytical Services, only 3.5 percent of all open-end equity funds outperformed the market (as measured by the S&P 500 Index) from the end of 1993 to the end of 1998. Over the decade that ended in 1998, only 10 percent of the funds outperformed the market and this was the decade that had the longest bull market in history.

The message is clear: If you buy a mutual fund, the chances are you will do significantly worse than the S&P 500. Whatever their success, managers use variations of two basic investment approaches (schools): fundamental analysis and technical analysis. The third school does not require an active manager, thus I call this the school of "passive management." The balance of this chapter explores the advantages and limitations of these three schools as an approach for strategic market investing.

SCHOOL OF FUNDAMENTAL ANALYSIS

Investors who use fundamental analysis to buy (or sell) stock are called fundamentalists. Fundamentalists fall into two groups: the first is interested in *value investing* and the second is interested in *growth investing*. Value fundamentalists analyze companies, industries, and the economic and market environments to identify stocks that are undervalued at their current market prices. Growth fundamentalists try to identify companies with high growth potential before that potential is reflected in the market value.

VALUE FUNDAMENTALISTS

Value fundamentalists examine every nook and cranny of a company's financial statement. Among other things, they evaluate companies based on some combination of earnings momentum, relative price strength, price–earnings/growth ratios, cash flows, dividend yields, revisions of analysts' earnings estimates, valuation levels, and their earnings prospects in the context of their industry. The purpose of this detailed analysis is to get an idea of the stock's real worth. If the real worth is significantly below the stock's market value, the value fundamentalist concludes that the stock has no significant downside risk and eventually will rise to its proper market value. The legendary Warren Buffet set an all-time record by compounding money at 22 percent for 20 years as a value investor.

With the thousands of companies to review, evaluation of financial statements is a monstrous task to accomplish manually. Value fundamentalists who are computer proficient may construct a computer program model to perform this task, or they may hire a computer programmer to construct an elaborate computer model to account for various economic, corporate, or market factors. The increase in computing power has allowed for an unemotional, statistical analysis of a huge volume of fundamental information. The model can be made to rank stock from best to worst based on expected performance, theoretically removing subjective biases and other limitations that humans might bring to the process. Value fundamentalists may go a step further with another computer program, the terminator, that eliminates the weak companies and builds a portfolio that conforms to specific risk factors. The question has been asked, "Are there limits to the complexity of models one can build?" The answer is, "Cost and time are the only limits to building computer models that filter the data to meet specific requirements."

GROWTH FUNDAMENTALISTS

Growth fundamentalists seek out companies that are expected to enjoy rapid growth based on the anticipated earnings growth of shares that are undervalued. These companies are usually, although not always, younger, smaller companies in emerging industries that carry a higher degree of risk than do established companies. They usually do not pay big dividends, since their earnings are reinvested to finance their rapid growth. Growth fundamentalists have their legend as well; the celebrated Peter Lynch, formerly of Fidelity's Magellan Fund, who garnered average annual returns of 29 percent compounded over a 10-year period.

Growth companies require meticulous and constant analysis. There are dramatic gains to be made in some growth stocks, although more efficient, computerized markets have reduced the number of what Lynch called 10-baggers, but risk increases significantly as well.

HOW WELL DOES FUNDAMENTAL ANALYSIS WORK?

It is safe to assume that at least 90 percent of all stock research in this country is based on a fundamental approach, with a small minority of investors concerned exclusively with the technical approach (covered next). In the final analysis, there is no real substitute for a comprehensive understanding of a firm and a correct assessment of its prospects. The ability to uncover inside information or to accurately forecast a company's future earnings is an invaluable asset but of questionable legality. The stream of future earnings and dividends constitutes what a stock is ultimately worth to its investors. When these earnings and dividends are estimated precisely, true value is defined. All that remains is to purchase those stocks priced beneath their true value and to sell them when they become priced in excess of that value. But few individual investors can afford to devote the time and money required for such value analyses, and those that can, find the value estimation task exceedingly difficult, if not impossible.

Hundreds of millions of dollars are spent on Wall Street each year to estimate company values, their growth potential, and to formulate investment decisions. Judging by historical portfolio experiences of large investors (e.g., mutual funds, pension funds, bank trust departments) who have been able to devote the necessary effort to analyzing fundamentals, it must be extremely difficult to estimate true value or growth potential. Why? Because very few of these fundamentalists have been able to *consistently* derive better than average investment results, and in recent years most have underperformed the market.

There is a good reason for this underperformance. Aside from occasional leaks of inside information (which the Securities and Exchange Commission is vigorously trying to eliminate), most fundamental analysts have access to and analyze the same information. Such basic measures as debt/equity ratios, current assets ratios, historical sales and earnings growth rates, dividend payout ratios, yields, price–earnings ratios, and the like are commonplace and overused. In most cases any predictive value they might have is incorporated into current stock prices so rapidly as to eliminate their usefulness. If any of these measures do have some residual value, it is probably only at the bullish extreme. Companies that appear to be exceptionally undervalued might be isolated for further analysis and then purchased if the undervaluation is confirmed by other factors: subjective or objective, fundamental or technical.

Stock price changes are caused by three factors. The first is a properly recognized change in value. This change in value, as previously noted, is within the realm of fundamental analysis but it is so difficult to measure that it may be eliminated from further consideration.

The second factor is a more or less erroneous change in investors' perceptions of value. Since value is based on what will occur in the future (future earnings, future dividends), it would seem at first glance that with each passing moment the marketplace should logically develop a newer and keener perception of it. But in fact an infinite future always lies ahead and value always retains its basic elusiveness; it never becomes easier to estimate merely with the passage of time.

Then, there is the third factor, which may turn out to be the most important one—investors are creatures of emotion. They remember the price they paid for a stock and this can influence their decisions of when and at what price to sell that stock.

So what to do? Well, consider investing in an index fund or index stock. If you can't otherwise beat the average, you can meet it (and outperform most other mutual funds) by investing in a market index stock or fund. This approach is examined under the school of efficient markets.

SCHOOL OF TECHNICAL ANALYSIS

Technical analysis is a very broad topic because there are so many varieties of this type of analysis. In general, technical analysis attempts to predict future stock prices by analyzing past stock prices. In effect, it asserts that tomorrow's stock price is influenced by today's price. That is a very appealing assertion, because it eliminates the need to perform fundamental analysis. No longer does the investor have to be concerned with earnings, ratios, estimating growth, and appropriate discount rates. Instead, "technicalists" need only keep a record of specific market factors, such as price changes, volume, momentum, and trends.

In contrast to fundamental analysis, which is the determination of value and the purchase or sale of stocks whose price deviates from value, technical analysis is based on two very different premises: (1) subjective estimates of value are simply too imprecise, and are thus effectively irrelevant, and (2) future price fluctuations may be predicted through analysis of historical price movements, resistance and support relationships, and other factors that impact directly on price. Technical analysis is devoted to studies of resistance and support for a company's stock (and to the market as a whole) and to those statistics that are related to price and volume.

For ease of presentation, I have broken down the school of technical analysis into two groups: *chartists* and *market timers*.

CHARTISTS

Chartists are primarily interested in specific information on individual stocks, such as the closing price and the volume of transactions. Chartists are guided by historical chart patterns created by the movements of the stock prices, looking for indications of what is going to happen next. Some of these patterns are known by such picturesque names as "head and shoulders," "double tops," "triangles," "gaps," and "rising bottoms." Chartists also look for cyclical patterns, hoping to spot relationships that appear ready to repeat themselves. This information is then summarized in a variety of forms, such as charts and graphs, which in turn tell the chartist when to buy and sell the securities being charted.

Chart Types and Their Utilization

The three standard types of charts are the bar, line, and point and figure. In each case the amount of information available and its intended use determine the type of chart chosen to record price activity.

The *bar* chart is the most commonly used technical tool. It is simple to construct as it portrays the high, low, and closing prices of a particular stock or stock market average for a particular time period chosen. In the latter regard, bar charts are kept either on a daily, weekly, or monthly basis. The type of bar chart will, of course, be predicated on the time horizon of the investor.

A bar chart is illustrated in Figure 8.1. In this example, the high, low, and weekly closing price of a large-cap stock fund are plotted over a three-year timeframe from August 1997. The figure also contains two moving averages (running through the price curve). The solid line is a 13-week moving average and the dashed line is a 39-week moving average. Notice how the 13-week moving average follows the price movement of the stock much closer than the 39-week moving average, which lags the rises and drops of the actual price changes. This lag is because of the way the mov-

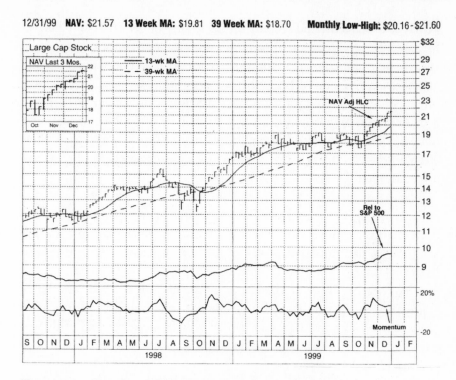

12/31/99 **NAV:** $21.57   **13 Week MA:** $19.81   **39 Week MA:** $18.70   **Monthly Low-High:** $20.16 - $21.60

Figure 8.1   Bar chart of a large-capitalization stock fund.

(*Source:* "Large Cap Stock" Mutual Fund, *Mutual Fund Guide*, Fidelity Investments, special 1999 year-end issue, p. 50.)

ing average is calculated. The 13-week moving average has one-third the number of terms in the average. In addition, at the bottom of the figure, a *relative strength* plot and a *momentum* plot are denoted. These types of plots and their utility will be discussed later in this chapter.

The *line* chart's primary use is to denote the trend of a single statistic. For example, the daily closing price of a stock, a weekly group statistic, or a monthly economic figure would most often be plotted on a line chart basis. In Figure 8.1, if you connected all the weekly closing prices and eliminated the vertical lines that connected each week's high and low, this would be a three-year weekly line chart whose group statistic would be the price trend of all large-cap stocks.

Both the bar chart and the line chart can be plotted on graph paper using one of two types of scales: the arithmetic or the semilog delineation.

The type of scale depends greatly on the desires of the chartist. Chartists who wish to analyze stock price movements on a percentage basis would keep their graphs on a semilog basis. Long-term trend analysis is often more useful on a semilog (geometrical) price scale. Other chartists desire simple short-term trend analysis or stock price movement in terms of points rather than percentages. Thus, for them, a straight arithmetic scale suffices. There are positive and negative factors for each approach, most often hinging on the price level of the stock and the amount of price history under study.

To many, the point and figure approach is a bit more mysterious, and indeed to some, the mastering of the technique of maintaining a *point and figure* chart is a cumbersome chore. The basic difference in a point and figure graph is that there is no distinct depiction of volume trends as there is in the bar chart.

Like the bar chart, a number of different types of point and figure graphs are used depending on the chartist's time horizon or investment philosophy. Whereas a bar chart depicts a daily, weekly, or monthly specific price range, a point and figure chart illustrates trades only as they occur, and in their sequence.

The essence of point and figure charts, which are also called X–O charts, seeks to identify changes in resistance and support by watching changes in security prices. If a stock's price goes up, that movement is caused by support and the chart is constructed by putting an X on the chart (in the X column for that day) when the price rises by an arbitrary value, such as $1 or $2. If the price remains stable there is no entry in the chart. However, if there is an *increased* shift in resistance, the price drops, and an O is entered on the chart (in the O column for that day) to indicate a downward price change of the $1 or $2 value.

When setting up an X–O chart, time is placed on the horizontal axis and dollars on the vertical axis. The dollar unit selected depends on the value of the stock. It is interesting that purchases and sales appear to be made at the wrong times. When an X is entered, it is after the stock has already increased in price. Conversely, when an O is entered, it is made after the stock has declined. The rationale for this behavior rests primarily in the belief that the charts indicate new trends. During an upward trend each high is higher than the preceding high price, and each low is also higher than the preceding low price. Obviously, if you buy this stock and hold it, the return will be positive over this period. However, the return may be increased by judiciously buying at each low, selling at each high, and repeating the process when the cycle within the trend is repeated.

As the chart progresses day after day, a set of lines can be drawn connecting the highs of each day and the lows of each day. The purpose of these lines is to isolate the buy and sell opportunities. The bottom lines suggest a price level that generates support for the stock; that is, this is a good time to buy the stock. Technical analysis asserts that when the price of the stock approaches a support line, the number of purchases will increase, which will stop further price declines. Hence, the approach of a stock's price toward a support level suggests that a buying opportunity is developing. Should the price reach the line and start back up, then you should buy the stock. The opposite occurs at the top line that represents a resistance. Since the price of the stock has risen to that level, more investors will want to sell their stock, which will thwart further price advances. Accordingly, you should sell the stock when the price reaches a line of resistance. After the stock has been sold, you should wait for the price to decline at the level of price support to repeat the cycle.

MARKET TIMERS

Sometimes technical analysts are specifically interested in the market as a whole and use special technical methods that are designed to indicate the general direction of the market. These analysts are called market timers. Market timers look at the market trends and volume thus creating moneymaking opportunities to determine an opportune time to buy or sell the market. Various types of market timers use specific approaches to determining when the market is a good time to buy and the right time to sell. One type of market timer believes that if the number of stock issues rising in price exceeds the number of declining issues by a certain amount for a certain length of time, the market is headed up for a while. This advance–decline theory is also said to work to the downside.

Another type of market timer espouses the Dow theory. The Dow theory, named after one of the founders of Dow Jones, is one of the most widely followed methods of technical analysis. It holds that a significant market move, up or down (a bull or bear market), is underway when a change in the primary direction of the DJIA, is confirmed by the Dow

Jones Transportation Index (which is composed of 20 transportation industry stocks moving in the same direction at the same time). Disciples of the Dow theory do not claim that it will predict a change in the market direction, just that it will confirm it in time for attentive investors to take advantage of the primary trend.

There are several problems with the Dow theory. The first is that it is not a theory but an interpretation of known data. It does not explain why the two averages should be able to forecast future stock prices. In addition, there may be a considerable lag between the actual turning points and those indicated by the forecast. It may be months before the two averages confirm each other, during which time individual stocks may show substantial change.

The accuracy of the Dow theory and its predictive power has been the subject of many debates. W. Gordon tested 20 Dow cycles between July 12, 1897, and October 24, 1967 and determined that the average gain in price over those 20 cycles was 38 percent.[1]

STOCK AND MARKET TRENDS

You may not want to get too involved in all the possible applications of technical analysis. In fact, you may just want to use charts as nothing more than a road map of the market or a particular stock. Trend lines constitute a very important element of charting theory. Trend line analysis of price movements in a stock market chart can aid you in at least examining where on the route you will be making a commitment. Trend lines are drawn on a price chart by connecting two points. An uptrend line connects two or more interim low prices with a straight line in an upward slope. A downtrend line connects two or more price peaks in a downward direction. Depending on the duration of the chart, short-, intermediate-, and long-term price trends can be so delineated.

Chartists like to construct channels. A channel requires two trend lines drawn parallel to each other, one on each side of the price figures plotted on the chart. A simple observation of a stock's chart channel can reveal the precise point in trend when an alert for a trading commitment should be made. According to trend analysis theory, a stock is expected to remain within its channel; if it does not it becomes a "breakout"—on the upside (a bullish indicator) and to the downside (a bearish indicator).

As simple as it is, a trend line can be a powerful technical tool to the novice and professional alike. "The trend is your friend," is the positive cliche to the old "don't fight the trend" slogan. Trend lines give guidance to the short-term trader and the longer-term investor. The trader can use trend progressions for the establishment of a stop-loss order while the investor can let his or her profits run using the elementary trend line approach. Trend lines can also keep the "bottom fisher" from entering the market too early and getting caught in the final declining phase—the "blowoff"—of the stock's free fall. A stock cannot go up until it stops going down, and the breaking of down trend lines will be the first clue that negative momentum is waning.

Stock (and market) trends often tend to accelerate at or near the end of a move. On the upside, the acceleration of support can be likened to the "everyone's got to own 'em" stage. On the downside, the familiar climactic "washout" occurs. Some investors refer to these respective trends as the greed and fear stages.

SUPPLY AND DEMAND FORCES AT WORK

The mere violation of a trend line is not the sole reason a technical analyst becomes concerned. It's the implied change in the resistance or support trend lines behind the shift that is meaningful. An uptrend, by definition, is a series of higher lows followed by higher highs, in that sequence. A downtrend is, of course, the opposite progression. Staying with the uptrend, let's more fully define the higher lows, higher highs progression in terms of resistance and support terms. Who creates the higher low? The higher high?

It is simple logic that a buyer (demand) is the force creating the higher lows in an uptrend. And the persistence of support (demand), over time is what creates the higher low pattern. On the resistance side, the seller (supply) is actually profiling a bullish bent. How? The seller is selling at progressively higher levels. So, an uptrend is not just a series of higher lows and higher highs but actually the portrayal, over time, of the supply–demand forces at work. Therefore, they are bullish signs of support (demand for the stock—buyers) and resistance (suppliers of the stock—sellers). Once these forces begin to change their style, for whatever reason, the technical analyst will be alerted by trend violations. Uptrend violations will most often be spotted by the support factor first giving a clue of change. The higher lows will not follow through. Then the technical analyst will look for signs of a change in the resistance side, which will manifest itself by a change in the progression of the higher highs. Lower highs, followed by lower lows, will be the complete evidence of a trend change from positive to negative.

Remember that stocks often look *expensive* in bull markets, yet they can continue to climb. Stocks often look *cheap* in major bear trends, but they can get cheaper. Trend analysis, while very simple from a supply–demand view of the market, provides an important discipline for letting profits run and cutting losses short.

RELATIVE STRENGTH

One of the oldest approaches of technical analysis and still one of the most widely used is *relative strength*. As the term signifies, action of a stock or a group of stocks is often compared to the market as a whole, so that it can be determined whether the stock is acting better or worse than the market.

Making money in a bull market is not difficult. If the general trend is upward, you would have much better than a 50 percent chance that a dart thrown at a stock table would result in the choice of a winner. In these days of competitive performance on the professional level, relative performance has taken on an even more important aspect. Professional portfolio managers must demonstrate their ability to outperform the market or else investors will invest their funds in an index fund that is guaranteed to emulate the market with little or no management fee. Such passive portfolio management has grown extensively in recent years for at least a portion of pension assets.

Technicians often apply relative-strength analysis first to the market's groups, believing that a strong group is a prerequisite to picking a strong stock. Academic research supports this view. There is an old cliche that a rising tide lifts all boats. Although you can pick a good-acting stock from a broad relative-strength stock screen, it's a lot easier if the tide of the group's behavior is rising.

Many different mathematical computations may be used to calculate relative strength, but the simplest (and most common) is when the daily (or weekly) close of a stock (or group) is divided by a market average or index. Most often, this index is the S&P 500. The result can be related to a specific time period to result in a ratio. If this ratio moves up or down over a period of time, it will indicate whether the stock is acting better or worse than the general market trend. A stock that is moving laterally while the market is trending lower possesses a strong relative-strength curve. A stock that is moving laterally as the market moves laterally possess a flat relative strength, indicating that the issue is acting in line with the general market trend.

Many times, the technical analyst will use relative strength to determine future market leadership or the pending loss of market leadership. Groups that act well during the tail end of a bear market often emerge as the new bull market's leaders. Leaders in a bull market may show signs of losing that status if relative-strength divergence begins to profile a mature trend. Simply said, if the absolute price index of a group goes on to make a bull trend high without the relative numbers confirming, a change in the group's trend may not be far off.

THE WORTH OF TECHNICAL ANALYSIS

Technical analysis is the art of identifying patterns from a chart of the price movement of a particular security or market. Technical analysts believe that profits above the market's overall rate of return can be earned by predicting future price movements based on past patterns. But the past is not necessarily prologue and history rarely repeats itself exactly. Investors who use a market-timing approach exclusively have about the same record of beating the averages as other professionals. Nonetheless, the investor who doesn't make a point of becoming familiar with these techniques is missing out on an opportunity to enhance returns.

Investors tend to allow themselves to be caught up in the market atmosphere of the moment, be it greed, panic, fear, or even apathy. All those fundamentalists looking at the same factors at the same time tend to move prices to extremes. Thus, prices tend to move in trends, and trend following (one of the basic precepts of technical analysis) has a valid theoretical basis. One reason for great sustained bull market trends is doubtless the plethora of optimistic earnings reports. These normally emerge after an economic upswing is well in progress. Investors tend to jump aboard those issues exhibiting the greatest fundamental improvement and bid them up to greater extremes. Such situations offer profit opportunities to technicians trading with prevailing price trends. At the same time, they ultimately spell doom, both for the fundamentalists who bought stocks at the high and for the not inconsiderable number of technicians who bought earlier for purely technical reasons but then fell in love with the fundamentals at the peak. The true technical analyst throws in the towel when prices begin to fall. Fundamentalists just think stocks are cheaper and are therefore better buys than ever. By the time the fundamental news turns sour and the reasons for the decline are widely understood, the process is usually ready to reverse itself. A similar situation, then, works during bear markets as well. Thus, technical indicators are frequently useful in the timing process. There is indeed an abundance of technical stock selection systems. Of course, not all of them work all of the time. (Some, frankly, don't work at all.)

SELECTION STRATEGIES

A caveat worth remembering at this point is that *something* always works best. Computers make it easy to test everything and find the *something* that worked best in the past. But if what works best doesn't have a sound theoretical and practical basis, it is probably meaningless.

Another very important consideration is that different market environments dictate different stock selection strategies. For example, the purchase of stocks priced far below book value per share was very profitable in the 1940s and 1950s. But during the soaring 1960s such systems became relatively unprofitable and new issues, conglomerates, and glamour stocks caught on. Relative-strength analysis also has its place, but it is a useful tool only during certain phases of the market cycle.

SCHOOL OF EFFICIENT MARKETS

Economics teaches that financial markets with many participants, that is, buyers and sellers who can enter and exit freely, will be competitive. In a free and open marketplace virtually anyone may purchase and sell stocks and bonds. In the United States, many firms, including banks, insurance companies, and mutual funds, compete for investors' funds. U.S. financial markets are perhaps the most competitive of all markets in the world. In addition to expecting a return on their investments, investors also bear risks, that is, the possibility of loss or the uncertainty of returns.

FINANCIAL MARKETS TEND TO BE VERY EFFICIENT

Security prices depend on future cash flows, such as interest or dividend payments. If new information suggests that these flows will be altered, the market rapidly adjusts the security's price. Thus, an efficient financial market implies that a security's current price embodies all the known information concerning the potential return and risk associated with the particular security. If a stock is undervalued and offers an excessive return, investors would seek to buy it, which would drive the price up and reduce the return that subsequent investors would earn. Conversely, if the stock is overvalued and offers an inferior return, investors would seek to sell it, which would drive its price down and decrease the return to subsequent investors. The fact that there are sufficient informed investors means that a stock's price will reflect the investment community's consensus regarding its true value and that the expected return will be consistent with the amount of risk the investor must bear to earn that return.

The concept of an efficient financial market has an important and sobering consequence. Efficient markets indicate that investors (or at least the vast majority of investors) cannot expect, on average, to beat the market *consistently*. Of course, that does not mean an individual will never select a stock that does exceedingly well. Individuals can earn large returns on particular stocks, as the stockholders of many companies know. What the concept of efficient markets implies is that you cannot consistently select those individual companies that earn abnormally large returns.

The converse is also true. If you cannot expect to outperform the market consistently, you should not expect to consistently underperform the market either. Of course, some stocks may decline in price and inflict large losses to your portfolio, but efficient markets imply that you will not always select the stocks of companies that fail. If you are so unfortunate, you will soon lose your money and will no longer be able to participate in the stock market.

The bottom line of the efficient market theory implies that you should, over an extended period of time, earn neither excessively positive nor excessively negative returns. Instead your returns should mirror the returns earned by the stock market as a whole and the risk that you are willing to bear. Although security prices and returns are ultimately determined by the interactions of buyers and sellers, there really is very little that you can do to affect a stock's price. Instead, you should select among the various alternatives to build a portfolio that is consistent with your financial goals and the risk level you are willing to bear.

THE THEORY BEHIND EFFICIENT MARKETS

Some individuals boast that they can use a valuation model, or P/E ratios, or some other technique to outperform the market on a risk-adjusted basis. Notice the use of the phrase "risk-adjusted basis." Bearing more risk implies the individual should earn a higher return than the market. To outperform the market and earn an excess return, the investor must do better than the return that would be expected given the amount of risk.

As previously stated, investors who are adherents of the efficient market theory cannot expect to *outperform the market consistently* on a risk-adjusted basis over an extended period of time. Being an occasional winner is not what is important to efficient market theory followers. Being a consistent winner is, because that would be an anomaly. Anomalies are discussed in depth later in this chapter.

Random Walk or Efficient Market Theory?

Academicians have to continue to publish to maintain their position or rank in the university environment. One way to do this is to rename an existing theory by a new catchy name, such as calling the efficient market theory the *random walk theory*. The random walk theory is based on the same premises as the efficient market theory: (1) security prices reflect all available information concerning a company, and (2) security prices change very rapidly in response to new information. As we have seen, a security's price fully incorporates known information and prices change rapidly; academicians say that these changes will follow in a random walk over time. The random-walk term implies that changes in price are unpredictable and *patterns* formed in line charts, bar charts, or in point and figure charts are accidental. If price changes do follow a random walk, trading rules are useless, and various techniques, such as fundamental analysis, technical analysis, moving averages, or any other strategy, cannot lead to superior security selection.

The choice of the term *random walk* by academicians to describe the pattern of changes in security prices is unfortunate for two reasons. First, it is reasonable to expect that over a period of time, stock prices will rise. Unless the stock return is entirely the result of dividends, stock prices must rise to generate a positive return. In addition, historically, stock prices tend to rise over time as companies and the economy grow.

Second, the phrase *random walk* is often misinterpreted as meaning that security values, for example, stock prices are randomly determined, an interpretation that is totally incorrect. Actually, it is the *time of occurrence* or *when* the price change occurs that is random. Stock prices themselves are rationally and efficiently determined by such fundamental considerations as earnings, interest rates, dividend policy, industry type, and economic environment. Changes in these variables are quickly reflected in a stock's price. All known information is embodied in the current price, and only new information will alter that price. New information has to be unpredictable; if it were predictable, the information would be known and stock prices would have already adjusted based on that information. Hence, new information must be random, and stock prices should change randomly in response to that information. If changes in stock prices were not random and could be predicted, then some investors could consistently outperform the market, that is, earn a return in excess of the expected return given the amount of risk; hence, security markets would not be efficient.

The Stock Price Is Always Right

Since the efficient market theory maintains that the current price of a stock properly values the company's future growth and dividends, then today's price is a true measure of the stock's worth. However, according to the school of fundamental analysis, that analysis is designed to determine if the stock is over- or underpriced; but the efficient market theory states that this effort is futile because the stock is neither. If prices were not true measures of the company's worth, an opportunity to earn excess returns would exist. Investors would recognize these opportunities and take advantage of the mispricing and would consistently outperform the market on a risk-adjusted basis by purchasing undervalued stock or shorting overvalued stock.

Academicians have established the efficient market theory as the cornerstone for all modern financial investment courses taught in today's business schools. You just cannot pass basic Finance 101, receive an MBA degree, obtain a license as a stockbroker, or be certified as a financial planner (CFP) or financial analyst (CFA) unless you give credence to the efficient market theory. Well, perhaps you don't have to swear to the credibility of the theory but you do have to pass the final examination using its concepts.

Rapidity of Price Adjustments

For security markets to be efficient, security prices must adjust rapidly. The efficient market theory asserts that the market prices adjust rapidly as new information is disseminated. In the electronic world of the Internet, cell phones, and 24-hour availability of stock market results on television, financial information is instantaneously disbursed to the investment community. The market then adjusts security prices in accordance with the impact of the news on the company's future earnings and dividends. By the time the individual investor learns of the information, security prices probably have already changed. Thus, the investor will not be able to profit from acting on the information.

If the market data were not so efficient and prices did not adjust almost instantaneously, some investors would be able to adjust their holdings and take advantage of differences in investors' knowledge. Consider the example of an expected merger of two companies that had abruptly terminated. If some investors knew that the agreement had been terminated but others did not, the former could sell their holdings to those who were not informed. The price then may fall over a period of time as the knowledgeable sellers accepted progressively lower prices in order to unload their stock. Of course, if a sufficient number of investors had learned quickly of the termination, the price decline would have been a free fall as these investors dumped their stock in accordance with the new information. If an investor were able to anticipate the termination of the merger before it was announced, that individual could avoid the free fall. Every year, there are cases where some investors sell their shares just prior to an announcement, but it is also evident that some individuals bought those shares.

VERSIONS OF THE EFFICIENT MARKET THEORY

The competition among investors, the rapid dissemination of information, and the speed with which security prices adjust to this information produce efficient financial markets in which an investor cannot expect to consistently outperform the market. Instead, investors can expect to earn a return that is consistent with the amount of risk they bear.

Although financial academicians agreed that financial markets were efficient, they were not quite sure how efficient. The degree of efficiency is important because it determines the value the individual investor places on various types of analysis to select securities. Academicians responded by establishing three versions or forms of the random walk or efficient market theory: the weak, the semistrong, and the strong. All three embrace the general belief that—except for the long-term trends where the stock market will advance—future stock prices are impossible to predict.

The weak version attacks the underpinnings of technical analysis; it says you cannot predict future stock prices on the basis of past stock prices. Studying past price behavior, patterns, and other technical indicators of the market will not produce superior investment results. Technical indicators do not produce returns on securities that are in excess of the return that is consistent with the amount of risk borne by the investor.

The semistrong and strong versions argue against many of the beliefs held by Fundamental analysts. The semistrong form asserts that the current price of a stock reflects all of the public's information concerning the company. This knowledge includes both the company's past history and the information learned through studying a company's financial statements, its industry, and the general economic environment. Analysis of this data cannot be *expected* to produce superior results. The implication here is that even if fundamental analysis produces superior results in some cases, it will not produce superior results over many investment decisions.

By far, the most research and the most interest lie with the semistrong version of the efficient market theory. Studies of strategies that use publicly available information such as the data found in a company's financial statements have generally concluded that this information does not produce superior results. Prices change very rapidly once information becomes public, and, thus, the security's price embodies all known information. If an investor could anticipate new information, for example, the "whisper number" of a firm's expected earnings, and act before the information became public, that individual might be able to outperform the market, but once the information becomes public, it rarely can be used to generate superior investment results.

The strong version frankly states that nothing—not even unpublished developments—can be of use in predicting future prices; everything known, or even knowable, has already been reflected in present prices. Thus, not even access to inside information can be expected to result in superior investment performance. Once again, the implication here is that even if an individual acts on inside information, which in some cases produces superior results, that these results cannot be expected and that success in one case will tend to be offset by failure in other cases. So, over time, the investor will not achieve superior results.

This conclusion rests on a very important assumption: Inside information cannot be kept inside! Too many people know about the activities of a company. Of course, most investors do not have access to inside information or at least do not have access to information concerning a number of companies. An individual may have access to privileged information concerning a company for which he or she works. But, the use of such information for personal gain is illegal. To achieve continuous superior results, the individual would have to have a continuous supply of correct inside information and to use it illegally. Probably few, if any, investors have this continuous supply, which may explain why both fundamental and technical analysts watch sales and purchases by insiders as a means to glean a clue as to the *true* future potential of the company as seen by its management.

Knowledge of this inefficiency, however, may have led to its demise; in other words, the inefficiency corrected itself. Insiders must register their trading activity with the Securities and Exchange Commission (SEC). Since the SEC publishes an Official Summary of Insider Trading, noninsiders can track purchases and sales by insiders and act accordingly. Once individuals start to follow such a strategy, the inefficiency may disappear. One study found that a strategy of buying after insider purchases and selling after insider sales failed to produce a return that was large enough to overcome the commissions associated with the trading strategy. Thus, unless the investor had minimal transaction costs (a few large mutual funds may have sufficiently small transaction costs), the strategy did not produce excess returns. This result supports the strong form of the efficient market theory.

ANOMALIES OF THE EFFICIENT MARKET THEORY

Although the evidence generally supports market efficiency, academia has established the three versions to explain away the degrees of efficiency, which raises an interesting question. If the financial markets are not completely efficient what are the exceptions? This question has led to the identification of exceptions referred to as *anomalies*. A market anomaly is a situation or strategy that cannot be explained away but would *not be expected* to happen if the efficient market theory were completely true. For example, if buying shares in companies that announced a stock split led to excess returns, such a strategy would imply that security markets are not entirely efficient.

In his book on investments,[2] H. B. Mayo references papers and studies that identify six anomalies of the efficient-market theory:

1. *Price–earnings effect*. The price–earnings effect indicates that portfolios consisting of stocks with low price–earnings ratios have a higher average return than portfolios with higher price–earnings ratios.

2. *Small-firm effect*. The small-firm effect, also known as the small-cap effect for small capitalization companies, suggests that returns diminish as the size of the company increases. Size is generally measured by the firm's market value, that is, the product of the stock outstanding and its net asset value. If all common stocks on the New York Stock Exchange are divided into five groups, the smallest quintile (the smallest 20 percent of the total companies) has tended to earn a return that exceeds the return on investments in the stocks that comprise the largest quintile, even after adjusting for risk.

3. *January effect*. Studies have found that the small-firm effect occurs primarily in January, especially the first five trading days. This

anomaly is referred to as the January effect. The January effect is often explained by the fact that investors buy back stocks in January after selling for income-tax reasons in December. And there is some evidence that within a size class those stocks whose prices declined the most in the preceding year tended to rebound the most during January.

4. *Neglected-firm effect.* The neglected-firm effect suggests that small companies, which are neglected by large financial institutions, tend to generate higher returns than those companies favored by financial institutions. By dividing companies into the categories of highly researched stocks, moderately researched stocks, and neglected stocks (based on the number of institutions holding the stock), researchers have found that the last group outperformed the better-researched companies. This anomaly is probably another variation of the small-firm effect that the market gets less efficient as companies get smaller. Since large financial institutions may exclude these companies from consideration, their lack of participation reduces the market's efficiency.

5. *Day-of-the-week effect.* Presumably there is no reason to anticipate that day-to-day returns should differ except over the weekend when the return should exceed the return earned from one weekday to the next. However, research has suggested that the weekend does not generate a higher return but a lower return. If this anomaly is true, it implies that investors anticipating the purchase of stock should not buy on Friday but wait until Monday. Investors anticipating the sale of stock should reverse the procedure. If this anomaly is true, it should be erased by investors selling short on Friday and covering their positions on Monday (i.e., an act of arbitrage should erase the anomaly). The existence of the anomaly is generally resolved by asserting that the excess return is too small to cover transaction costs.

6. *Value Line Investment Survey effect. Value Line* ranks all the stocks that it covers weekly into five groups ranging from those most likely to outperform the market during the next 12 months (i.e., stocks ranked 1) to those that are likely to underperform the market during the next 12 months (stocks ranked 5). Several studies have found that using the Value Line ranking system, that is, se-

lecting stocks ranked 1 generates an excess return, hence, the *Value Line* effect. Once again, the smaller companies tended to generate the largest excess return. Although the amount of this excess return differed among the various studies, its existence is inconsistent with the efficient-market theory. However, it may be exceedingly difficult for the individual investor to take advantage of this anomaly since the *Value Line* rankings change weekly, which would require substantial transaction costs as investors would frequently adjust their portfolios.

While most evidence supports the efficient market theory, the conclusion indicates that there appear to be exceptions. Perhaps the observed exceptions are the result of flaws in the research methodology. Furthermore, any evidence supporting a particular inefficiency cannot be used to support other possible inefficiencies; it applies only to the specific anomaly under study.

Using the Anomalies of Efficient Market Theory

Before you rush out to take advantage of these alleged inefficiencies, Mayo reminds us of five sobering considerations:

First, the empirical results are only consistent with inefficiencies; they do not prove their existence. Second, for the investor to take advantage of the inefficiency, it must be ongoing. Once an inefficiency is discovered and investors seek to take advantage of it, the inefficiency will probably disappear. Third, transaction costs are important, and the investor must pay the transaction costs associated with the strategy. Fourth, the investor still must select individual issues. Even if small companies outperform the market in the first week of January, the individual investor cannot purchase all of them. There is no assurance that the selected stocks will be those that outperform the market in that particular year. Fifth, for an anomaly to be useful for an active investment strategy, its signals must be transferable to the individual investor. Just because the *Value Line* rankings produce excess returns in an empirical study does not mean that the individual investor may be able to receive the information rapidly enough to act upon it. The anomaly may exist for those investors with the first access to the information, but not to all investors who receive the recommendations.[3]

UTILITY OF THE EFFICIENT MARKET THEORY

Ultimately, you must decide for yourself the degree of efficiency and whether the anomalies are grounds for particular strategies. If you have a proclivity toward active investment management, you may see these anomalies as opportunities. If you prefer more passive investment management, you may see them as nothing more than interesting curiosities.

An efficient market implies that investors and financial analysts are using known information to correctly value what a security is worth. You may not be able to use public information to achieve superior investment results because the investment community is already using and acting on that information. It is this very fact that investors as a group are competent and are trying to beat each other that helps to produce efficient markets.

The efficient market theory applies to an individual's portfolio and indicates that you could randomly select a diversified portfolio of securities and earn a return consistent with the market as a whole. Furthermore, once the portfolio has been selected, there is no need to change it. This buy-and-hold-forever strategy has the additional advantage of minimizing commissions. The problem with this strategic investment technique is that it fails to consider the reasons an investor saves and acquires stock and other assets. The goals behind the portfolio are disregarded, and different goals require different portfolio construction strategies. Furthermore, goals and conditions change with time, which in turn requires changes in your portfolio. When your goals or financial situation change, your portfolio should be altered in a way that is consistent with the new goals and conditions.

The importance of the efficient market theory to the individual investor is not the implication that investment decision making is useless. Instead, it brings to the foreground the environment in which you must make decisions. The theory should make you realize that investments in securities may not produce superior returns. Rather, you should earn a return over a period of time that is consistent with the return earned by the market as a whole and the amount of risk borne by you. This means that you should devote more time and effort to the selection of your investment goals and the types of securities to meet those goals than to the analysis of individual securities. Since such analysis cannot be expected to produce superior returns, it takes resources and time away from the important questions of why you save and invest.

WORTH OF THE EFFICIENT MARKET THEORY

The efficient market theory can be condensed into five axioms:

1. Investors cannot expect to outperform the market *consistently* on a risk-adjusted basis. (Bearing *less* risk implies that the investor should earn a lower return than the market. The converse is also true.)
2. For security prices to be efficient, security prices must adjust rapidly.
3. Since security prices, in rapid response to new information, reflect all available information concerning the company's stock, price changes are unpredictable and patterns formed are accidental. Thus, the next move in a series of stock prices is unpredictable on the basis of past price behavior.
4. Trading rules are useless, and various techniques, for example, charting, moving averages, or other advertised techniques, cannot lead to superior security selection or outperform the market consistently.
5. The current price of a stock efficiently values the company's *future* growth and dividends. (Stock prices themselves are rationally and efficiently determined by the five pillars of the market: dividend policy, earnings, interest rate, inflation rate, and the company's valuation, that is, price-to-earnings ratio).

Y-PROCESS VERSUS EFFICIENT MARKET THEORY

Normally, it would be unfair and misleading to assert that any one stock selection system or portfolio management strategy is always the right one or the wrong one. The efficient market theory notwithstanding, this book is predicated on a unique technical approach that supplements the efficient market theory. The efficient market theory establishes the generally accepted baseline for the stock market investment strategy. In Chapter 9, I present another approach to stock market investing, which, if proven accurate, is the seventh anomaly to the six efficient market theory anomalies already documented. The anomaly is called the Y-Process anomaly or, for short, the Y-Process.

Chapter 9

The Y-Process Strategy

The Y-Process Uses a Market Model That
Forecasts Crucial Market Turns

STOCK MARKET FORECASTING

Mathematics is one of the fundamental tools of the physical scientist; the means by which physicists and chemists can describe the motions and interactions of atoms and molecules. Social sciences, such as psychology and sociology, involve so many parameters that mathematical equations are not very useful in describing or predicting the behavior of people or groups. Since forecasting stock market turns is in the same category as the social sciences, to be successful, one would have to predict the behavior of investors.

The Y-Process model is founded on two quintessential market concepts: (1) the law of supply and demand, and (2) that stock prices tend to move in trends. For the stock market dynamics of supply and demand to function effectively requires an efficient and competitive marketplace where buyers and sellers meet in an auction process. In this marketplace, there is a buyer for every seller of stocks. But one of these forces is usually more influential since the market is a discounting mechanism, meaning that events, which affect a stock's price, are usually discounted in advance with movements that are the result of *informed* buyers and sellers at work. It is because of this supply and demand behavior that *price formations* evolve due to the convictions of all types of investors—fundamentalists, speculators, technicians, buy-and-hold-and-prayers—putting their money to work based on their established convictions.

TREND WATCHING

A saying often heard on Wall Street is "The trend is your friend." The Y-Process is a model that synthesizes the precursors of change in the market's trend, that is, whether a bull market or bear market is in process. The Y-Process's greatest feature is its ability to detect the transition from bull to bear or from bear to bull very close to these major cyclical turning points.

Two factors are used in determining this transition: the market's *trend* and *moving average*. Technical analysts use trend analysis of stock price movements to aid investors in examining the market's direction and determining the time when the market changed direction. For example, Standard & Poor's (S&P) 500 Index's trend for the decade from 1989 through 1998 is illustrated in Figure 9.1. This decade, the most bullish in stock market history, depicts the market's continual uptrend with some zigs and zags along the way. On January 1, 1989 the S&P 500 was 280 points; it closed at 1,229 on December 31, 1998—an outstanding growth of 339 percent. This growth rate calculates to a 15.9 percent annualized return for those 10 years, the equivalent of doubling your investment every 4.33 years.

Observation of the market's upward trend shows that two major downturns occurred, one in 1990 and the other in 1998. The 1990 free fall (from 367 to 315) was about a 14 percent drop but did not qualify as a bear market; it was only a moderate *correction*. Bears require a loss of 20 percent or more. The 1998 downdraft (from 1,187 to 974) was of shorter duration but a greater loss—about 18 percent—qualifying as a *severe correction* (losses of 15 percent or more).

Reading Market Trend Line Charts

Reading the numbers of Figure 9.1 can be deceiving. The years are plotted on the horizontal axis using a linear scale (equally spaced), but, on the vertical axis, the prices are plotted nonlinearly (not equally spaced). The primary reason for this approach is to compress the data into a small space. However, there is an advantage for the investor. A one-inch vertical rise at the low S&P numbers has the same *percentage gain* as a one-inch vertical

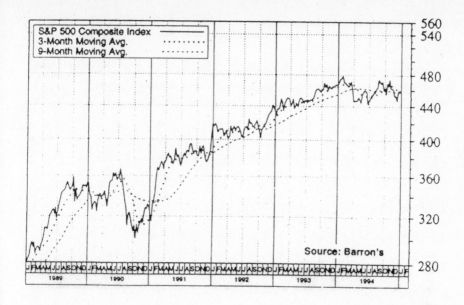

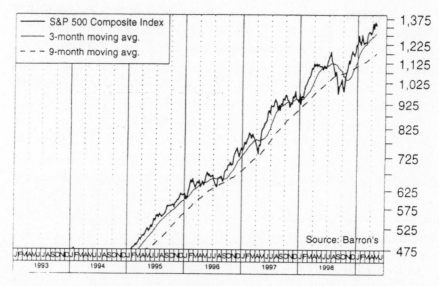

Figure 9.1   S&P 500 Index with three- and nine-month moving averages
(1989–1998). The three-month moving average speed is much
greater than the nine-month moving average speed and
therefore follows the index much closer.

rise at the high numbers. This provides the investor the ability to easily compare price gains on a percentage basis. For example, from January 1, 1989 to May 1989, a 40-point price rise (280 to 320) is a 14.3 percent gain; this is a one half-inch vertical rise. Ten years later, when the S&P 500 is at 1,075, a one half-inch vertical rise is also 14.3 percent gain but the point gain is almost four times greater: 153 points (1,075 to 1,229).

TREND FOLLOWING MOVING AVERAGES

Also displayed in Figure 9.1 are the three-month and nine-month moving averages. A moving average is really a *mathematical trend line*. The primary purpose of a moving average (a process used in statistical mathematics) is to smooth out the numbers of the data points in order to modify minor and irregular fluctuations.

Moving averages can be created using any number of days, weeks, or months. The time duration chosen affects the moving average *speed*. Moving averages can be calculated using different time periods, such as, a 10-day moving average for the short term, a 65-day moving average for the intermediate term, or a 200-day moving average for the long term. The greater the number of time periods that are used, the more sluggish the moving average becomes. Thus, a 13-month average is much faster (closer to the actual number) than the more sluggish 39-month moving average.

Moving averages for the same total time duration can be calculated using different time lengths as well. For example, a 3-month moving average can be calculated using either a 65-day or a 13-week time length. Both are equal to three (stock market) months since the market is open only five days per week (except for holidays). Similarly, a 9-month moving average can be calculated using either a 200-day or a 39-week time length. In both of these cases the smaller the number of days or weeks, the greater the speed or the greater the tracking accuracy.

Moving Average Systems

The array of moving average systems is almost unlimited. Some are based on moving average's rising or falling; others on the relationships between two, three, or more moving averages of different lengths, for example, daily, weekly, monthly, and the multidimensional array of all possibilities.

To make matters even more complex, there are many types of moving averages and various techniques for calculating them.

All moving averages can be categorized into three basic types: simple, weighted, and exponential. A simple moving average is calculated merely by adding the closing prices of the number of days under question and dividing by the number of days. For example, a 200-day moving average would be the sum of the closes for the previous 200 market days divided by 200. This simple moving average treats all entries equally.

The weighted and exponential moving averages place more emphasis on the more recent price activity. Many market students use the weighted or exponential varieties, because they believe that the more recent price action is more important than the price of 25, 50, or 200 days ago.

The three-month and nine-month moving averages presented in Figure 9.1 are the simple type. The nine-month moving average consists of successive averages of its 39 most recent week's closing number. Just add up the latest 39 prices and divide the total by 39. With each subsequent week, the newest closing number is incorporated into the average and the oldest 39-week's number is dropped so that the 39 most recent periods are always measured and all others are excluded. In your review of Figure 9.1 note that the speed of the three-month moving average is much greater than the nine-month.

Stock Market Forecasting Using the Moving Average Trend Line

Although moving averages are primarily used for smoothing out irregularities in a series of market numbers, they can also be useful as the basis to formulate a stock market (or stock portfolio) forecasting system. Trading with moving averages, as the Y-Process does, will never position the investor in the market at precisely the correct time because, by its very makeup, a moving average lags the numbers it tracks.

A close examination of Figure 9.1 indicates that when the moving average trend line is penetrated by the index, the market trend changes direction in both the intermediate and long term. For example, in July 1990 and August 1990, both three-month and nine-month moving averages were violated to the downside, and again were penetrated on the upside in November 1990 and January 1991, respectively. Notice that in both cases, these penetrations occurred after the peak or valley had been reached and that the speedier the moving average the earlier the penetration. Notice how long it took the S&P 500 Index to get back to the previous peak in July 1990—about seven months.

Had you sold the S&P 500 Index when the three-month moving average trend line was first violated to the downside and bought it back when it was penetrated on the upside, you would have saved the 11 percent opportunity cost. In this case, had you exited the market in July 1990 and reentered it in October 1990 you would have made a profit instead of taking a loss during this same period.

One of the conditions of using moving averages in market trading is the risk of whipsaws (false trades). Whipsaws are directly correlated to the speed of the moving average, that is, the greater the speed, the greater the potential of whipsaws. Likewise, the speedier the moving average, the smaller the opportunity cost to the downside and the greater the gain on the upside. The limitations of whipsaws in the Y-Process will be amplified in Chapter 10.

SEARCHING FOR THE OPTIMUM Y-PROCESS NUMBER

The simple moving average is subject to criticism on two counts. First, it assigns equal weight to each of its numbers. It seems logical that recent numbers are more relevant and are more important in the average. Second, as the moving average moves through time, its fluctuations are dependent only on two numbers; the one being added and the one being dropped. Moving-average systems that reduce these adverse effects are called weighted or exponential moving average systems. Both weighted and exponential systems are based on the assignment of greater weight to more recent observations and lesser weight to older numbers.

The weighted moving average is simple but time consuming to calculate. For example, in a 10-day weighted moving average, you take the current day's number and multiply it by 10, the day before times 9, the day before that times 8, and so on. The final number is then divided by the sum of the multipliers for the 10-day period, which would be x divided by 55.

The exponential moving average, which is akin to the weighted version, is simpler to calculate because only two numbers are used in a daily calculation, today's price and the previous day's exponential moving average. A smoothing constant is first determined to be used in each day's calculation.

To calculate the smoothing constant, divide the number 2 by 1 plus the number of days you wish to smooth. For example, in a 10-day exponential moving average, 2 is divided by (1 + 10) or 11; this equals 0.18 for the smoothing constant. The smoothing constant is multiplied by each day's closing stock price minus the previous day's exponential moving average; this result is then added to the prior day's exponential moving average, which provides the new exponential moving average.

Determining the optimum moving average system for the Y-Process required an extensive search. Just the number of combinations and permutations of variants of time duration (called *speed*) and the weight assigned to each observation were overwhelming.

The search for the optimum Y-Process number would have failed had it not been for two technologies. First, affordable high-speed computers that had mammoth storage capabilities. Second, modern, highly capable, computer-processing technology made it possible to develop a computer program to automatically search the various combinations and permutations of the many moving average systems and speed for the optimum value.

THE RESULTS OF THE SEARCH

The results of my search led to an exponential moving average system and a 16-week speed. The baseline portfolio used for the search was the S&P 500 Index. This index was chosen because its database was extensive and available, and it is the preferred stock market benchmark of most market professionals. I selected the index's closing price each Friday as the marker (data point) for the Y-Process number.

The Y-Process number is unique because all other moving average numbers lag the market. The Y-Process number provides the buy-in value of the stock, fund, or exchange-traded fund (ETF) in the event that the market continues to rise. In addition, the Y-Process is a unique *moving average trend line* for Y-Process investors because it forecasts a sell signal for the following week if the S&P 500 ETF penetrates the Y-Process number to the downside. If the S&P 500 ETF penetrates the Y-Process number on the upside, this forecasts a positive change in the market's trend, and this number is a buy signal.

GOING LONG THE MARKET

What happens after the bear market has run its course? Once the bear is exhausted, it retrenches. Ultimately the ETF's price rises until the Y-Process number is penetrated on the upside, signaling a new positive market trend. Simply put, once the market price penetrates the Y-Process number on the upside, you should take an aggressive position by buying shares of the stock, fund, or ETF that you are tracking. This step is called "going long the market." With an upside penetration, the market starts retracing its steps, backing and filling on the way up, until it exceeds its previous market high value, signaling a new bull market phase. This upward moving momentum could take a few weeks or even years before the market reaches and exceeds its previous market high. This point defines a new bull market.

THE RISK INDEX

In addition to the Y-Process number (Y_1) there is an another number that is of interest to Y-Process users. This second number tells the investor how far away he or she is from the dreaded bear market onslaught. This number is called the risk index or R. The risk index is defined as the percentage drop that the market would have to go through before it violates the Y-Process number to the downside. The results of the Y-Process derivation are provided in Equations 9.1 and 9.2. If you are unsure of what the equation mathematical symbols represent, refer to Mathematical Symbols in the Glossary.

$$Y_1 = (P * C_1) + (Y_2 * C_2) \tag{9.1}$$

$$R = [(P - Y_1) * C_3] \div P \tag{9.2}$$

where the moving average speed is sixteen weeks and:

$C_1 = 0.1177$ (smoothing constant)
$C_2 = 0.8823$ (a constant)
$C_3 = 100$ (a constant)
Y_1 = the Y-Process number for next week
Y_2 = last week's Y-Process number
R = next week's risk index (expressed in percent)
P = this week's closing price (Friday)

CALCULATING Y_1 AND R WHEN YOU KNOW Y_2

To assist you in the exercise of calculating Y_1 and R, I have developed Worksheet 9.1. The worksheet is divided into two parts; the left side contains the first six months of year 2000, the weekly closing values of the S&P 500, P, and the calculated values for Y_1 and R. The right side is the area where you are challenged to duplicate these Y_1 and R values using Equation 9.1 to determine Y_1 and Equation 9.2 to determine R. Use all the data on the left side for the equations. To ease your burden, I have calculated Y_1 and R in the table for the first row (week ending January 7). To assist you even further, I have provided you the equations with the solutions for Y_1 and R:

$$Y_1 = (1441.41)(0.1177) + (1402.39)(0.8823) = 1406.99 \qquad (9.3)$$

$$R = [(1441.41 - 1406.99)(100)] \div 1441.41 = 2.39 \qquad (9.4)$$

CALCULATING Y_1 AND R WHEN YOU DO NOT KNOW Y_2

As an exercise, use Worksheet 9.2 to calculate the Y-Process numbers and the risk indexes found in the Table 9.1. Use Equation 9.1 to determine Y_1 and Equation 9.2 to determine R.

This case assumes that you want to calculate the Y-Process number and risk index for a new stock that you want to track from scratch, that is, you do not have the previous week's Y-Process number. In this situation, the solution is to use this week's closing price (P) for Y_2. This is done for the first week only. After that, Y_2 will be available. Note that I developed

Worksheet 9.1 Calculating Y-Process Number (Y_1)[1] and Risk Index (R)[2] for Year 2000 Knowing (Y_2)

Date (Friday close)	S&P 500 (ETF) P	Y-Process number = Y_1	Risk Index (%) R	P = S&P 500 (ETF), P	Y-Process number = Y_{1}	Risk Index (%) R
12/31/99	1469.25	1402.39	3.63	xxxx	xxxx	xxxx
1/7/00	1441.47	1406.99	2.39	1441.47	1406.99	2.39
1/14/00	1465.15	1413.83	3.50	1465.15		
1/21/00	1441.36	1417.07	1.68	1441.36		
1/28/00	1360.16	1410.37	−3.69	1360.16		
2/4/00	1424.37	1412.02	0.87	1424.37		
2/11/00	1387.12	1409.09	−1.58	1387.12		
2/18/00	1346.09	1401.68	−4.13	1346.09		
2/25/00	1333.36	1393.36	−4.52	1333.36		
3/3/00	1409.17	1395.36	0.97	1409.17		
3/10/00	1395.07	1395.42	−0.02	1395.07		
3/17/00	1464.47	1403.54	4.16	1464.47		
3/24/00	1527.46	1418.13	7.16	1527.46		
3/31/00	1498.58	1427.60	4.74	1498.58		
4/7/00	1516.35	1438.04	5.16	1516.35		
4/14/00	1356.56	1428.45	−5.30	1356.56		
4/21/00	1434.54	1429.17	0.37	1434.54		
4/28/00	1452.43	1431.91	1.41	1452.43		
5/5/00	1432.63	1431.99	0.04	1432.63		
5/12/00	1420.96	1430.69	−0.69	1420.96		
5/19/00	1406.95	1427.90	−1.49	1406.95		
5/26/00	1378.02	1422.03	−3.19	1378.02		
6/2/00	1477.26	1428.53	3.30	1477.26		
6/9/00	1456.95	1431.87	1.72	1456.95		
6/16/00	1464.46	1435.71	1.96	1464.46		
6/23/00	1441.48	1436.39	0.35	1441.48		
6/30/00	1452.82	1438.32	7.4	1452.82		

[1]Equation 9.1: $Y_1 = (P * C_1) + (Y_2 * C_2)$
[2]Equation 9.2: $R = [(P - Y_1) * C_3] \div P$

Worksheet 9.2   Calculating Y-Process Number (Y_1)[1] and Risk Index (R)[2] for Year 2000 Not Knowing (Y_2)

Date (Friday close)	S&P 500 (ETF) P	Y-Process number = Y_1	Risk Index (%) R	P = S&P 500 (ETF), P	Y-Process number = Y_1	Risk Index (%) R
12/31/99	1469.25			xxxx	xxxx	xxxx
1/7/00	1441.47	1406.99	2.39	1441.47	1441.47	
1/14/00	1465.15	1413.83	3.50	1465.15		
1/21/00	1441.36	1417.07	1.68	1441.36		
1/28/00	1360.16	1410.37	−3.69	1360.16		
2/4/00	1424.37	1412.02	0.87	1424.37		
2/11/00	1387.12	1409.09	−1.58	1387.12		
2/18/00	1346.09	1401.68	−4.13	1346.09		
2/25/00	1333.36	1393.36	−4.52	1333.36		
3/3/00	1409.17	1395.36	0.97	1409.17		
3/10/00	1395.07	1395.42	−0.02	1395.07		
3/17/00	1464.47	1403.54	4.16	1464.47		
3/24/00	1527.46	1418.13	7.16	1527.46		
3/31/00	1498.58	1427.60	4.74	1498.58		
4/7/00	1516.35	1438.04	5.16	1516.35		
4/14/00	1356.56	1428.45	−5.30	1356.56		
4/21/00	1434.54	1429.17	0.37	1434.54		
4/28/00	1452.43	1431.91	1.41	1452.43		
5/5/00	1432.63	1431.99	0.04	1432.63		
5/12/00	1420.96	1430.69	−0.69	1420.96		
5/19/00	1406.95	1427.90	−1.49	1406.95		
5/26/00	1378.02	1422.03	−3.19	1378.02		
6/2/00	1477.26	1428.53	3.30	1477.26		
6/9/00	1456.95	1431.87	1.72	1456.95		
6/16/00	1464.46	1435.71	1.96	1464.46		
6/23/00	1441.48	1436.39	0.35	1441.48		
6/30/00	1452.82	1438.32	7.4	1452.82		

[1]Equation 9.1: $Y_1 = (P * C_1) + (Y_2 * C_2)$
[2]Equation 9.2: $R = [(P - Y_1) * C_3] \div P$

141

Worksheet 9.3 Calculating Y_1 and R (Year 2000)

Date (Friday close)	S&P 500 (ETF) P	Y-Process number = Y_1	Risk Index (%) R	P = S&P 500 (ETF), P	Y-Process number = Y_1	Risk Index (%) R
1/3/00	1455.22	1402.48	3.62	1455.22		
1/10/00	1441.47	1407.07	2.39			
1/17/00	1465.15	1413.90	3.50			
1/24/00	1441.36	1417.13	1.68			
1/31/00	1360.16	1410.43	−3.70			
2/7/00	1424.37	1412.07	0.86			
2/14/00	1387.12	1409.13	−1.59			
2/21/00	1346.09	1401.71	−4.13			
2/28/00	1333.36	1393.67	−4.52			
3/6/00	1409.17	1395.49	0.97			
3/13/00	1395.07	1395.44	−0.03			
3/20/00	1464.47	1403.57	4.16			
3/27/00	1527.46	1418.15	7.16			
4/3/00	1498.58	1427.62	4.74			
4/10/00	1516.35	1438.06	5.16			
4/17/00	1356.56	1428.47	−5.30			
4/24/00	1434.54	1429.18	0.37			
5/1/00	1452.43	1431.92	1.41			
5/8/00	1432.63	1432.00	0.04			
5/15/00	1420.96	1430.70	−0.69			
5/22/00	1406.95	1427.91	−1.49			
5/29/00	1378.02	1422.04	−3.19			
6/5/00	1477.26	1428.54	3.30			
6/12/00	1456.95	1431.88	1.72			
6/19/00	1464.46	1435.71	1.96			
6/26/00	1441.48	1436.39	0.35			
7/3/00	1452.82	1438.33	1.00			

the solution to this case by empirical analysis. I found that it takes at least 16 to 20 weeks before the Y_1 number gets close to the expected value, that is, Y_1 never quite converges to the exact number; it is always off by a few tenths. The technical reason for this disparity is that the P replacement for Y_2 doesn't have the series of historic values that are imbedded in the actual Y_2 number, hence, the lack of total convergence.

PRACTICE CALCULATING Y_1 AND THE RISK INDEX

As an exercise, try duplicating in Worksheet 9.3 the Y-Process values and the risk numbers found in Table 9.1. Use Equation 9.1 to determine Y_1 and Equation 9.2 to determine R. There are two cases you should practice. The first is when you know Y_2, that is, last week's Y-Process number. In the second case, assume that you do not know Y_2 for the previous week.

THE Y-PROCESS AT WORK

An example of implementing the Y-Process is provided here by assuming an investment in the S&P 500 ETF from January 1, 2000 through December 31, 2000. Table 9.1 contains each week's S&P 500 ETF closing price (P), Y-Process number (Y), and risk index (R). The table uses Equation 9.1 and 9.2 to calculate Y_1 and R.

During the first six months listed in Table 9.1, the ETF had 15 weeks of price decline from the previous week. You can see these losses by scanning down the S&P 500 ETF column. Note, however, when scanning down the risk index column that there are only nine negative risk numbers. The reason for this disparity is the way risk is calculated in Equation 9.2. Risk can only become negative when Y_1 is greater than P. A change from a positive risk index to a negative one indicates that the market's trend was penetrated to the downside sometime during that week. This signals the investor to move from an aggressive position in the ETFs to a defensive position out of the ETFs and into the money market (T-bills or the equivalent). Likewise, a change in the risk index from a negative to a positive number during the week, for example, January 28 and February 11 through February 25, and those weeks that follow with negative signs signal the investor to move from a defensive position to an aggressive position, that is, buying the ETFs.

Table 9.1 Using Y-Process Strategy to Optimize Returns and Minimize Market Risk

Year Friday	S&P 500 ETF (P)	Y-Process Number Y_1	Risk Index (R, %)	Year Friday	S&P 500 ETF (P)	Y-Process Number Y_1	Risk Index (R, %)
12/31/99	1469.25	1402.39	3.63	7/7/00	1478.90	1443.10	2.42
1/7/00	1441.47	1406.99	2.39	7/14/00	1509.98	1450.97	3.91
1/14/00	1465.15	1413.83	3.50	7/21/00	1480.19	1454.41	1.74
1/21/00	1441.36	1417.07	1.68	7/28/00	1419.89	1450.35	0.86
1/28/00	1360.16	1410.37	-3.69	8/4/00	1462.93	1451.83	1.36
2/4/00	1424.37	1412.02	0.87	8/11/00	1471.84	1454.18	1.20
2/11/00	1387.12	1409.09	-1.58	8/18/00	1491.72	1458.60	2.22
2/18/00	1346.09	1401.68	-4.13	8/25/00	1506.45	1464.23	2.80
2/25/00	1333.36	1393.36	-4.52	9/1/00	1520.77	1470.89	3.28
3/3/00	1409.17	1395.36	0.97	9/8/00	1494.50	1473.67	1.39
3/10/00	1395.07	1395.42	-0.02	9/15/00	1465.81	1472.74	-0.47
3/17/00	1464.47	1403.54	4.16	9/22/00	1448.72	1469.91	-1.46
3/24/00	1527.46	1418.13	7.16	9/29/00	1436.51	1465.98	-2.05
3/31/00	1498.58	1427.60	4.74	10/6/00	1408.99	1459.27	-3.57

Date				Date		
4/7/00	1516.35	1438.04	5.16	10/13/00	1374.13	1449.26	-5.46
4/14/00	1356.56	1428.45	-5.30	10/20/00	1396.93	1443.10	-3.31
4/21/00	1434.54	1429.17	0.37	10/27/00	1479.58	1435.62	-4.06
4/28/00	1452.43	1431.91	1.41	11/3/00	1426.69	1434.57	-0.55
5/5/00	1432.63	1431.99	0.04	11/10/00	1365.98	1426.50	-4.43
5/12/00	1420.96	1430.69	-0.69	11/17/00	1367.72	1419.58	-3.79
5/19/00	1406.95	1427.90	-1.49	11/24/00	1341.77	1410.42	-5.12
5/26/00	1378.02	1422.03	-3.19	12/1/00	1315.23	1399.22	-6.39
6/2/00	1477.26	1428.53	3.30	12/8/00	1369.89	1395.77	-1.89
6/9/00	1456.95	1431.87	1.72	12/15/00	1312.15	1385.92	-5.62
6/16/00	1464.46	1435.71	1.96	12/22/00	1305.97	1376.51	-5.40
6/23/00	1441.48	1436.39	0.35	12/29/00	1320.28	1369.89	-3.76
6/30/00	1452.82	1438.32	7.4	12/31/00	1320.28	1364.06	-3.32

In the second half of year 2000, Table 9.1 displays how badly the market rally stumbled. There were 16 consecutive weeks of price decreases from September 8 through December 29. This resulted in the ETF's loss of 174.22 points, which is the equivalent of a moderate correction (–11.66 percent). The worst was yet to come. The ETF continued to drop, week after week, and into the year 2001. The new year provided no relief for the buy-and-hold investor. The ETF continued to plummet and by April 6, 2001, it reached its nadir with a value of 1,128.40. This meltdown passed through the severe correction phase and stopped only a few tenths of a percent from grizzly bear market territory with a –24.55 percent plunge.

As demonstrated in the previous example, the Y-Process trading strategy is both simple to use and cost-effective. Essentially, the Y-Process is a buy low and sell high approach to investing. You may smile at this often-used market cliché, but that is essentially how the Y-Process works. It's a momentum-following algorithm that generates a sell signal when, close to its peak, the market momentum slows, turns, and reverses direction. The Y-Process detects this reversal before most professional money managers realize that it has occurred. The same action happens when you are out of the market, but in the opposite direction. All the investor has to do is to go on autopilot and follow the Y-Process trading rules for any stock, fund, or ETF that he or she owns.

The Y-Process is extremely cost-effective as well. In the previous example, just for the year 2000, you would have been long the ETFs for 27 weeks and in the money market for 25 weeks. In this circumstance, your total gains are composed of two parts. First, what you gained when you were in the ETFs while they were rising in price; and, second, when the Y-Process number was violated, you gained when you pulled your funds out of the ETFs and into the money market. In our case, that occurred 25 weeks out of the 52-week year.

ACCOUNTING FOR DIVIDEND PAYOUT IN THE Y-PROCESS EQUATIONS

Most firms earn a profit and they can retain or distribute those earnings as cash dividends, usually on a regular quarterly basis. When a stock (ETF or fund) goes "ex dividend" or "x-div," that stock trades exclusive of any dividend payment.

For Y-Process users, this could be a significant disruption between this week's Y-Process number, Y_1, and last week's Y-Process number, Y_2. The size of the disruption is directly proportional to the amount of the dividend. Consider the case where the stock pays a cash dividend that represents 5 percent of the firm's Friday's closing price (P). If this dividend is not properly accounted for, it could signal a sell order if the Y-Process number is violated to the downside.

The approach I use to neutralize the x-div effect is to subtract the x-div amount from the previous closing prices of the stock for the past 16 weeks (as a minimum). As a result, this requires a recalculation of the Y_1 for each week that was changed. The reason for choosing 16 weeks is because this is the moving average speed in the Y-Process equation. For greater understanding about this accounting, the reader should go back and reread the section entitled "Searching for the Optimum Y-Process Number.

USING THE SPREAD AS A Y-PROCESS EFFECTIVENESS EVALUATOR

I use the term *spread* as a way of evaluating the effectiveness of two different stock market investment strategies. For example, in Table 9.1 for the first six months of 2000, you were out of the ETFs and in the money market for 9 weeks. During that time, the money market paid the equivalent of T-bill rates, that is, 6.08 percent per annum. Hence, you gained 1.05 percent in interest (6.08 percent * 9/52 = 1.05 percent). From September 15 to the end of the year 2000, the risk indexes were negative. Therefore, you would have been out of the ETFs and in the money market for 16 consecutive weeks. As a result, your money market funds grew 1.87 percent (6.08 percent * 16/52 = 1.87 percent). For the year your total money market gain was 2.92 percent (or 1.87 percent plus 1.05 percent).

At this point I would like to compare two different investment strategies. The first is a buy-and-hold-forever investor (Bahf) and the second is a Y-Process investor (Ypro). If you were a Bahf during the year 2000, you would have suffered a loss of –10.14 percent. The return for the Ypro market timer was a gain for the year of 11.29 percent. When comparing the two market investment strategies, that is, the Bahf and the Ypro investor, the spread is a significant differential of 21.43 percent in favor of the Ypro investor (or 11.29 percent minus –10.14 percent equals 21.43 percent).

There is a caveat to this significant net Ypro gain. The analysis does not take into account transaction costs or tax costs. If your account was a tax-deferred type, then any capital-gains tax cost would be deferred until you withdraw your funds.

Y-PROCESS TRADING RULES

When using the Y-Process market timing strategy, there are three rules that the investor should use when trading stock. I use the term "stock" as a generic term for stock, mutual funds, and ETFs. These rules were empirically developed to conform to the method that was used during the 71 years of back testing. The first rule pertains to selling stock. The second rule pertains to buying back a stock that you just sold or previously owned, and the third rule pertains to buying new stock.

- *Rule one.* When a stock you own drops in value violating its Y-Process number to the downside, you *must* sell that stock as soon as possible after the violation.
- *Rule two.* You may not buy back the same stock in the same week that you sold it. However, you may buy another stock or leave your money in the money market or equivalent.
- *Rule three.* When you buy a stock, you should buy it at or above the Y-Process number. To buy is your *option*; it is *not a requirement.* Just because you have been tracking a stock and its price rises above the Y-Process number does not obligate you to buy that stock or any stock for that matter.

WHY THE Y-PROCESS WORKS SO WELL

The Y-Process works so well because of two fundamental factors: First, all trading decisions are the automatic result of the price action of the stock market without any consideration of fundamental, economic, or political factors. Although theorems, yield curves, and advance/decline lines are valuable instruments, in the end, a market rises or falls on the unpredictable and unquantifiable emotions of humans. That's worth remembering, especially now, when many of the world's markets are newly liberated; and many of the 3 billion investors are feeling, for the first time, the power of the popular will.

Second, the ability to convert human sentiment into numbers that, in turn, can be manipulated by a computer. It is the computer's use of market price action that is caused by trades of individual investors in a free and open marketplace: For each buyer (demand) there must be a seller (supply). Hundreds of millions of shares are traded each day and at the close of the business day, the market's final price provides the consensus of the day's sentiment. An analogy is that of a daily Gallup poll of all stock buyers and sellers. A small change in the market's closing number would indicate that the consensus is slightly bullish or bearish, whereas a large change would indicate a very bullish or bearish mood.

The market is truly a caldron for all human emotions. The market ebbs and flows because of investor's dreams and hopes, disappointments and failures, and reactions to world events. The complete spectrum of investor emotions can be aggregated into swings between anxiety and confidence, with occasional side trips to euphoria and fear. Still, these market drivers do not preclude the development of a computer model that takes advantage of the very statement of sentiment (demand–supply differential) that the market makes each day. The paradox is that the Y-Process's empirically derived mathematical formula eliminates the very basis that drives the market—human emotion. The Y-Process's model that embodies this capability reduces investor's risk, increases stock market profits, and provides superior returns.

There is an old market adage that raises an additional concern: "The only thing constant about the stock market is change." Market timers hope that the patterns in the system will work in the future. I confidently believe that, as history has amply demonstrated, human emotion will not change; it is the one constant in the stock market that we can count on.

A close examination of Figure 9.1 indicates that when the moving average trend line is penetrated by the index, the market trend changes direction in both the intermediate and long term. For example, in July and August 1990, both three- and nine-month moving averages were penetrated to the downside and were penetrated again on the upside in November 1990 and January 1991, respectively. Notice that in both cases, these penetrations occurred after the peak or valley had been reached and that the speedier the moving average the earlier the penetration. Notice how long it took the S&P 500 Index to get back to the previous peak in July 1990—about seven months.

Chapter 10

Validating the Y-Process

*Managing Your Stock Portfolio Using the Y-Process
Enables You to Consistently Outperform an
Unmanaged Portfolio at Reduced Risk*

BACK TESTING

The question posed in this chapter is: "How can I prove that the Y-Process equations consistently provide superior market results while simultaneously reducing my risk?" The results in Tables 10.1 and 10.2 provide detailed empirical evidence that the Y-Process consistently outperforms the stock market. I use the Standard & Poor's (S&P) 500 Index as the stock market's benchmark for measuring these results.

The technique used to verify the Y-Process model is the same as that used by engineers and scientists when they want to measure the effect that a new design or computer program model has on an existing process. The term engineers use for this comparative evaluation is called back testing. At its simplest, back testing is a side-by-side comparison of stock market results by two investors. The first investor is a buy-and-hold-forever (Bahf) investor, who buys $1,000 of the S&P 500 on the American Stock Exchange (AMEX) as an exchange-traded fund (ETF); its symbol is SPY. The second investor, I call Ypro, also invests $1,000 in this ETF but uses the Y-Process model to time when to buy and when to sell the SPY. The rules that Ypro uses for investing are simple. Either she is totally invested in the ETF or, when designated by the Y-Process model, she sells her ETF and moves her money into a money market, that is, the equivalent of a

Treasury bill. Both Bahf and Ypro invest their $1,000 in SPYs on January 2, 1930, and every year thereafter they compare the value of their assets. This back testing comparison continues for 71 years and terminates on December 31, 2000

SINGLE-YEAR COMPARISON AND RESULTS OF BACK TESTING

Table 10.1 contains the S&P 500 ETF for 1930. It presents the index's weekly closing price, the Y-Process number, and the risk index for each of the 52 weeks. Note that Bahf's annual return for the year was negative, that is, −27.74 percent, whereas Ypro had an exceptional year by comparison, with a positive 14.23 percent return. The spread between the two is a whopping 41.97 percent.

You can see in the table that Ypro had two round turns for the year. A round turn is defined as a complete trading loop, that is, a combination of buying and selling the same number of shares of the ETF. In the table, the first sale occurs during the last week in April. Ypro sold her ETF at the Y-Process number of 24.00. This is when the ETF passed down through the 24.00 Y-Process number providing a significant four-month profit of 12.97 percent. The funds from the sale are moved into a money market (equivalent to T-bills) that yields 1.22 percent annually.

In accordance with the three Y-Process trading rules (defined in Chapter 9), when the Y-Process number is penetrated again, this time on the upside, the funds are moved out of the money market and are used to buy back the ETF. Table 10.1 indicates that Ypro bought back her ETF in three weeks at 23.97. However, Ypro received more ETFs for the same amount of money. Shortly thereafter Ypro again sells her shares at 24.04 due to a Y-Process downturn during the first week in June, netting Ypro a gain of 0.32 percent. Ypro remains sidelined for the rest of the year. Ypro nets an annual return of 16.43 percent (excluding any fees, taxes, and trading costs) and is very pleased because she made a significant profit compared to Bahf who *lost* 21.37 percent for the year.

The interesting fact about the Y-Process is that when you sell your ETF, it does not predict how long you will be out of the market. What the Y-Process does do is to project, one week in advance, a Y-Process number that, when penetrated, signals a market turn with a high probability.

Table 10.1 S&P 500 Index for 1930

Date (Friday)	S&P 500 Index Price	Y-Process Number	Risk Index (%)	Ypro Buy (B) or Sell (S)	Y-Process Values	Annual Return (AR)[a] (%)	Total Return (ATR)[b] (%)	Δ ATR	Year	Bahf S&P 500 Index ATR (%)	Ypro Y-Process ATR (%)
1/3/30	21.23	21.18	0	B0	21.23			Δ ATR	1930	−21.37	16.43
1/10/30	21.55	21.23	1.51		1930 S&P 500 =	−27.74	−21.37	6.37%	1931	−37.00	5.82
1/17/30	21.31	21.24	0.34		Y-Process =	14.23	16.43	2.20%	1932	−7.89	38.20
1/24/30	22.04	21.33	3.20		1930 T-bill =	1.22			1933	50.97	75.99
1/31/30	22.79	21.51	5.63		Div =	6.37			1934	32.11	14.90
2/7/30	22.97	21.68	5.61		Market Risk =	34.62			1935	44.90	54.43
2/14/30	23.35	21.88	6.29		Rnd Turns =	2.0			1936	32.11	34.54
2/21/30	22.92	22.01	3.99						1937	−30.97	6.34
2/28/30	23.38	22.17	5.18						1938	28.42	33.70
3/7/30	23.59	22.34	5.31						1939	−21.37	16.43
3/14/30	23.45	22.47	4.17								
3/21/30	24.29	22.69	6.60								
3/28/30	24.85	22.94	7.67								
4/4/30	25.54	23.25	8.96								
4/11/30	25.84	23.56	8.83								
4/18/30	25.75	23.82	7.50								
4/25/30	25.32	24.00	5.22	B0'	23.98 rate =	12.97					
5/2/30	23.57	23.95	−1.61	S1							
5/9/30	23.69	23.92	−0.98	S1'	RoR/T-bill =	0.07					
5/16/30	24.28	23.97	1.29	B1	23.94						
5/23/30	24.03	23.98	0.22								
5/30/30	24.49	24.04	1.84	B1'	24.02 rate =	0.32					
6/6/30	23.52	23.98	−1.96	S2							
6/13/30	22.26	23.78	−6.83								
6/20/30	20.25	23.37	−15.39								

(continued)

153

Table 10.1 (continued)

Date (Friday)	S&P 500 Index Price	Y-Process Number	Risk Index (%)	Ypro Buy (B) or Sell (S)	Y-Process Values	Annual Return (AR)[a] (%)	Total Return (ATR)[b] (%)	Year	Bahf S&P 500 Index ATR (%)	Ypro Y-Process ATR (%)
6/27/30	19.18	22.88	−19.27							Round Turns
7/4/30	20.25	22.57	−11.46				Mkt Risk			
7/11/30	20.55	22.33	−8.68				34.62%	1930		Turns = 2.0
7/18/30	21.77	22.27	−2.30				13.46%	1931		Turns = 2.5
7/25/30	21.5	22.18	−3.17				23.08%	1932		Turns = 3.5
8/1/30	21.11	22.06	−4.49				59.62%	1933		Turns = 4.0
8/8/30	20.27	21.85	−7.79				40.38%	1934		Turns = 4.0
8/15/30	20.7	21.72	−4.91				75.00%	1935		Turns = 1.0
8/22/30	20.79	21.61	−3.94				88.46%	1936		Turns = 2.0
8/29/30	21.37	21.58	−1.00				26.92%	1937		Turns = 2.5
9/5/30	21.34	21.56	−1.02				42.31%	1938		Turns = 2.5
9/12/30	21.5	21.55	−0.24				38.46%	1939		Turns = 6.0
9/19/30	20.68	21.45	−3.73							
9/26/30	19.43	21.22	−9.19					Ave Round Turns For 30s		3
10/3/30	19.42	21.01	−8.17					Ave Round Turns For 40s		3.15
10/10/30	18.11	20.67	−14.12					Ave Round Turns For 50s		2.35
10/17/30	17.16	20.26	−18.05					Ave Round Turns For 60s		2.9
10/24/30	17.74	19.96	−12.53					Ave Round Turns For 70s		3.65
10/31/30	16.94	19.61	−15.76					Ave Round Turns For 80s		3.4
11/7/30	16.09	19.2	−19.31					Ave Round Turns For 90s		3.8
11/14/30	16.89	18.93	−12.06					70 Years Average Round Turns		3.18
11/21/30	17.2	18.73	−8.87							
11/28/30	16.85	18.51	−9.83							
12/5/30	16.43	18.26	−11.16							
12/12/30	15.43	17.93	−16.22							
12/19/30	15.39	17.64	−14.59							
12/26/30	14.85	17.31	−16.56							
12/31/30	15.34	17.08	−11.34		S2'	RoR/T-bill =	0.73%			

[a] AR excludes dividends but includes T-bill interest.
[b] ATR includes dividends and interest.

154

SEVENTY-ONE YEARS OF BACK-TESTING RESULTS

To portray the 71 years' results in table format would take up an excessive number of pages in this book. Instead, I have included appendixes that contain the first year of each of the six remaining decades. These exhibits use the same format as Table 10.1. The upper right corner of each exhibit contains a summary of the annual total returns for the S&P Index and compares it with a Y-Process managed S&P ETF. Also included are the market risk and round turns for each year.

Table 10.2 contains a summary of annual returns from 1930 through 2000. The table compares the performance of Bahf, the buy-and-hold-forever investor, who uses the S&P 500 ETF with the performance of Ypro, the investor who uses a Y-Process-managed ETF. The table also provides two sets of annualized returns (5 and 10 year) for Bahf and Ypro. In addition, the table contains the annual risk Ypro takes during the time she is in the ETF for each year. The risk number provides the percentage of 52 weeks that Ypro remained in the ETF. The last column in the table provides the number of round-turn trades Ypro made during the year. The greater the number, the more transaction costs that Ypro has to pay. In 1954 Ypro had no transaction costs because she stayed fully invested for the year and thus had the same annual return as Bahf. In 1994, however, Ypro made eight round turns (a maximum for the 71 years). Even with all these trades, Ypro still outperformed Bahf by fivefold.

In analyzing Table 10.2 data, four assumptions must be established:

1. *Statistically relevant annual returns.* The difference between the annual returns of Ypro and Bahf must be equal to or greater than 1.5 percent to be statistically relevant. Anything less is considered a stalemate and is not used in the calculation for over- or underperformance relative to Bahf.

2. *Straight line between closing values.* The stock price change on consecutive Fridays is a straight line between the two closing values. The reason for this is to simplify the mathematical solution of determining when the Y-Process number is penetrated. This simplifying assumption allows the date and time of penetration to be determined by *interpolation*, a mathematical technique used by many analysts and mathematicians that estimates a value between two known values.

Table 10.2   Seventy-One Years of Back Testing

Year	S&P 500 Annual Returns (%)	Y-Process-Managed Annual Returns (%)	Unmanaged S&P 500 Five-Year Return Annualized (%)	Y-Process-Managed S&P 500 Five-Year Return Annualized (%)	Unmanaged S&P 500 Ten-Year Return Annualized (%)	Y-Process-Managed S&P 500 Ten-Year Return Annualized (%)	Annual Reduction in Risk Using the Y-Process Risk (%)	Number of Round Turns per Year Using the Y-Process	Y-Process Minus S&P 500 Annual Returns (%)
1930	-21.37	16.43					63.46	2	37.80
1931	-37.00	5.82					86.54	3	42.82
1932	-7.89	38.20					76.92	4	46.09
1933	50.97	75.99					40.38	4	25.02
1934	-1.19	14.90	-7.41	28.05			59.62	4	16.09
1935	44.90	54.43					25.00	1	9.53
1936	32.11	34.54					21.54	2	2.43
1937	-30.97	6.34					73.18	3	37.31
1938	28.42	33.70					47.69	3	5.28
1939	-.01	17.99	11.15	28.37	1.45	28.21	61.54	6	18.00
1940	8.95	8.63					71.15	5	-.32
1941	9.67	7.60					69.23	3	-2.07
1942	18.42	23.89					40.38	1	5.47
1943	24.70	29.37					36.54	4	4.67
1944	18.63	17.97	15.92	17.19			15.38	5	-.66

1945	34.53	32.29					9.62	3	-2.30
1946	-7.26	9.84					57.69	3	17.10
1947	5.52	9.38					61.54	4	3.86
1948	5.49	15.45					51.92	5	9.96
1949	17.05	21.63	10.20	17.41	13.03	17.30	48.08	1	4.58
1950	28.98	28.87					13.46	2	-.11
1951	22.39	23.81					25.00	3	1.42
1952	17.07	17.93					26.92	4	.86
1953	-.78	5.32					50.00	3	6.10
1954	49.30	48.49	22.31	24.09			1.00	0	-.81
1955	30.01	32.11					5.77	2	2.10
1956	6.35	13.72					48.08	5	7.37
1957	-9.83	10.36					59.62	2	20.19
1958	41.24	38.73					13.46	2	-2.51
1959	11.54	13.78	14.45	21.22	18.32	22.65	23.08	1	2.24
1960	.38	9.49					55.77	5	9.11
1961	25.95	24.65					7.69	3	-1.30
1962	-8.43	14.02					59.62	2	22.45
1963	21.93	21.50	10.35	16.95			7.69	1	-.43
1964	15.92	15.73					7.69	2	-.19
1965	12.00	14.36					21.15	2	2.36
1966	-9.52	6.17					67.31	4	15.69
1967	23.12	24.44					13.46	4	1.32
1968	10.62	17.23					26.92	4	6.61

(continued)

Table 10.2   (continued)

Year	S&P 500 Annual Returns (%)	Y-Process-Managed Annual Returns (%)	Unmanaged S&P 500 Five-Year Return Annualized (%)	Y-Process-Managed S&P 500 Five-Year Return Annualized (%)	Unmanaged S&P 500 Ten-Year Return Annualized (%)	Y-Process-Managed S&P 500 Ten-Year Return Annualized (%)	Annual Reduction in Risk Using the Y-Process Risk (%)	Number of Round Turns per Year Using the Y-Process	Y-Process Minus S&P 500 Annual Returns (%)
1969	-7.93	9.38	4.91	14.14	7.60	15.54	76.92	4	17.31
1970	3.51	23.25					61.54	1	19.74
1971	13.80	19.59					34.62	5	5.79
1972	18.30	20.15					19.23	7	1.85
1973	-13.91	7.84					69.23	3	21.75
1974	-24.47	13.35	-1.96	16.70			88.46	3	37.82
1975	35.63	41.63					25.00	3	6.00
1976	22.92	13.40					21.15	3	-9.52
1977	-6.59	9.27					80.77	4	15.86
1978	6.34	19.94					51.92	2	13.60
1979	15.02	21.16	13.75	21.79	5.61	18.63	28.85	4	6.14
1980	30.31	36.53					23.08	2	6.22
1981	-4.32	16.64					63.46	6	20.96
1982	19.64	36.72					51.92	2	17.08
1983	21.57	26.30					25.00	4	4.73

1984	5.90	16.66	13.94	26.25			55.77	5	10.76
1985	30.07	33.47					19.23	3	3.40
1986	18.04	22.47					19.23	3	4.43
1987	5.60	33.29					28.85	3	27.69
1988	15.90	16.53					42.31	6	.63
1989	30.38	29.98	19.63	26.97	16.75	26.61	7.69	2	-.40
1990	-2.90	12.44					65.38	5	15.34
1991	29.24	33.76					17.31	5	4.52
1992	7.30	8.81					21.15	4	1.51
1993	9.76	9.92					11.54	5	.16
1994	1.33	8.31	8.41	14.27			48.08	8	6.98
1995	36.35	36.35					1.00	1	.00
1996	22.27	22.69					11.54	2	.42
1997	32.55	34.74					13.46	2	2.19
1998	27.85	34.95					21.15	2	7.10
1999	19.55	23.13	26.97	30.06	17.33	21.91	18.31	4	3.58
2000	-10.14	11.29					47.27	6	21.43
71-Yr Ave (geo mean) =				28.73			3.32		

Note: An average of 39.3% less risk is the equivalent of 20.5 weeks out of the market. On average there are 3.2 round-turn trades per year over the 71 years analyzed. The Y-Process underperformed the S&P 500 for 1941 (2.1%), 1945 (2.3%), 1958 (2.5%), and 1976 (9.5%).

3. *Intraweek whipsaws.* Because of the straight-line assumption between consecutive Fridays, intraday and intraweek whipsaws cannot occur using historical data. However, in actuality, whipsaws do happen in the market, and they can have a significant impact when using the Y-Process as your investment strategy. I have developed certain rules to mollify the impact of whipsaws when using the Y-Process. These rules were discussed in detail in Chapter 9.

4. *Transaction costs, fees, or taxes.* For the purpose of comparing apples with apples, the analysis does not take into account transaction costs, fees, or taxes. Since these costs can be significant in reducing the returns, the topic of cost containment is covered in Chapter 11.

CONCLUSIONS FROM 71 YEARS OF BACK TESTING

Table 10.3 summarizes the empirical results of back testing 71 years of the ETFs. Using the first assumption of the boundary conditions established earlier, 15 years of return stalemates, that is, ties, are excluded. An analysis of the remaining 56 years of returns indicates that the Y-Process *outperforms* Bahf in 52 of the 56 years, yielding an accuracy of 93 percent in successfully calling market turns to increase investors' profits. These statistics are startling!

In examining Bahf's and Ypro's returns in detail, Bahf had 15 years of negative annual total returns of greater than 1.5 percent. This compares to *none* for Ypro. In the 71 years of back testing, there were only four years—1941, 1945, 1958, and 1976—that Ypro underperformed Bahf and three of those were less than a 2.5 percent difference. The significance of these outstanding Y-Process results cannot be overstated.

Table 10.2 provides two columns of additional attributes. The first is a measure of Y-Process's risk exposure. The smaller the number, the lower the risk. The second is the average number of round turns it takes to obtain the Y-Process's outstanding annual gains. The costs involved for an average of three round-turn trades is small relative to the gains obtained.

Table 10.3   Using the Y-Process-Managed S&P 500 versus Using a
Passive Strategy

Number of ties of the Y-Process-managed S&P 500 and the buy-and-hold S&P 500 Index[a]	15
Number of times the Y-Process-managed S&P 500 *outperformed* the S&P 500 Index	52
Number of times the Y-Process-managed S&P 500 *underperformed* the S&P 500 Index	4
Number of years (1930 through 2000)	71
Number of *negative* annual total returns of the S&P 500 in 71 years	17
Number of *negative* returns of Y-Process-managed S&P 500 in 71 years	0
Reduction in risk exposure of the Y-Process-managed S&P 500 in 71 years.	28%
Market risk of the benchmark S&P 500 in 71 years	100%
Average number of round turns per year using the Y-Process in 71 years.	3.30

[a]A tie occurs if the difference between the Y-Process-managed S&P 500 and the S&P 500 Index returns is less than ±1.5%.
Note: This table has been updated to include 2000.

RISK AVERSION USING THE Y-PROCESS

There are many ways of defining risk, and there are elements of risk in every investment. In essence, anything that causes your investment to be-have differently from what you would expect can be called risk. Because risk is not one-dimensional, there is no single definition or measurement that can provide an accurate picture of an investment's total risk for every person. For the purpose of this book, I define risk, for Y-Process users, as the percentage of time you are in the market each year. Thus, any time you are in the stock market you are at 100 percent risk, and when you are out of the stock market and in the money market (T-bills or equivalent) you are at zero risk.

A group of numbers at the top center of Table 10.1 contains a summary of the 1930's ETF's statistics. One of these is "market risk," which has a value of 34.62 percent. Using my definition of risk, 34.62 percent repre-sents 18 weeks of being in the ETF during the year, while ensconced in T-bills for the balance of the year. The money market interest accumulated from the 34 weeks while out of the ETF is added to the dividends received from ETF ownership during the 18 weeks of being in the ETF during that time.

Y-PROCESS VERSUS EFFICIENT MARKET THEORY

Chapter 8 discussed the three schools that are followed today for investors to make a profit. Before the advent of the efficient market theory, most market analysts were divided between the two schools: fundamental analysis and technical analysis. Fundamental analysts look to basic economic factors to estimate the intrinsic value (the expected risk and return) of any given security. The school of technical analysis uses mechanical rules to look for recurring patterns in such things as trading volume, price movements, and odd-lot trading. From these patterns, the results of opinions and actions of those in the market, technical analysts hope to determine the beginnings of a change in prices and to profit from that change. Technical analysts believe that the markets' opinion is summed up in the behavior of investors. This behavior is reflected in the prices and the enthusiasm with which the stocks are bought (volume). Technical analysts hope to improve their investment returns by trading on what they believe is investor's lack of historic perspective: They believe investors overbuy, oversell, and repeat their mistakes.

In the school of efficient markets, rule one states that investors cannot expect to beat the averages consistently. Technically, back testing results demonstrated that the Y-Process did not consistently outperform the market over the years *if* one uses the definition of 100 percent of the time. However, one of Webster's definitions of consistent is "marked by harmony, regularity, or steady continuity." Since Ypro outperformed Bahf 93 percent of the time over a 71-year time span, I consider this pretty consistent. Moreover, Ypro *never had a losing year*, whereas Bahf had 17 losing years. These statistics are very compelling and dependable enough to provide the Y-Process investor with a strategic investment tool that exceeds by far a strategy of buying and holding the market.

The efficient market theory dampened enthusiasm for technical analysis for a period of time. I believe that the Y-Process form of technical analysis will be discovered and used by investors for market timing of their individual portfolios. The distinguishing and yet paradoxical feature of the Y-Process is that it is based on the fundamental premise of the efficient market theory; that is, each firm's security valuation is efficiently established because the marketplace is open to all investors and information flows quickly without restrictions to all investors.

CAN THE EFFICIENT MARKET THEORY COEXIST WITH THE Y-PROCESS?

The efficient market theory cannot coexist with the Y-process. This may surprise you after the previous statement about the market's efficiency in setting a security's value. The empirical results of back testing the Y-Process have provided sufficient evidence that an investor who uses the Y-Process can time the market. Interestingly, when including ties, a Y-Process market timer has a 94 percent chance (67/71) to be equal to or to be outperforming the market based on historical evidence.

THE PROBLEMS WITH THE EFFICIENT MARKET THEORY

A reexamination of the efficient market theory indicates that its problems rest with (1) a poor choice of terminology, and (2) a quantum jump in conclusions. The derivation of the efficient market theory started with a sample model of a stock's valuation, which suggested that its value depends on a firm's earnings, its dividend policy, and the investors' required rate of return. According to this dividend-growth model, future dividends should be discounted back to the present to determine a stock's value. An alternate to the dividend-growth model is the use of price–earnings ratios (P/Es) and forecasted earnings to determine if the stock should be purchased. Both the dividend-growth model and the use of P/Es place emphasis on future earnings and dividends. Risk is also incorporated into the valuation of stock through the application of the capital-asset pricing model (CAPM). The CAPM suggests that the greater the risk, the more investors expect as a return on their investment.

Financial securities are bought and sold in competitive financial markets. This competition as well as the rapid dissemination of information among investors and the rapid changes in security prices result in efficient security markets. The efficient market theory suggests that the individual investor cannot expect to consistently outperform the market on a risk-adjusted return.

The previous two paragraphs illustrate that the problems with the efficient market theory are first, that a firm's stock value is based on future earnings and dividends, which seems logical. Next, in the second paragraph, we jump to "efficient security markets," which is undefined but the reader probably assumes they pertain to all the individual firms' stock because they have been "bought and sold in competitive financial markets." This also seems logical. However, the next step takes a major leap; a hypothesis called the "efficient market theory," which states that "the investor cannot expect to consistently outperform the market." What is this *market* that the hypothesis refers to? Is it the sum of all the firms' stocks listed on the exchanges or is it the Dow Jones Industrial Average (DJIA), the S&P 500 Index, or some other index? Does efficient market mean that if individual firms are efficient then the sum of all firms—*the market*—has to be efficient? Apparently it does according to the efficient market theory.

If this is the case, how could back testing of the Y-Process outperform the market? There are two reasons for Y-process's success. The first is that the "efficient market theory" is a misnomer. It really should be labeled the "efficient securities theory" because the efficiencies apply to a firm's security not to the *market* as a whole. The second reason is that the Y-Process does not treat the market as if it were an individual firm's stock. If the market were treated like a stock, what would the market's valuation be? What dividend policy would the market have? What are the investors' required rates of return? If we could determine the S&P 500 Index's earnings or the Wilshire 5000 Index's earnings, would they be meaningful numbers? These are interesting questions, especially when using the S&P 500 Index as the market's proxy. It is a capitalization-weighted index. This means that the largest companies have the most impact on the S&P 500 Index.

CAN THE Y-PROCESS BEAT THE MARKET?

All the mathematics thus far fly in the face of rule one of the efficient market theory: "You cannot beat the market consistently." Now we may quibble over the exact definition of consistency but by the ground rules previously established, the Y-Process successfully outperformed the market

52 out of 56 years in the last 71 years—excluding ties. Moreover, a tally of the average annual total returns over the last 40 years indicates that the Y-Process had a momentous advantage in returns over a passive (buy-and-hold) strategy—20.7 to 11.8 percent.

WHY THE Y-PROCESS OUTPERFORMS THE MARKET

The Y-Process can call market turns successfully because it treats the S&P 500 ETF different from a stock in that it has characteristics and parameters that are different from an individual firm's stock. The ETF's earnings, dividend policy, and growth potential are meaningless when it comes to determining whether the market's trend is about to change. What is important is how the market's ETF translates investor's emotions into numbers.

Eliminating Emotion

The heart of the Y-Process's market model is its use of price momentum, which is caused by the trades of individual investors or money managers. For the market to work there must be a buyer for each seller and vice versa. Billions of shares are traded each day and at the close of the business day the market's final price provides the consensus of the day's sentiment. A small change in the market's closing number would indicate that the consensus is *slightly* bullish or bearish, whereas a large change would indicate a *very* bullish or bearish mood.

The market is truly a caldron for all human emotions; it is the ebb and flow of all dreams and fears, euphoria and anxiety, hopes and disappointments, reactions to world events, and especially to Federal Reserve Board announcements. But, this does not preclude the development of an investment model that takes advantage of the very *statement of sentiment* that the market makes each day. The Y-Process is a technical model that reduces investor's risk, increases stock market profits, and provides superior returns. The paradox here is that the Y-Process model *eliminates* the very basis that drives the market, that is, *human emotion.*

In sum, this chapter provides sufficient empirical evidence that the Y-Process outperforms the market on a consistent basis, and that this outperformance results in greater returns. Does this prove that the school of efficient markets is flawed? It must, because axiom one of the efficient market theory says, "You cannot beat the market consistently."

A New Version of the Efficient Market Theory

Is there another way out of this dilemma for those who want to keep both the efficient market theory and the Y-Process? Perhaps, but the Y-Process must be considered as another anomaly. Unfortunately, the Y-Process cannot be explained away as were the previously described six anomalies of the efficient market theory. Academia created a home for the six anomalies that has been recognized thus far and identified in Chapter 8. The home for the Y-Process anomaly is with the three versions of the *efficient market theory*: (1) the strong form, (2) the semistrong form, and (3) the weak form.

However, the Y-Process does not fit in any of these forms. At this stage, there is no mathematical proof other than empirical back testing that the Y-Process challenges the efficacy of the efficient market theory. I don't believe financial academicians are prepared to admit a paradigm shift in their fundamental dogma. However, the back testing results presented in this book are hard to deny, much less to refute. In order to retain the efficient market theory *and* explain the consistent outperformance capability of the Y-Process, I propose a new version of the efficient market theory—the fourth version—the *very weak form*.

The very weak form of the efficient market theory asserts that a unique market-timing program called the Y-Process performs superior investment results. The Y-Process derives its data only from the stock portfolio's past history. When this data is applied to the Y-Process model (Equations 9.1 and 9.2 in Chapter 9), the portfolio's Y-Process number and risk index are determined in the following week's market. When the portfolio's value causes the risk index to change its sign from a negative to a positive value or from a positive to a negative value, this causes a Y-Process trading signal to be issued. An investor trading on this signal will, with a high likelihood, obtain superior market results.

However, before you rush out to take advantage of the very weak form of the efficient market theory, you should remember five sobering considerations:

1. The empirical results are only that; they do not *prove* the Y-Process's success.

2. Total transaction costs are important. These costs include fees, commissions, sale charges, and taxes (if applicable) on dividends and capital gains. You must pay the transaction costs associated with this strategy and it is possible that transaction costs could exceed any excess return. (These costs are discussed in Chapter 11.)

3. You must still select a stock market index or mutual fund or create your own portfolio. There is no assurance that the ETF or mutual fund selected or the portfolio created will outperform the market benchmark in that particular year although the probability is high if the ETF or mutual fund selected is the S&P 500 benchmark or an S&P 500 mutual fund.

4. For this very weak form to be useful for an active investment strategy, its signal must be transferable to you in a *timely fashion* to act on it.

5. For anyone to take advantage of the inefficiency, it must be ongoing. Once the inefficiency is discovered and enough investors seek to take advantage of it, there is a possibility that the inefficiency *may* disappear. (This anomaly is discussed in Chapter 11.)

In conclusion, I believe that in today's cost-conscious stock market environment and with the easy availability of stock market data such as closing prices, the Y-process overcomes all of these negatives. I also believe that the Y-Process will be officially accepted by academia, but not necessarily as the seventh anomaly to the efficient market theory.

Chapter 11

The Devil Is in the Details

*That Old Adage "The Devil Is in the Details"
Applies When Trying to Optimize Your Gains*

Investors entering the new millennium may be wealthier but many won't be all that wiser. Financial experts say we should acquire a host of stocks and bonds and then focus on the performance of the entire portfolio rather than on the individual stocks and bonds. In theory, it is a smart strategy: By buying a slew of investments, some of which will soar while others are sinking, we should get healthy returns with less violent portfolio swings. The problem is, this method doesn't correspond to people's intuition of how to build portfolios. The notion that we should consider portfolios as a whole and focus only on the risk and return of the *overall* portfolio is good advice, but it is advice that investors find hard to take.

What's our problem? We tend to divide our money into different mental accounts. We fret about each investment's performance, rather than focusing on our whole portfolio. And we aren't consistent about risk. With some money, we yearn for safety. With other money, we hunger for riches. Sure, we could fight these instincts. But it makes more sense to incorporate these mental quirks into our portfolios.

If you find stock investing really nerve-racking, you might want to buy a mutual fund that offers one-stop shopping. These funds combine a host of stocks from a variety of market sectors, so they provide a globally diversified portfolio in a single mutual fund. This way you don't have to be emotionally attached to each stock in that fund and somebody else will diversify the fund for you. Buying this type of fund means fewer investments and all you see is the big picture.

Most investors do not build one portfolio, as the experts suggest. Instead, we build many portfolios, each designed to meet a different goal. We earmark some money for emergencies, while other money gives us a chance to dream about being rich, and so we buy the hottest issues and lottery tickets. We behave like the main character in *The Three Faces of Eve*, a story of a woman who suffered from multiple-personality disorder, where there are three people inside of us, each pulling in a different direction. The problem is how do we mediate among these personalities.

One way is to divide your money into three mental accounts. There is your emergency money, which is in a money market fund. There is your retirement money and a college portfolio for the kids, and this money is mostly in well-diversified stock funds. Then there's your fun-money account. This mental accounting isn't ideal; but the resulting portfolio should meet both your psychological and investment needs, as long as you are careful. In particular, watch out for two pitfalls.

First, make sure your overall mix of stocks, bonds, and cash investments makes sense for someone of your age and risk tolerance. For instance, if your pot of emergency money is too big and your retirement nest egg relatively small, you may unintentionally end up with too many conservative investments.

Second, don't let your hunger for "blowout" returns hurt the rest of your portfolio. Your best bet is to designate a small portion of your portfolio as "fun money." Build speculative investing as a legitimate activity and put in enough safeguards so that if you take a high-stakes gamble that doesn't work out, you don't end up hurting other sectors of your portfolio.

In pursuit of both safety and riches, many investors combine ultraconservative investments with investments that are extraordinarily risky. In a modified form, you can also use this notion within your stock portfolio. The idea is to own a core portfolio of an index fund, so that you guarantee that part of your stock market money earns the market's return. Then, to give yourself a shot at beating the market, you add a smattering of a Y-Process-managed stock exchange-traded funds (ETFs). This pursuit of safety and riches is known as the "core and satellite" approach. It is a good example of downside *protection* and upside *potential*, even though the core doesn't really have a floor in absolute dollar terms. If you use the Y-Process to manage both the core fund and the satellite ETFs, you have a greater potential to enhance all returns and further reduce risk.

UNDERSTANDING AND PROFITING FROM EXCHANGE-TRADED FUNDS

Investing in ETFs, varieties of mutual funds that unlike regular funds trade throughout the day on stock exchanges, gives you a lot of flexibility. ETFs are a good strategy for the average individual investor who wants to trade actively while still reaping the benefits of diversification. In June 2001, it was estimated that investors big and small collectively had $73 billion invested in ETFs. These funds have surged in popularity in the past few years, though they remain just a tiny part of the $7 trillion mutual fund industry. As an example of their popularity, investors bought $8.9 billion of new ETF shares in March 2001, up from $3.2 billion in February and $2.3 billion in January.

What's the appeal? Like index mutual funds, ETFs offer investors diversified portfolios tracking the S&P 500 Index, for example, or specialized portfolios tracking such thin market slices as only biotechnology stocks, Malaysian issues, or U.S. real estate investment trusts.

ETFs have been around since 1993. "Spiders," "iShares," "Diamonds," "sTrack," along with other fanciful named offerings, for example, "HOLD-ERs" and "Cubes," form a new class of securities. ETFs owe their popularity to the success of index investing. In the five years from 1994 through 1999, the average U.S. closed-end equity fund has returned 30 percent, compared to 15 percent for its actively managed rival. When you consider that ETFs are essentially index funds that trade like stocks, it is easy to understand why they have already attracted $25 billion in assets, which may be the only thing about ETFs that's easy to understand.

IS AN ETF A CLOSED-END FUND?

The typical ETF product is not a closed-end fund; it is a hybrid. As with a closed-end fund, you buy shares in a stock ETF from another shareholder on the open market, rather than from the fund company itself. And because you buy through a brokerage company, you pay a commission on the purchase, whether you choose a full-service firm, one of the bargain basement discount firms, or one of the online organizations.

WHAT YOU ARE BUYING WHEN YOU BUY AN ETF

What you're buying is a fund designed to track one of several indexes: SPDRs (pronounced spiders for Standard and Poors Depository Receipts) track the S&P 500 Index; Cubes, so named because they trade under the symbol QQQ that tracks the NASDAQ 100 Index, which tracks the top 100 companies in the NASDAQ Composite Index; Diamonds are pegged to the Dow Jones Industrial Average (DJIA), taking the name from three letters in DJIA; Select Sector SPDRs trade individual indexes, such as those devoted to financial services, energy, and technology. And then there are the Barclays' iShares, which track the single-country indexes maintained by Morgan Stanley Capital International (MSCI), against which most international fund managers measure their performance. Both Select Sector SPDRs and iShares will be discussed in greater detail in Chapter 12.

ETFS COST LESS THAN INDEX FUNDS

To a large extent, ETFs function like their open-end and closed-end relatives except they are often less costly. For example, whereas the closed-end Japan Equity Fund, has an expense ratio of 1.19 percent, the Japan ETFs weigh in at 26 basis points lower, that is, 0.93 percent. SPDRs boast an actual expense ratio of just 17 basis points a year according to Morningstar, well below the 0.83 percent average for stock index funds and even a hair below the Vanguard's 500 Index Fund's cheap 0.18 percent expense ratio. It is expected that ETF costs have to go lower now that a new comer, Barclays, went public with their iShares in the spring of 2000. When the British banking behemoth Barclays joined, their current lineup of 61 ETF products included a fund pegged to the S&P 500 in a clear attempt to take business away from Vanguard and the other brokerages that have this index as a fund, and they entered the market with an expense ratio as low as 0.08 percent, a good example of the value of competition in an open and free marketplace.

Generally, fund performance closely tracks the comparable index. So Barclays' iShares MSCI Canada Index Fund, for instance, lost 11 percent through the first week in May 2001, while the MSCI Canada Index was down 13.29 percent in U.S. dollars. Meanwhile "streetTracks," a Morgan Stanley Internet Index Fund, sponsored by State Street, had lost 23 percent through the same period in May and the Morgan Stanley Internet Index was down 26.3 percent.

DIVIDEND DRAG

Interestingly, in 1998, the Vanguard 500 Index Fund returned an average annual 23.97 percentage points, nearly 20 basis points *more* than the SPDR, even though the two products have identical expense ratios, and presumably identical holdings. Is it possible that all index funds are not created equal? Yes, you can add significant value by actively managing the fund and executing your trades efficiently by reducing dividend drag, which is one of the facets of Spiders that is seldom discussed.

Technically registered as a "unit investment trust (UIT)," rather than a mutual fund, a SPDR distributes dividends to shareholders the third Friday of every quarter. But, the SPDR's 500 companies pay their dividends more frequently than that. Because of the UIT structure, however, the SPDR is required to hold dividends it receives as cash rather than reinvest them into the fund, as a mutual fund can. This is why the index fund can outperform the index it tries to replicate every time. You can say, "Oh, the difference is just 20 basis points a year." But, over time, this compounded growth can be significant.

A recent example of dividend drag is a comparison of the SPDRs and the S&P 500 Index which it seeks to replicate. In 1999, the SPDR trust closed its fiscal year with a 27.54 percent return that underperformed the Index by 32 basis points for the same period. Eighteen of those 32 basis points were the SPDRs expense ratio and the 14 basis point balance was dividend drag.

DO ETFS ALWAYS OFFER TAX SAVINGS?

ETFs often offer tax savings but not always. One of the confusing aspects of ETFs is that while the products are all touted as more tax efficient than mutual funds, they are also touted as appealing to short-term traders because ETFs are constantly being repriced during the day, whereas mutual funds calculate their net asset value only once each day at the close of the trading day.

Further, ETFs are more tax efficient than mutual funds, if sometimes narrowly. For the five years through 1998, owners of SPDR shares kept 95.84 percent of their return after paying taxes compared with 95.45 percent for Vanguard 500 shareholders. It's true that pretax returns on Spiders were lower, due to dividend drag, but Barclays' S&P products will take care of that problem. Unlike Spiders, iShares are legally structured as a mutual fund, allowing them to reinvest dividends rather than hold dividends as cash.

Furthermore, most of the ETF products now available are structured as mutual funds, making dividend drag not that much of a drag. This change came about as the Securities and Exchange Commission granted "exemptive relief" after many ETFs petitioned it to bypass certain restrictions that generally apply to mutual funds. Owners of ETF shares are now allowed to sell their shares short, an option not available to mutual fund shareholders. Chapter 12 discusses this attribute and uses it as the cornerstone of a tax-saving strategy.

PAYMENT IN KIND ENHANCES TAX EFFICIENCY

Payment in kind is a sophisticated strategy to eliminate unrealized capital gains. Mutual funds are expected to be ready, at any time, to give shareholders cash in exchange for their shares. ETFs, however, regularly redeem shares for a basket of stocks being turned in and can issue shares in exchange for a similar basket.

From a practical standpoint, this feature doesn't matter to individual investors. After all, you're not buying or redeeming your shares from the fund company, and, in fact, the in-kind payments apply only to blocks of at least 50,000 shares. For SPDRs, that would represent about $7.5 million at today's prices. However, it is precisely that in-kind feature that makes ETFs so tax efficient. If a large shareholder in your mutual fund decides to redeem his or her shares, your fund manager will almost certainly have to sell securities to raise the necessary cash, soaking you and your fellow remaining shareholders with not only the transaction cost but also, and more painfully, the taxable capital gains he may have to distribute.

By contrast, if a large owner of SPDRs, Fidelity, for example, decides to sell some of its shares, it bundles up 50,000 of them into a redemption unit and hands this unit over to the fund, receiving a bunch of stock in return. Because the fund didn't sell this stock, but only swapped it, no taxes or capital gains are involved.

And it gets better. Every day, ETFs publish a list of the stocks, and proportions of those stocks, that it will hand over in exchange for a redemption unit. While it is limited to stocks in its index, within that limitation it can arrange the basket however it likes. And it still gets better. The ETF can identify not only the stocks it wishes to sell, but also the specific shares.

Table 11.1 contains an interesting comparison of the advantages and limitations of investing in ETFs and index mutual funds. One of the areas that the table does not comment on is the customer service an investor gets when calling a mutual fund representative using the fund's handy 1-800 telephone number.

TAKING CONTROL OF BROKERAGE COMMISSIONS

Broker's costs reduce your profits. For day traders, broker's costs can be a dominant factor. There are no round-turn costs when trading certain no-load funds, but this is not the case when trading ETFs or individual firm securities. By using a discount broker, you can get advertised stock trades that cost as low as $10 per round turn.

Even in large brokerage firms, such as Fidelity Investment Company, the cost of trading stocks and ETFs is very competitive. At this writing, the total round-turn cost for Fidelity is a fixed fee or $33, that is, $15 when buying and $18 when selling up to and including 1,000 shares. The prerequisite is that you must be a *preferred* client (a minimum of 12 trades per year) and you must trade online via the Internet. This round-turn cost is relatively small when considering the round-turn cost of trading 1,000 shares of a high value stock. For instance, the $33 round-turn cost of trading 1,000 shares of $100 per share stock is 3.33 basis points (0.0333 percent). This is a rather low cost for the value of the transaction. There is an

Table 11.1 Comparison of Exchanged-Traded Funds and Index Mutual Funds

Exchange-Traded Funds	Index Mutual Funds
Tax-Efficiency	
Extremely high, due to the low turnover associated with index structure and the lack of redemption-induced sales.	83% (Average)
Expense Ratio: Domestic[a]	
0.18%–0.65%	0.15%–1.5%
Expense Ratio: International[b]	
0.95%–1.43%	0.97% (Average)
Available for Short-Selling	
Yes	No
Pricing	
Continuous	Once a day
Portfolio Disclosure	
Continuous	Twice a year
Where to Buy	
From any brokerage	From a brokerage, a fund supermarket, or directly from the fund company, depending on the fund
Sales Charge to Trade	
Yes, nominally from $5 to $15 for up to 1,000 shares per trade depending on your discount broker and if you use the Internet to place the order.	Varies
Minimum Investment	
Most ETFs sell for under $100	Average of $2,000

[a]Most domestic ETFs trade at 18 basis points, a few at 25; Select Sectors SPDRs, which track industrial indexes, have an expense ratio of approximately 65 basis points.
[b]The Malaysia ETFs product has an unusually high (1.43%) expense ratio due to that country's capital controls.
Source: Based on data from Morningstar.

additional cost of $5 per trade if you place your trade at other than a "market order."

In comparison, trading the same number of shares using a "representative-assisted transaction," will cost a preferred client $145, that is, $71 when buying and $74 when selling. For limit and stop orders add $5 per trade.

OPTIMIZING TRADE ORDER TYPE

To buy or sell a security you must place an order through a stockbroker, which can be done by mail, phone, electronically (via the Internet), or in person. To complete an order, four essential questions must be answered: (1) the price that you want to sell or buy the security, (2) the number of shares that you want to buy or sell, (3) the type of order, and (4) the time in force. Each of these items is discussed in turn. There are three types of buy and sell orders: market orders, limit orders, and stop orders.

MARKET ORDERS

When you place a *market order*, you are instructing your broker to buy or sell securities for your account at the *next available price*. A market order remains in effect for only the day. When your stockbroker receives your market order, she forwards it to the specialist (market maker) at the appropriate stock market, for example, American Stock Exchange, New York Stock Exchange, or NASDAQ. There may be market orders ahead of yours, so the specialist (market maker) enters your order in queue in his book. As the specialist fills the orders, you move up in the queue until your market order is executed by *matching* your shares to buy (or sell) to another investor's order for shares to sell (or buy).

The advantage of a market order is that you are guaranteed a prompt execution of all your shares, as long as the security is actively traded and market conditions permit but *not at a specific price*. The disadvantage of selling shares using a market order in a down market is that your order may be filled at a price considerably below the market value on the stock screen at the time you placed it. Some academics call this price difference slippage.

LIMIT ORDERS

Limit orders are inherently "or better" orders. The advantage of placing a limit order to buy makes the stock eligible to be purchased *at or below* your limit price, but *never above it.* The same advantage holds for placing a limit order to sell except that it makes the stock eligible to be sold *at or above* your limit price, but *never below it.*

There are also disadvantages to limit orders. Orders at each price level are filled in a sequence that is determined by the rules of the various exchanges. But there can be no assurance that all orders at a particular price limit (including yours) will be filled when that price is reached. The reason? Such orders are subject to the existence of a market for that security. Thus, the fact that your price limit was reached does not guarantee an execution. In other words, you run the risk that the price will "run away" from your limit, because there were no buyers (or sellers), therefore, your trade won't be executed.

STOP ORDERS

Stop orders are used to buy or sell a stock *after* the stock has reached the stop price that you enter in your order. Stop orders are used in conjunction with loss and limit orders. Thus, there are two types of stop orders: stop loss orders and stop limit orders.

A buy or sell stop loss order automatically becomes a market order when the stop price is reached. A buy or sell stop limit order automatically becomes a limit order when the stop price is reached.

A buy stop order is generally used when you're "short the market" and you want to "cover your short" position.

For a Y-Process investor to *buy* a stock using a *stop loss order*, place your stop loss order at or above the current market in accordance with the Y-Process number. When the stop price is reached, the stop loss order automatically becomes a market order to buy. Similarly, to *sell* a stock, place your *stop loss order* at or below the current market. When the stop is reached, the stop loss order automatically becomes a market order to sell. In both cases, there is slippage potential when selling (or buying) shares using a market order. That is, your sell (or buy) order may be filled at a price well below (or above) the market value at the time the stop was reached.

When you place a limit order to buy, that stock is eligible to be purchased at or below your limit price but never above it. When you place a limit order to sell, that stock is eligible to be sold at or above your limit price but never below it.

A stop limit order automatically becomes a limit order when the stop price is reached. Like any limit order, a stop limit order may be filled in whole, in part, or not at all, depending on the number of shares available for sale or purchase at the time. In these cases, there is no slippage possible. But there is a possibility that the price will "run away" from your stop price. If this were to happen, it would most likely happen in thinly traded stocks.

Stop Limit Orders Are Recommended for Y-Process Investors

I recommend the use of stop limit orders when you buy or sell stocks, because a limit order defends against poor execution of trades. If you are buying, place your stop limit at or just above the current asked price; the shares will be bought at this level or lower. If you are selling, put your limit at the current bid price or just below; the stock will be sold at this stop price or higher. There is always the risk that the price will run away from your limit, and your trade won't be executed, but I have never experienced such a situation in many years of trading.

TIME IN FORCE

Time in force is a term that describes the duration of a buy or sell order. There are six types of time-in-force entries: (1) day, (2) good until cancelled, (3) fill or kill, (4) immediate or cancel, (5) on the open, and (6) on the close. You may place an order good only for the day on which the order is entered or for an open-ended period that ends when it is executed, or when you cancel, or when it expires, that is, normally 120 calendar days after the order is placed. An order may be placed before the market opens and with a criterion that it must be executed at the opening price. At any time prior to the close, you may enter an order with a criteria that it must be executed at the closing price.

Limit orders for more than 100 shares or for multiple round lots (200, 300, 400, etc.) may be filled completely or in part until completed. It may take more than one trading day to completely fill a multiple round lot order unless the order is designated as either a *fill or kill* (fill the order immediately or cancel it), or an *immediate or cancel* (fill the whole order or any part immediately, and cancel any unfilled balance).

An investor who places a *good until cancel order* when placing buy or sell stop orders can go on vacation without anxiety. This approach will mechanically control the process of either entering the market or selling the market as calculated using the Y-Process equations for the Y-Process value. However, these stop orders are valid for one week because the Y-Process requires weekly updates. Even if the investor is on vacation, the prudent thing to do to preserve your capital is to follow the rules—update each stock in your portfolio and reenter the new stop orders.

THE EFFECT OF SHORT-TERM WHIPSAWS ON Y-PROCESS INVESTORS

If the Y-Process has an Achilles' heel it is whipsaws. Whipsaws generally happen in a sideward moving market and occur around the Y-Process transition of buying or selling. The term whipsaw is jargon for the financial effect of a rapid upward price movement followed by a rapid decline. A whipsaw contains three attributes: (1) there must be round-turn trade involved, (2) the round turn must occur in a short period of time, and (3) the round-turn trade must result in a loss.

When using the Y-Process trading strategy, being whipsawed is a sell signal quickly followed by a buy signal or vice versa. A whipsaw is when a round-turn trade occurs within one month of the original buy order. If the whipsaw occurs within the same week (intraweek), this I define as *a short-term whipsaw* (previously called a false alarm).

Being whipsawed can be devastating to some investors in any of three ways. First, it can be monetarily detrimental because whipsaws cause an investor to be exposed to financial risk on both the up- and downside of a round-turn transaction. It is possible that you are subjected to a double market loss through trying inopportunely to recoup a loss by a subsequent buy-back of the same security at a higher price than you sold it, and in a round-turn trade there is always the additional cost of the round-turn commissions.

Second, being whipsawed may have a severe negative psychological effect greater than the financial loss because it can cause you to lose faith in the Y-Process. One of the primary advantages of the Y-Process is that it provides the investor with a nonemotional means of buying and selling stocks. Once you build a confidence factor that you will always protect your downside risk exposure with the Y-Process, it becomes almost mechanical to buy and sell stocks and ETFs.

Third, the whipsaw can have other deleterious financial effects from a federal income tax standpoint. The financial impact in taxable brokerage accounts can be much greater than the round-turn cost because trading stock held for less than 12 months is a short-term transaction and that would cause a short-term capital gain.

PRESERVATION OF CAPITAL RULE

As previously discussed, back testing the S&P 500 index was used to verify and validate the utility of the Y-Process in beating the market. The back testing technique only allowed a single trade per week, because the database used contained only week-ending stock prices. In other words, *intraweek* whipsaws could not occur in the 3,500 weeks tested because the test examined the change in price from Friday to Friday. However, using the Y-Process in buying and selling index funds and ETFs in the stock market real-time, short-term intraweek whipsaws can and do occur because stock market prices vary continuously on a daily basis. Moreover, in real-time stock markets, short-term whipsaws are not limited to intraweek; they can and have occurred within the same day. These are called intraday whipsaws.

To replicate the stunning success of the 71 years of the back tested Y-Process, I developed a *preservation of capital rule* to prohibit short-term (intraday or intraweek) whipsaws from occurring in the real-time market utilization of the Y-Process. The preservation of capital rule allows a single sell trade per week for a given stock portfolio, ETF, or index fund. For example, if you buy an ETF on Monday and its price violates the Y-Process number any time during the week, you must sell it as soon as that event occurs. In accordance with the preservation of capital rule, the earliest you can repurchase this ETF is after the close of business on Friday or the following Monday. In the worst case, if you sell out on a Monday morning, the preservation of capital rule prohibits you from buying back until after Friday's close, even though the market may have recovered within a few hours on the Monday you sold out.

Chapter 12

Stretch Your Gains:
Reach for Higher Returns

*A Strategy That Aims for Higher Returns Does
Not Have to Mean Higher Risk*

Financial academics argue that any strategy that aims for higher returns means higher risks. They also caution investors to limit aggressive investments to a small portion of a well-diversified portfolio and *never* to use money they can't afford to lose.

For the experienced, sophisticated Y-Process investor, this chapter presents the view that there is nothing wrong with reserving a portion of your portfolio to aim for higher returns. Even a few percentage points difference in return can have a big impact on how fast your money grows. For example, at the market's historical average return of about 11 percent a year, it takes a little over six and one-half years for your stake to double. Not bad; but if you can earn five percentage points more, or 16 percent yearly, your investment will double in four and one-half years (all before taxes of course).

Four strategies that use the Y-Process in an aggressive and unique manner that could earn advanced investors 16 percent or more returns annually over the next five or more years are described here. Not all of these strategies will be right for you, but the better you understand them, the more likely you will be able to select the right choice for you.

INTERNATIONAL STOCK EXCHANGE-TRADED FUNDS

Indexing is known for its market-tracking performance. Index mutual funds are linked to the S&P 500 Index, Dow Jones Industrial Average, NASDAQ 100 or some other benchmark. When you buy an index fund, you know your return will match that of the index it was tracking (less commissions and taxes).

As described in Chapter 11, international stock exchange-traded funds (ETFs), a first cousin of index funds, are being traded on the American Stock Exchange (AMEX). This provides you with the ability to purchase a benchmark of a country as easy as that of a domestic company stock or fund. Since 1990, combined U.S. and international indexed mutual fund assets have increased greater than 31-fold. Investing only in the U.S. markets passes up about 60 percent of the world's equity market.

One reason for the popularity of international ETFs is that they work like index funds, yet trade like stocks. You can track their performance real time just like a stock, and easily buy or sell during the trading day, through your broker or online. But unlike stock, you are not buying a single company, you're buying an entire stock index and getting the diversification of owning stock in many companies. Unlike most managed funds, international ETFs offer an approach to investing that provides lower fees and expenses and important tax efficiencies. A single share lets you buy or sell the largest and most actively traded companies on each of the 17 country's stock exchanges, all in one security.

iShares is an AMEX-traded fund consisting of 19 foreign markets and their major local market indexes, such as Germany's DAX and Japan's Nikkei 225. Table 12.1 contains a complete list of 37 NASDAQ/AMEX indexes. The table includes the 19 countries and Hong Kong, their local market indexes, and the symbol used to trade iShares. These iShares

Table 12.1   Thirty-Seven NASDAQ/AMEX Indexes and Symbols

Index	*Symbol*
Major U.S. Indexes	SPDRs "S&P Depository Receipts" (SPY) SPDRs "Mid Cap-400" (MDY) NASDAQ 100 Shares "Cubes" (QQQ) DOW-30 "Diamonds" (DIA)
Internet Indexes	Internet Index (Emerging Mkts Telecom) (ETF) Merrill Lynch Internet Index (HHH)
Sector Spiders	Basic Industries (XLB) Consumer Staples (XLP) Cyclicals/Transportation (XLY) Energy (XLE) Financials (XLF) Industrials (XLI) Technology (XLK) Utilities (XLU)

iShares (Barclays MSCI Benchmark Shares)	*Local Market*	
	Symbol	*Index*
	Australia (EWA)	All Ordinaries
	Austria (EWO)	ATX
	Belgium (EWK)	BEL-20
	Brazil (EWZ)	BELFOX
	Canada (EWC)	TORONTO 35
	France (EWQ)	CAC
	Germany (EWG)	DAX
	Hong Kong (EWH)	Hang Sang
	Italy (EWI)	BCI
	Japan (EWJ)	Nikkei 225
	Malaysia (EWM)	KLSE
	Mexico (EWW)	IPC
	Netherlands (EWN)	EOE
	Singapore (EWS)	Straits Times
	South Korea (EWY)	Soul
	Spain (EWP)	IBEX
	Sweden (EWD)	OMX
	Switzerland (EWL)	SMI
	Taiwan (EWT)	SMI
	United Kingdom (EWU)	FTSE

provide individual investment results that correspond to the price and yield performance of their publicly traded securities, in the aggregate, as compiled by Morgan Stanley Capital International Index.

ADVANTAGES AND LIMITATIONS OF ETFs

Because you must pay a commission each time you trade, stock ETFs are not appropriate for investors using a dollar-cost-averaging strategy or any similar discipline involving regular purchases of shares. The comparatively low share price of ETFs offers an opportunity for cash-strapped investors to gain exposure to other areas, such as the international arena and specialized portfolios of specific industry sectors that might otherwise be out of reach because of minimum investments demanded by many mutual funds. But, it's possible that the commissions on ETFs will eat into your return sufficiently unless you're prepared to invest a large enough sum to amortize them. The high costs involved make a very good case for you to trade using a computer. Trading via the Internet provides most investors a significant discount in trading costs. This discount is enhanced considerably if your brokerage firm registers you as an active trader. Over time, the money saved should be sufficient to pay for the cost of the computer and the Internet interface.

Foreign Investments Involve Greater Risks Than U.S. Investments

As with any investment, share price and return on foreign investments will fluctuate. The risks of foreign investments also include unstable political climates and economic uncertainties as well as the risk of currency fluctuations. When foreign securities are sold and converted back into U.S. dollars, the value of the dollar may have risen or declined, depending on what has happened in the foreign exchange markets. When trading iShares, however, the daily conversions are already built in and the value of the daily share price is listed in U.S. dollars.

Three Classic Advantages of Foreign Securities

The first advantage is investing in economies experiencing economic growth generally found in countries referred to as emerging markets. The second advantage is more obvious; it is risk reduction through diversification using global markets. The third advantage is in obtaining excess returns due to certain inefficiencies of foreign markets.

It is this last advantage that is both intriguing and risky. According to the school of efficient markets, higher returns can be achieved by bearing more risk, that is, purchasing assets whose returns tend to be more *volatile* than the U.S. markets as a whole. Market inefficiencies suggest that astute investors and those who also manage their portfolio using the Y-Process may be able to isolate a foreign market that is under- or overvalued. If this is true, then the opportunity for excess returns exists.

TRADING FOREIGN SECURITIES TAKES DISCIPLINE

Investing in iShares is ideal for the disciplined Y-Process investor who has the stamina to dart in and out of the market using the Y-Process equations provided in Chapter 9. If foreign ETFs sound intriguing, soul-searching is recommended because it takes plenty of discipline to invest in them. Because some of these countries are thinly traded, stop loss or limit orders are essential to prevent you from going into free fall while you're not looking. Of course, this could be beneficial if you're on the short side which you can do with ETFs.

INVESTING IN SECTOR FUNDS

Have you ever wished that you had owned some of those cyber stocks or technology stocks when they were the rage? Most sane investors conclude that the risks are too monumental to invest anything more than a small amount of "mad" money in such a narrow niche. Yet, while funds that focus on a particular industry are often quite volatile, the payoffs can be worthwhile.

If an investor started with $10,000 and earned just average returns in the top-performing sector for each of the 10 years beginning in 1989, his or her money would have grown to an outstanding $1.1 million, a compound return of 60 percent a year. Of course the risks are high, too. If that same investor had purchased the worst-performing sector for those 10 years, he or she would have just $768 left; this is the equivalent of a compounded return of –23 percent each year.

Table 12.1 contains 37 different types of index and sector funds. Clearly these funds are not for everyone. That's why index and sector funds tend to attract market timers. For the investor who has the discipline to manage his or her stock portfolio using the Y-Process, index and sector funds provide the potential of large returns while downside risk is significantly reduced. If the investor follows the Y-Process's risk index alert, the timing of the sell signal will reduce risk and maximize returns.

EVALUATING SECTOR FUNDS

There are several ways to evaluate a fund's historical performance. The investor can look at the cumulative total percentage change in value, the average annual percentage change, or the growth of a hypothetical $10,000 investment. *Total returns* reflect the change in value of an investment, assuming reinvestments of the fund's dividend income and capital gains (the profits earned on the sale of securities that account for those sales charges, commissions, and trading fees).

Cumulative total returns show the fund's performance in percentage terms over a set period, for example, 1 year, 5 years, and 10 years. The investor can compare the funds to a baseline to evaluate relative performance. Many investors use the S&P 500 Index as the baseline.

Average annual total returns take the fund's cumulative return and show the investor what would have happened if the fund had performed at a constant rate each year.

BUYING SECTOR FUNDS

If you're interested in sector investing, there are two approaches. The first approach buys a special class of ETFs—select sector SPDRs. Table 12.1 contains the 9 select SPDR sectors presently traded on the AMEX.

The second approach uses brokerage companies that deal in sector funds. The largest selections are offered by Fidelity, with 38 sector funds, Rydex, with 14, and Invesco and Morgan Stanley, with 11 apiece. Rydex and Invesco are load free, whereas Fidelity and Morgan Stanley impose sales charges. Moreover, Fidelity also imposes a penalty of 0.75 percent on trading the sector within 90 days of the initial purchase. Table 12.2

Table 12.2 **Fidelity Sector Funds' Cumulative Returns for Year-to-Date Ended April 1, 2001**

Sector Fund Name	Cumulative Total Return, YTD (%)
Air Transportation	−3.01
Automotive	+10.24
Biotechnology	−25.01
Brokerage & Investment Management	−6.98
Business Services & Outsourcing	+0.93
Chemicals	+4.95
Computers	−14.58
Construction and Housing	+5.26
Consumer Industries	−2.18
Cyclical Industries	+2.75
Defense & Aerospace	+0.79
Developing Communications	−17.81
Electronics	−2.53
Energy	+3.31
Energy Services	+9.11
Environmental Services	−0.29
Financial Services	−6.91
Food & Agriculture	−6.92
Gold	+8.02
Health Care	−15.67
Home Finance	−4.82
Industrial Equipment	+4.22
Industrial Materials	+7.54
Insurance	−7.32
Leisure	+9.99
Medical Delivery	−8.59
Medical Equipment & Systems	−8.95
Multimedia	+8.14
Natural Resources	+3.39
Networking and Infrastructure	−33.73
Paper & Forest	+5.95
Retailing	+1.76
S&P 500	**−5.09**
Software & Computer Services	−5.32
Technology	−18.89
Telecommunications	−11.89
Transportation	+7.33
Utilities Growth	−1.24

provides the cumulative returns of Fidelity's 38 select portfolios for the year ended April 1, 2001.

Fidelity has a unique and cost-savings exchange privilege when trading its sector funds. A special *Select Money Market* portfolio has been created as a "parking place" for each exchange out of one of the select equity portfolios. This money market exchange privilege is ideally suited for the Y-Process investor since fees do not apply to exchanges out of the Select Money Market. Three percent fees once paid do not have to be paid again as this loaded money stays within the sector fund family.

BUYING ON MARGIN

Another way to use the capabilities of the Y-Process in pursuit of higher returns and reduced risk is to buy funds on margin, that is, partly with money borrowed from your broker. Buying on margin boosts both your risk and your potential reward. This strategy is not in the domain of investors who have tax-deferred stock portfolios. Tax-deferred accounts such as IRAs or other types of retirement plans generally are prohibited from buying on margin by Securities and Exchange (SEC) rules.

Here's how buying on margin works: Suppose you are thinking of buying 100 shares of an ETF priced at $10 a share for $1,000. Instead of paying cash, you set up a margin account at your brokerage firm and purchase $2,000 of ETF shares, borrowing the extra $1,000. If the share price grows 50 percent, to $15, the investment rises to $3,000. After paying back the $1,000 you owe the broker, you would have $2,000 left for a 100 percent profit (less interest on the loan). That is twice what you would have made paying cash. Thanks to that boost, and even with the typical 7.5 to 9 percent interest that brokers charge for margin loans, your ETF shares would need to earn only about 11.5 percent a year for you to double your stake in five years, as opposed to the 15 percent you'd need without leverage.

Buying on margin can be a curse, though. If your stock plummets, that leverage will magnify your losses instead of your gains. Brokerages generally let you borrow up to half the cost of a fund, the most allowed by Federal Reserve Board rules. Past that, rules vary. Fidelity customers get a margin call, meaning that they either have to put up more cash or sell some of their position if the equity in an account dips below 30 percent of the market value of the securities. Schwab won't make that call until total equity dips below 30 percent.

For Y-Process investors, buying on margin is less of a threat of "losing your shirt" by being caught in a downside plunge. The reason being that you get advance notice of a potential decline or correction when the Y-Process number is violated.

THE MARKET-NEUTRAL POSITION

Sophisticated investors are always on the lookout for strategies to increase *net* gains. The market-neutral position achieves that goal by selectively hedging your exposure to reduce taxes. Ordinary income and short-term capital gains are taxed at the top federal rate. And today's tax law requires that you pay short-term capital gains at your standard tax rate schedule, that is, 15 percent, 28 percent, 31 percent, or 39 percent. The 1997 tax law allows investors to pay a long-term capital gains tax at a *fixed* 20 percent rate for securities held a minimum of one year from the date of purchase. Commencing January 1, 2001, for securities held for five years, the tax rate is 18 percent for those in the higher tax bracket and 8 percent for those in the 15 percent tax bracket.

Depending on your tax bracket, this can significantly increase your after-tax returns. Thus, if you are in the 28 percent tax bracket, you will save an additional 8 percent in taxes; a much more significant 20 percent saving could occur for securities held a minimum of 12 months if you are in the 39.1 percent tax bracket.[1] As Ben Franklin said, "A penny saved is a penny earned." In this example, if you owned fund "X," its return has been increased by 19.6 percent by holding it for a year and one-half.

How a Market-Neutral Position Works

As a Y-Process investor you get a signal to sell your securities. Instead of selling fund X that you've owned for almost 12 months in a taxable account—providing a short-term capital gain profit—you try to hold on for an additional 6 months. To do this, you establish a market-neutral position. How? By shorting the equivalent dollar amount of an *alias fund*, which we will call fund "Z." Fund Z has a high correlation to fund X. R^2 is a mathematical measurement, called a correlation coefficient, that provides information on how closely your fund's performance matches the performance of a benchmark index, such as fund Z. R^2 is a proportion that ranges between 0.00 and 1.00. An R^2 of 1.00 indicates perfect correlation to the benchmark index, that is, if X goes up 10 percent so does Z. If X goes down 3.5 percent so does Z. At the other end of the spectrum, a 0.00 R^2 indicates a zero correlation. Hence, the lower the R^2, the less the fund's performance tracks the benchmark index, Z.

Extending Your Gains Using R^2

Let's assume you own the ETF known as Spider, symbol SPY. You have a significant short-term capital gain. If you can hold your Spider for another six months, you will be able to make the critical time of holding the spider for 12 months, thus making your gains taxable at the fixed long-term capital gains rate of 20 percent. Unfortunately, your Y-Process indicator has just signaled that a downturn is imminent. You normally would sell out your position, but you have been told that Diamonds, symbol DIA, has a high R^2 to Spiders, a correlation of about 0.86. You decide to short an equal dollar amount of Diamonds against your Spider. This market-neutral position allows you to ride out the potential six-month meltdown, preserving most of your gains because, as your Spider drops in value, your (shorted) Diamonds increase in value at an 86 percent rate. Not a perfect match, but if you hold on for six months, you can convert your Spider's gain to a fixed 20 percent long-term capital-gain tax rate, with a net saving of 19.6 percent in taxes.

To complete the transaction, when your Spider reaches the critical maturity date, you sell it and you simultaneously cover your Diamonds short position closing out this transaction. Gains made on Spiders are paid at the long-term rate and any gains/losses on Diamonds are short-term capital gains/losses. If you have insufficient funds to perform this transaction, try borrowing money from your broker by margining the Spider shares.

Why go through all this trouble? Why not just short the Spiders? The reason is that the Internal Revenue Service (IRS) disallows this procedure if the intent is to establish a long-term capital gain (which is exactly what our market-neutral position strategy is all about). The IRS has a term for this: "shorting against the box" that is, taking a short position on a stock you already own. However, if an investor shorts a similar type of equity, such as an alias stock or fund that is not substantially the same as the equity the investor is holding, then the IRS does not consider this to be a short against the box.

The key to this market-neutral position strategy is (1) finding the appropriate high correlation stock, mutual fund, or ETF, (2) knowing when to implement the short position on this stock, and (3) knowing when to cover the short position. Steps 2 and 3 are relatively easy for the sophisticated investor who uses the Y-Process, because the Y-Process model signals the investor of the potential downturn/upturn in a timely fashion to allow a short/cover of the alias stock.

FINDING A HIGH CORRELATION ALIAS STOCK

Most stock portfolios and mutual funds can be correlated to a stock ETF. Many services provide this information free and most mutual funds contain correlation data (R^2) in their prospectuses. Data can also be obtained by contacting the organization or broker directly. For funds that invest primarily in common stocks of foreign markets, the fund will provide the correlation statistics on request.

AN EXAMPLE OF A MARKET-NEUTRAL POSITION

Suppose you own a large position in Singapore, an international mutual fund. When your Y-Process number has been violated, indicating that your prospects for the Singapore market are dim, you could sell your fund, but if you're sitting on major gains in a taxable account, that sale would trigger a tax bill. Instead, you could hedge your exposure by shorting the Singapore iShares fund—a proxy for the Singapore market—avoiding the big tax bill that would result in selling your long-held international fund shares. When the Y-Process signals an upward potential, you should cover your short position, pay a relatively small capital-gains tax on that gain and maintain your long-term gains in your taxable Singapore account until you reach the fixed-rate tax bracket.

Unfortunately, there is no free lunch. Why? Because you must pay short-term capital-gain tax on any gain made on your short position. However, *you can have your cake and eat it too.* How? This requires a two-step process. First, take the profits made on the short sale and buy additional shares of the stock. Next, at tax time, sell a sufficient number of these "just bought shares" to pay the tax. Make sure to stipulate to your broker (in writing) before selling these shares that they *were last in and will be first out.* This total procedure assumes that the market returns to the upside. Why else would you cover your short position?

The market-neutral strategy has two significant advantages: First, it gains time toward meeting your 18-month objective, and second, it pays the short-term capital gain tax with short-term capital gain money made on the short sale. Unfortunately, this cake may be bittersweet. There is a possibility that the market will rise above the shorted value after you sold short and before you cover your short position. But, even in this case, the gain on your long position offsets the loss on your short position *and* the IRS allows this as an investment tax loss that reduces your income tax.

Epilogue: Some Reflections on Our Ride to Beat the Bear

We are now at the end of our ride. Let's look back for a moment and see where we have been. All investors want to invest in the market, make lots of money, and retire wealthy. But, all investors do not possess the same experience or skill level to accomplish that feat. As a result, I found it convenient to divide this book into separate parts for each investor's skill level: novice, intermediate, and experienced.

Novice investors are normally short on the four essentials of correct stock market investing: goal setting, determination of risk tolerance level, understanding the concept of the time value of money, and understanding the notion of opportunity cost. In Part One, novices learned about these essentials and about the different types of investment vehicles. They were introduced to index funds, money market funds, and the advantages and limitations of load versus no-load mutual funds. For novices to climb the investment skill ladder, they must become more astute about controlling their investment costs. To close the gap, Part One also covered the concept of buying the stock market's benchmark (i.e., the Standard & Poor's 500) and using index funds to limit risk and enhance returns.

Part Two included topics to enable the intermediate investor to become a more effective manager of his or her portfolio, with renewed confidence to make risk–reward decisions. A majority of intermediate investors are long-term, buy-and-hold, investors with diversified portfolios pursuing their journey of wealth building to support a comfortable retirement. This, as explained in Part Three, is not the way to go. As intermediate investors, new students learned about the 13 prevalent mistakes in investing decision making and how to overcome them. They learned the art of finding the right benchmarks and how to interpret returns. To match their goals, performance expectations, and investment style, they determined whether to invest in traditional mutual funds or take advantage of exchange-traded funds. With that information under their belts, they were ready to learn what it takes to become an advanced (sophisticated) investor.

For the sophisticated investor, Part Three developed the Y-Process, a stock market model that forecasts crucial market turns enabling the investor to reduce risk and enhance returns. The Y-Process synthesizes the precursors of change in the market's trend, that is, whether a bull market or bear market is in the making. For the sophisticated investor, the Y-Process's greatest value is its ability to generate a sell signal (or buy signal) very close to a crucial market turning point, even before most money managers know that this event is about to occur.

Now that you have completed the ride, I hope this book makes your investing life more enjoyable, less risky, and, above all, more profitable by continually beating the bear.

Appendix A

S&P 500 Index for 1940

Date (Friday)	S&P 500 Index Price	Y-Process Number	Risk Index (%)	Ypro Buy (B) or Sell (S)	Y-Process and T-Bill Rates	Annual Return (AR)	Annual Total Return (ATR)	Year	Bahf S&P 500 Index ATR (%)	Ypro Y-Process ATR (%)
1/2/40	12.63	12.49	1.11	S0	12.63			40	−8.95	8.63
1/5/40	12.66	12.51	1.17	'B1'	12.64 rate =	0.12%		41	−9.67	7.60
1/12/40	12.13	12.47	−2.78	S1				42	18.42	23.89
1/19/40	12.15	12.43	−2.32					43	24.70	29.37
1/26/40	12.15	12.40	−2.05					44	18.63	79.70
2/2/40	12.06	12.36	−2.50	S1'	RoR/T-bill =	0.00%		45	34.53	32.22
2/9/40	12.37	12.36	0.05	'B2'	12.36 rate =	2.52%	ATR	46	−7.26	9.84
2/16/40	12.29	12.36	−0.54	S2	1940 AR =	−15.29%	−8.95% 6.34%	47	5.52	9.38
2/23/40	12.23	12.34	−0.92		1940 Y-Proc AR =	6.80%	8.63% 1.83%	48	5.49	15.45
3/1/40	12.06	12.31	−2.08		1940 T-Bill =	0.01%	Mkt Risk = 28.8	49	17.05	21.63
3/8/40	12.20	12.30	−0.81		Div =	6.34%	Rnd Turns = 4.5			
									Mkt Risk	Rnd Turns
3/15/40	12.07	12.27	−1.68					40	28.85	4.5
3/22/40	12.13	12.26	−1.05					41	30.77	2.5
3/29/40	12.18	12.25	−0.57	S2'	RoR/T-bill =	0.00%		42	59.62	0.50
4/5/40	12.48	12.28	1.62	B3	12.26			43	63.46	4.0
4/12/40	12.32	12.28	0.29	B3'	12.28 rate =	0.19%		44	84.62	5.0
4/19/40	12.04	12.26	−1.80	S3				45	90.38	3.0
4/26/40	12.08	12.24	−1.30							

5/3/40	12.12	12.22	−0.86		46	42.31	2.5
5/10/40	11.76	12.17	−3.49		47	38.46	4.0
5/17/40	9.95	11.91	−19.71		48	48.08	4.5
5/24/40	9.16	11.59	−26.51		49	51.92	1.0

Date			
5/3/40	12.12	12.22	−0.86
5/10/40	11.76	12.17	−3.49
5/17/40	9.95	11.91	−19.71
5/24/40	9.16	11.59	−26.51
5/31/40	9.27	11.32	−22.08
6/7/40	9.34	11.08	−18.68
6/14/40	9.94	10.95	−10.17
6/21/40	9.91	10.83	−9.28
6/28/40	9.98	10.73	−7.52
7/5/40	9.94	10.64	−7.03
7/12/40	9.95	10.56	−6.12
7/19/40	9.97	10.49	−5.22
7/26/40	9.97	10.43	−4.62
8/2/40	10.25	10.41	−1.56
8/9/40	10.27	10.39	−1.21
8/16/40	9.84	10.33	−4.98
8/23/40	10.19	10.31	−1.23
8/30/40	10.50	10.34	1.54
9/6/40	10.85	10.40	4.16
9/13/40	10.31	10.39	−0.77
9/20/40	10.59	10.41	1.66
9/27/40	10.58	10.43	1.37

46	42.31	2.5
47	38.46	4.0
48	48.08	4.5
49	51.92	1.0

Average Round Turns for 1940s = 3.15

S3'	RoR/T-bill =	0.01%
B4	10.33	
B4'	10.39 rate =	0.65%
'S4'	10.40	
B5	RoR/T-bill =	0.00%
	10.40	

(continued)

Date (Friday)	S&P 500 Index Price	Y-Process Number	Risk Index (%)	Ypro Buy (B) or Sell (S)	Y-Process and T-Bill Rates	Annual Return (AR)	Annual Total Return (ATR)	Bahf S&P 500 Index ATR (%)	Ypro Y-Process ATR (%)	Year
10/4/40	10.78	10.48	2.82							
10/11/40	10.58	10.49	0.85							
10/18/40	10.72	10.52	1.89							
10/25/40	10.73	10.54	1.73							
11/1/40	11.08	10.61	4.26							
11/8/40	11.23	10.68	4.88							
11/15/40	11.17	10.74	3.84							
11/22/40	10.79	10.75	0.39	B5'	10.74 rate =	3.32%				
11/29/40	10.57	10.73	-1.49	S5						
12/6/40	10.53	10.71	-1.67							
12/13/40	10.69	10.70	-0.14							
12/20/40	10.41	10.67	-2.51							
12/27/40	10.44	10.65	-1.96							
12/31/40	10.58	10.64	-0.55	S5'	RoR/T-bill =	0.00%	10.58			

Appendix B

S&P 500 Index for 1950

Date (Friday)	S&P 500 Index Price	Y-Process Number	Risk Index (%)	Ypro Buy (B) or Sell (S)
1/3/50	16.66	16.21	2.69	B0
1/6/50	16.98	16.30	3.98	
1/13/50	16.67	16.35	1.93	
1/20/50	16.90	16.41	2.87	
1/27/50	16.82	16.46	2.11	
2/3/50	17.29	16.56	4.20	
2/10/50	17.24	16.64	3.45	
2/17/50	17.15	16.71	2.59	
2/24/50	17.28	16.77	2.92	
3/3/50	17.29	16.84	2.62	
3/10/50	17.09	16.87	1.30	
3/17/50	17.45	16.94	2.93	
3/24/50	17.56	17.01	3.11	
3/31/50	17.29	17.05	1.40	
4/7/50	17.82	17.14	3.81	
4/14/50	17.96	17.24	4.02	
4/21/50	17.96	17.33	3.53	
4/28/50	17.96	17.40	3.11	

Y-Process and T-Bill Rates

	Annual Return (AR)	Annual Total Return (ATR)	
		ATR	ΔATR
1950 AR =	21.78%	28.98%	7.20%
1950 Y-Proc AR =	22.64%	28.87%	6.23%
1950 T-Bill =	1.22%	Mkt Risk = 86.54	
Div =	7.20%	Rnd Turns = 2.0	

Year	Bahf S&P 500 Index ATR (%)	Ypro Y-Process ATR (%)
50	28.98	28.87
51	22.39	23.81
52	17.07	17.93
53	−0.78	5.32
54	49.30	48.49
55	30.01	32.11
56	6.35	13.72
57	−9.83	10.36
58	41.23	37.26
59	11.54	13.78

Year	Mkt Risk	Rnd Turns
50	86.54	2.0
51	75.00	3.0
52	73.08	4.0
53	50.00	3.0
54	100.00	0.0
55	94.23	2.0

5/5/50	18.22	17.50	3.95			
5/12/50	18.18	17.58	3.29			
5/19/50	18.68	17.71	5.18			
5/26/50	18.67	17.83	4.52			
6/2/50	18.79	17.94	4.51			
6/9/50	19.26	18.10	6.03			
6/16/50	18.97	18.20	4.04			
6/23/50	19.14	18.32	4.31	B0'	18.30 rate =	9.19%
6/30/50	17.69	18.24	-3.13	S1		
7/7/50	17.67	18.18	-2.87			
7/14/50	16.87	18.03	-6.85			
7/21/50	17.59	17.98	-2.20			
7/28/50	17.69	17.94	-1.44	S1'	RoR/T-bill =	0.14%
8/4/50	18.14	17.97	0.94	B1	17.96	
8/11/50	18.28	18.01	1.49			
8/18/50	18.68	18.09	3.17			
8/25/50	18.54	18.14	2.14			
9/1/50	18.55	18.19	1.92			
9/8/50	18.75	18.26	2.61			
9/15/50	19.29	18.38	4.70			
9/22/50	19.44	18.51	4.79			
9/29/50	19.45	18.62	4.26			

56	51.92	5.0
57	40.38	1.5
58	86.54	2.0
59	76.92	1.0

Average Round Turns for 1950s = 2.35

(continued)

Date (Friday)	S&P 500 Index Price	Y-Process Number	Risk Index (%)	Ypro Buy (B) or Sell (S)	Y-Process and T-Bill Rates	Annual Return (AR)	Annual Total Return (ATR)	Year	Bahf S&P 500 Index ATR (%)	Ypro Y-Process ATR (%)
10/6/50	20.12	18.80	6.56							
10/13/50	19.85	18.93	4.66							
10/20/50	19.96	19.05	4.56							
10/27/50	19.77	19.14	3.21							
11/3/50	19.85	19.22	3.16							
11/10/50	19.94	19.31	3.17							
11/17/50	19.86	19.38	2.44							
11/24/50	20.32	19.49	4.09							
12/1/50	19.66	19.51	0.76	B1'	19.50 rate =	8.59%				
12/8/50	19.40	19.50	-0.51	S2						
12/15/50	19.33	19.48	-0.78	S2'	RoR/T-bill = 19.50	0.07%				
12/22/50	20.07	19.55	2.58	B3						
12/29/50	20.43	19.66	3.78							
12/30/50	20.41	19.66	3.78	B3'	20.41 rate =	4.65%				

Appendix C

S&P 500 Index for 1960

Date (Friday)	S&P 500 Index Price	Y-Process Number	Risk Index (%)	Ypro Buy (B) or Sell (S)	Y-Process and T-Bill Rates	Annual Return (AR)	Annual Total Return (ATR)		Year	Bahf S&P 500 Index ATR (%)	Ypro Y-Process ATR (%)
1/1/60	59.91	58.35	2.60	B0					60	0.38	9.49
1/8/60	59.50	58.49	1.69	B0'					61	25.95	24.65
1/15/60	58.38	58.49	-0.18	S1	58.49 rate =	-0.023	ATR	ΔATR	62	8.43	14.02
1/22/60	57.38	58.36	-1.71		1960 AR =	-2.972%	0.378%	3.35%	63	21.93	21.50
1/29/60	55.61	58.04	-4.38		1960 Y-Proc AR =	8.005%	9.49%	1.48%	64	15.92	15.73
2/5/60	55.98	57.81	-3.26		1960 T-Bill =	2.930%	Mkt Risk = 44.23		65	12.00	14.36
2/12/60	55.46	57.54	-3.74		Div =	3.35%	Rnd Turns = 5.0		66	-9.52	6.17
2/19/60	56.24	57.39	-2.04						67	23.12	24.44
2/26/60	56.16	57.25	-1.94						68	10.62	17.23
3/4/60	54.47	56.93	-4.52						69	-7.93	9.38
3/11/60	54.24	56.62	-4.39							Mkt Risk	Rnd Turns
3/18/60	55.01	56.43	-2.59						60	44.23	5.0
3/25/60	55.98	56.39	-0.73						61	92.31	3.0
4/1/60	55.43	56.28	-1.53	S1'	RoR/T-bill =	0.0068			62	40.38	2.0
4/8/60	56.39	56.30	0.16	B1	56.30				63	92.31	1.0
4/15/60	56.43	56.32	0.20	B1'	56.31 rate =	0.0002			64	92.31	2.0
4/22/60	55.42	56.22	-1.44	S2					65	78.85	2.0
4/29/60	54.37	56.01	-3.01						66	32.26	3.5

Date						
5/6/60	54.75	55.86	-2.04			
5/13/60	55.30	55.80	-0.91	S2'	RoR/T-bill =	0.0028
5/20/60	55.83	55.81	0.03	B2'	55.81 rate =	0.0093
5/27/60	55.74	55.81	-0.13	S2'	RoR/T-bill =	0.0011
6/3/60	56.23	55.86	0.65	B3	55.82	
6/10/60	57.97	56.12	3.19			
6/17/60	57.44	56.28	2.02			
6/24/60	57.68	56.45	2.13			
7/1/60	57.06	56.53	0.93			
7/8/60	57.38	56.63	1.30	B3'	56.60 rate =	0.0141
7/15/60	56.05	56.57	-0.93	S3		
7/22/60	54.72	56.36	-2.99			
7/29/60	55.51	56.26	-1.36			
8/5/60	55.44	56.17	-1.32	S3'	RoR/T-bill =	0.0028
8/12/60	56.66	56.24	0.75	B4	56.22	
8/19/60	57.01	56.33	1.19			
8/26/60	57.60	56.49	1.93			
9/2/60	57.00	56.55	0.78	B4'	56.53 rate =	0.0056
9/9/60	56.11	56.51	-0.71	S4		
9/16/60	55.11	56.35	-2.25			
9/23/60	53.90	56.07	-4.02			
9/30/60	53.52	55.77	-4.21			
10/7/60	54.03	55.57	-2.85			
10/14/60	54.88	55.50	-1.12			
10/21/60	53.32	55.25	-3.61			
10/28/60	53.41	55.04	-3.04			

67	86.54	3.5
68	73.08	3.5
69	23.08	3.5

Average Round Turns for 1960s = 2.9

(continued)

207

Date (Friday)	S&P 500 Index Price	Y-Process Number	Risk Index (%)	Ypro Buy (B) or Sell (S)	Y-Process and T-Bill Rates	Annual Return (AR)	Annual Total Return (ATR)	Year	Bahf S&P 500 Index ATR (%)	Ypro Y-Process ATR (%)
11/4/60	54.90	55.02	-0.23	S4'	RoR/T-bill =	0.0051				
11/11/60	55.87	55.13	1.33	B5	55.04					
11/18/60	55.82	55.22	1.08							
11/25/60	56.13	55.33	1.43							
12/2/60	55.39	55.34	0.09							
12/9/60	56.65	55.50	2.03							
12/16/60	57.20	55.71	2.61							
12/23/60	57.44	55.92	2.65							
12/31/60	58.11	56.18	3.32	B5'	58.11 rate =	0.056				

Appendix D

S&P 500 Index for 1970

Date (Friday)	S&P 500 Index Price	Y-Process Number	Risk Index (%)	Ypro Buy (B) or Sell (S)	Year	Bahf S&P 500 Index ATR (%)	Ypro Y-Process ATR (%)
1/2/70	93.00	94.05	-1.13	SO'	70	3.51	23.25
1/9/70	92.40	93.87	-1.59		71	13.80	19.59
1/16/70	90.92	93.53	-2.87		72	18.30	20.15
1/23/70	89.07	93.01	-4.43		73	-13.91	7.84
1/30/70	85.02	92.08	-8.31		74	-24.47	13.35
2/6/70	86.33	91.41	-5.89		75	35.63	41.63
2/13/70	86.54	90.85	-4.98		76	22.92	13.40
2/20/70	88.03	90.53	-2.84		77	-6.59	9.27
2/27/70	89.50	90.41	-1.02		78	6.34	19.94
3/6/70	89.44	90.31	-0.97		79	15.02	21.16
						Mkt Risk	Rnd Turns
3/13/70	87.86	90.03	-2.47		70	38.46	0.5
3/20/70	87.06	89.69	-3.02		71	65.38	5.0
3/27/70	89.92	89.73	0.22		72	80.77	6.5
4/3/70	89.39	89.69	-0.34		73	30.77	2.5
4/10/70	88.24	89.53	-1.46		74	11.44	3.0
4/17/70	85.67	89.09	-3.99		75	75.00	2.5
4/24/70	82.77	88.35	-6.74				

Annual Total Return (ATR)

Annual Return (AR)	ATR	ΔATR
0.10%	3.51%	3.41%
21.94%	23.25%	1.31%
6.46%	Mkt Risk = 38.46	
3.41%	Rnd Turns = 0.5	

Y-Process and T-Bill Rates

1970 AR =	0.10%
1970 Y-Proc AR =	21.94%
1970 T-Bill =	6.46%
Div =	3.41%

5/1/70	81.44	87.55	-7.50
5/8/70	79.44	86.60	-9.02
5/15/70	76.90	85.47	-11.14
5/22/70	77.25	84.51	-9.40
5/29/70	76.55	83.58	-9.19
6/5/70	76.17	82.72	-8.60
6/12/70	74.21	81.72	-10.13
6/19/70	77.05	81.18	-5.36
6/26/70	73.47	80.28	-9.27
7/3/70	72.92	79.42	-8.92
7/10/70	74.57	78.86	-5.75
7/17/70	77.69	78.73	-1.34
7/24/70	77.82	78.63	-1.04
7/31/70	78.05	78.57	-0.67
8/7/70	77.28	78.43	-1.48
8/14/70	75.18	78.05	-3.82
8/21/70	79.24	78.20	1.31
8/28/70	81.86	78.64	3.94
9/4/70	82.83	79.14	4.46
9/11/70	82.52	79.55	3.60
9/18/70	82.62	79.92	3.27
9/25/70	83.97	80.40	4.25

SO'

B1

RoR/T-bill = 4.10%

78.20

76	78.85	3.0
77	19.23	3.5
78	48.08	2.0
79	71.15	3.5

Average Round Turns for 1970s = 3.2

(continued)

Date (Friday)	S&P 500 Index Price	Y-Process Number	Risk Index (%)	Ypro Buy (B) or Sell (S)	Y-Process and T-Bill Rates	Annual Return (AR)	Annual Total Return (ATR)	Year	Bahf S&P 500 Index ATR (%)	Ypro Y-Process ATR (%)
10/2/70	85.16	80.97	4.92							
10/9/70	85.08	81.46	4.25							
10/16/70	84.28	81.80	2.94							
10/23/70	83.77	82.04	2.06							
10/30/70	83.25	82.19	1.27							
11/6/70	84.22	82.44	2.12							
11/13/70	83.37	82.56	0.98							
11/20/70	83.72	82.70	1.22							
11/27/70	85.93	83.09	3.31							
12/4/70	89.46	83.85	6.27							
12/11/70	90.26	84.61	6.26							
12/18/70	90.22	85.28	5.48							
12/25/70	90.61	85.92	5.18							
12/31/70	92.15	86.66	5.96	BI'	92.15 rate =	17.84%				

Appendix E

S&P 500 Index for 1980

Date (Friday)	S&P 500 Index Price	Y-Process Number	Risk Index (%)	Ypro Buy (B) or Sell (S)	Y-Process and T-Bill Rates	Annual Return (AR)
1/2/80	105.76	106.06	-0.29			
1/4/80	106.52	106.13	0.37	B0	1980 AR =	25.77%
1/11/80	109.92	106.58	3.04		1980 Y-Proc AR =	33.04%
1/18/80	111.07	107.12	3.55		1980 T-Bill =	11.81%
1/25/80	113.61	107.90	5.03		Div =	4.54%
2/1/80	115.12	108.76	5.53			
2/8/80	117.95	109.85	6.87			
2/15/80	115.41	110.52	4.24			
2/22/80	115.04	111.06	3.46			
2/29/80	113.66	111.38	2.01			
3/7/80	106.90	110.86	-3.71%	B0'	111.28 rate =	3.10%
3/14/80	105.43	110.23	-4.56	S1		
3/21/80	102.31	109.31	-6.84			
3/28/80	100.68	108.31	-7.57			
4/4/80	102.15	107.59	-5.33			
4/11/80	103.79	107.16	-3.24			
4/18/80	100.55	106.39	-5.81			
4/25/80	105.16	106.25	-1.04			

Annual Total Return (ATR)

	ATR	ΔATR
	30.31%	4.54%
	36.53%	3.49%
	Mkt Risk = 76.92	
	Rnd Turns = 2.0	

Bahf

Year	S&P 500 Index ATR (%)	Ypro Y-Process ATR (%)
80	30.31	36.53
81	-4.32	16.64
82	19.64	36.72
83	21.57	26.30
84	5.90	16.66
85	30.07	33.47
86	18.04	22.47
87	5.60	33.29
88	15.90	16.53
89	30.38	29.98

Year	Mkt Risk	Rnd Turns
80	76.92	2.0
81	36.54	5.5
82	48.08	1.5
83	75.00	4.0
84	44.23	4.5
85	80.77	3.0
86	80.77	3.0

			SI'	RoR/T-bill =	2.50%
			B1	106.13	
5/2/80	105.58	106.19	-0.57		
5/9/80	104.72	106.02	-1.25		
5/16/80	107.35	106.19	1.08		
5/23/80	110.62	106.72	3.52		
5/30/80	111.24	107.27	3.57		
6/6/80	113.20	107.97	4.62		
6/13/80	115.81	108.91	5.96		
6/20/80	114.06	109.52	3.98		
6/27/80	116.00	110.30	4.92		
7/4/80	117.46	111.15	5.37		
7/11/80	117.84	111.95	5.00		
7/18/80	122.04	113.15	7.29		
7/25/80	120.78	114.06	5.57		
8/1/80	121.21	114.91	5.20		
8/8/80	123.61	115.95	6.20		
8/15/80	125.72	117.11	6.85		
8/22/80	126.02	118.17	6.23		
8/29/80	122.38	118.68	3.03		
9/5/80	124.88	119.42	4.37		
9/12/80	125.54	120.15	4.29		
9/19/80	129.25	121.23	6.20		
9/26/80	126.35	121.85	3.56		

87	71.15	2.5
88	57.69	6.0
89	92.31	2.0

Average Round Turns for 1980s = 3.4

(continued)

Date (Friday)	S&P 500 Index Price	Y-Process Number	Risk Index (%)	Ypro Buy (B) or Sell (S)	Y-Process and T-Bill Rates	Annual Return (AR)	Annual Total Return (ATR)	Year	Bahf S&P 500 Index ATR (%)	Ypro Y-Process ATR (%)
10/3/80	129.33	122.74	5.09							
10/10/80	130.29	123.64	5.10							
10/17/80	131.52	124.58	5.28							
10/24/80	129.85	125.21	3.57							
10/31/80	127.47	125.49	1.55							
11/7/80	129.18	125.94	2.51							
11/14/80	137.15	127.27	7.20							
11/21/80	139.11	128.68	7.50							
11/28/80	140.52	130.08	7.43							
12/5/80	134.03	130.56	2.59	B1'	130.49 rate =	22.95%				
12/12/80	129.23	130.42	–0.92	'S2'	RoR/T-bill =	2.95%				
12/19/80	133.70	130.82	2.16	B2						
12/26/80	136.57	131.51	3.71							
12/31/80	135.76	131.51	3.71	B2'	135.76 rate =	1.54%				

Appendix F

S&P 500 Index for 1990

Date (Friday)	S&P 500 Index Price	Y-Process Number	Risk Index (%)	Ypro Buy (B) or Sell (S)	Y-Process and T-Bill Rates	Annual Return (AR)	Annual Total Return (ATR) ΔATR	ΔATR	Year	Bahf S&P 500 Index ATR (%)	Ypro Y-Process ATR (%)
1/5/90	352.20	346.26	1.69	B0'	346.01 rate =	-2.09%	ΔATR	ΔATR	90	-2.90	12.44
1/12/90	339.93	345.55	-1.65	S1	1990 AR =	-6.56%	-2.90%	3.66%	91	29.24	33.76
1/19/90	339.15	344.83	-1.68		1990 Y-Proc AR =	11.17%	12.44%	1.27%	92	7.30	8.81
1/26/90	325.80	342.63	-5.16		1990 T-Bill =	7.51%	Mkt Risk = 34.62		93	9.76	9.92
2/2/90	330.92	341.28	-3.13		Div =	3.66%	Rnd Turns = 5.0		94	1.33	8.31
2/9/90	333.62	340.42	-2.04						95	36.35	36.35
2/16/90	332.72	339.54	-2.05						96	22.27	22.69
2/23/90	324.15	337.77	-4.20						97	32.55	34.74
3/2/90	335.54	337.54	-0.60	S1'	RoR/T-bill =	1.16%			98	27.85	34.95
3/9/90	337.93	337.62	0.09	B1					99	20.75	24.12
										Mkt Risk	Rnd Turns
3/16/90	341.91	338.16	1.10	B1'					90	34.62	5.0
3/23/90	337.22	338.08	-0.26	S2'	RoR/T-bill =	0.29%			91	82.69	5.0
3/30/90	339.94	338.33	0.47	B2	338.17				92	78.85	4.0
4/6/90	340.08	338.57	0.44						93	88.46	5.0
4/13/90	344.34	339.28	1.47	B2'	339.08 rate =	0.27%			94	51.92	7.5
4/20/90	335.12	338.83	-1.11	S2					95	100.00	0.5
4/27/90	329.11	337.72	-2.62	S2'	RoR/T-bill =	0.43%					

218

Date						
5/4/90	338.39	337.83	0.17			
5/11/90	352.00	339.53	3.54	B3	337.84	
5/18/90	354.64	341.34	3.75			
5/25/90	354.58	342.94	3.28			
6/1/90	363.16	345.35	4.90			
6/8/90	358.71	346.96	3.28			
6/15/90	362.91	348.87	3.87			
6/22/90	355.43	349.68	1.62			
6/29/90	358.02	350.69	2.05			
7/6/90	358.42	351.64	1.89			
7/13/90	367.31	353.52	3.75			
7/20/90	361.61	354.51	1.96	B3'	354.45	rate 4.92%
7/27/90	353.44	354.42	-0.28	S1		
8/3/90	344.86	353.33	-2.46			
8/10/90	335.52	351.27	-4.69			
8/17/90	327.83	348.54	-6.32			
8/24/90	311.51	344.22	-10.50			
8/31/90	322.56	341.70	-5.94			
9/7/90	323.40	339.58	-5.00			
9/14/90	316.83	336.94	-6.35			
9/21/90	311.32	333.96	-7.27			
9/28/90	306.05	330.71	-8.06			

96	88.46	2.0
97	84.62	2.0
98	78.85	2.0
99	82.69	3.0

Average Round Turns for 1990s = 3.5

(continued)

Date (Friday)	S&P 500 Index Price	Y-Process Number	Risk Index (%)	Ypro Buy (B) or Sell (S)	Y-Process and T-Bill Rates	Annual Return (AR)	Annual Total Return (ATR)	Year	Bahf S&P 500 Index ATR (%)	Ypro Y-Process ATR (%)
10/5/90	311.50	328.48	-5.45							
10/12/90	300.03	325.16	-8.38							
10/19/90	312.48	323.70	-3.59							
10/26/90	304.71	321.50	-5.51							
11/2/90	311.85	320.40	-2.74							
11/9/90	313.74	319.64	-1.88							
11/16/90	317.12	319.38	-0.71							
11/23/90	315.10	318.91	-1.21	S1'	RoR/T-bill =	2.74%				
11/30/90	322.22	319.33	0.90	B4	319.19					
12/7/90	327.75	320.35	2.26							
12/14/90	326.82	321.15	1.74							
12/21/90	331.75	322.43	2.81							
12/28/90	328.72	323.20	1.68							
12/31/90	330.22	324.06	1.87	B4'	rate =	3.46%				

Notes

INTRODUCTION

1. The 59 percent risk reduction is the mean value for the past 71 years—1930 through 2000.

CHAPTER 1

1. H. Markowitz, *Portfolio Selection: Efficient Diversification of Investments* (New York: Wiley, 1959).

CHAPTER 2

1. J. Siegel, *Stocks for the Long Run* (New York: McGraw-Hill, 1998).
2. Technically, the first great crash began in October 1929.
3. Inflation-adjusted returns measure the increase in purchasing power earned by the investor. The inflation-adjusted return is determined by the following equation: $[(1 + \text{nominal return})/(1 + \text{rate of inflation}) - 1] * 100\%$. Thus, for the period from 1930 to 1998, the inflation-adjusted rate is $[(1 + .104)/(1 + .031) - 1] * 100\% = 7.0805\% = 7.1\%$ (rounded).

CHAPTER 3

1. $9.3\% = (\$850 /\$915) \times 10$.
2. "Intelligent Investing," *Philadelphia Inquirer*, 27 Sept. 1998, p. 4.

CHAPTER 4

1. Cited in C. Willis, "The Ten Mistakes to Avoid with Your Money," *Money Magazine*, June 1990, pp. 86–92.
2. Ibid.
3. Ibid.
4. Ibid.

5. P. Lynch with J. Rothchild, *Beating the Street* (New York: Simon & Schuster, 1993), pp. 303–305.
6. A term coined by the author describing people who are lovers of "large, whole, round numbers."

CHAPTER 5

1. Large-capitalization (large-cap) firms are firms whose net present values times the number of shares are greater than $2 billion.

CHAPTER 6

1. SPDR from Standard & Poor's depository receipts, ticker symbol, SPY. SPDRs were created in February 1993.

CHAPTER 7

1. Recent history is taken from World War II through 1998, as presented in Table 7.2.
2. Alan Greenspan is Chairman of the Federal Reserve Board, which is sometimes referred to as the Fed.
3. Bearish is defined as fearful of falling stock market prices, probably from the adage about "selling the bearskin before catching the bear."
4. The Investment Company Institute recorded an outflow of $11.2 billion from stock mutual funds in August 1998, the first month in nearly a decade when there were net redemptions. From "Fund Track," *Wall Street Journal*, 17 Nov. 1998.
5. For those whose memories have faded, the Dow fell 48 percent from 381.17 on 3 Sept. 1929. Then they rallied back 48 percent to 294.1 by 17 May 1930—only to fall to a thudding 86 percent over the next two years, finally bottoming out at 41.2 on 8 July 1932.

CHAPTER 8

1. W. Gordon, *The Stock Market Indicators as a Guide to Market Timing* (Palisades Park, NJ: Investors' Press, 1968), p. 20

2. H. B. Mayo, *Investments: An Introduction* (Orlando, FL: Dryden Press, 1993), pp. 208–215.
3. Ibid., p. 216.

CHAPTER 10

1. *Merriam Webster's Collegiate Dictionary*, 10th ed., s.v. "consistent."

CHAPTER 12

1. The 1997 tax law set in motion a new five-year holding period commencing January 1, 2001, for securities purchased thereafter. For securities held for a minimum of five years, the tax rate is 18 percent for those in the higher tax brackets and 8 percent for those in the 15 percent bracket.

    The 2001 Tax Relief Act reduces all tax brackets over the next five years. Beginning in 2006, the new brackets will be 10 percent (this is an entirely new bracket), 15 percent, 25 percent, 33 percent, and 35 percent. The current highest bracket, 39.1 percent, steadily declines. In 2002/2003 it will be 38.6 percent; in 2004/2005, 37.6 percent; and in 2006 and thereafter, the maximum bracket drops to 35 percent.

Glossary

Active Management   An investment approach that seeks to exceed the average returns of the financial markets. Active managers rely on research, market forecasts, and their own judgment and experience in selecting securities to buy or sell.

Algorithm   A procedure for solving a mathematical problem using a computer program that is adept at performing repetitive operations.

American Stock Exchange (AMEX) Major Market Index   An index of 20 blue chip industrial stocks that closely track the changes in the Dow Jones Industrial Average. Fifteen of the stocks in the index are also included in the Dow Jones Industrial Average.

Asked   Price that someone is willing to accept for a security or an asset. In the stock market, the ask portion of a stock quote is the lowest price.

Asset Allocation Funds   Asset allocation funds have the ability to shift assets among asset classes (for example equities, bonds, and short-term instruments). Asset allocation funds take the concept of a private asset manager—a skilled professional who builds and manages a comprehensive portfolio for a client—and apply it to a mutual fund.

Asset-Backed Securities.   Bonds or notes backed by loan paper or accounts receivable originated by banks, credit card companies, or other providers of credit and often enhanced by a bank letter of credit or by insurance coverage provided by an institution other than the issuer.

Auction Market.   A market for securities, typically found on a national securities exchange, in which trading in a particular security is conducted at a specific location with all qualified persons at that post able to bid or offer securities against orders via outcry.

Average Annual Total Return.   Average annual total return is a hypothetical rate of return that, if achieved annually, would have produced the same cumulative total return if performance had been constant over the entire period. Average annual total returns smooth out variation in performance; they are not the same as actual year-by-year results.

Average Yield, 30-Day   Based on yield to maturity of a fund's investments over a 30-day period and not on the dividends paid by the fund, which may differ.

Balloons Final payments on a debt that are substantially larger than the preceding payments. Loans or mortgages are structured with balloon payments when some projected event is expected to provide extra cash flow or when refinancing is anticipated. Balloon loans are sometimes called partially amortized loans.

Basis Point One one-hundredth (1/100 or 0.01) of one percent. Yield differences among fixed-income securities are stated in basis points.

Bear Market   A market that declines 20 percent or more and lasts for one year or less. Two other bear market definitions created by the author and defined in this book are: Grizzly Bear Market and Kodiak Grizzly Bear Market. A Grizzly Bear Market is one that plunges 25 percent or more and lasts for one to three years before it returns to its prior peak. A Kodiak Grizzly Bear is the one that is the most fearsome and dreaded. It is one that meltsdown a gut-wrenching, wealth-ravaging, 30 percent or more and lasts for three or more years before it returns to its prior peak.

Bellwether Bond   For the U.S. market, it is the 30-year Treasury bond most recently offered by the government. Its performance is a benchmark for evaluating the bond market in general. Also called the long bond.

Beta   A measurement of a portfolio's sensitivity to market movements. It is a ratio of the portfolio's past price fluctuations compared to the fluctuations of a benchmark index, such as the S&P 500. The S&P 500 has, as a generally accepted standard, a beta of 1.0. A beta less than 1.0 indicates that the fund's share price has fluctuated less (positively or negatively) than the S&P 500 for any given move in the index. The correlation measure R^2 should always be considered before beta to determine the validity of the comparison; a beta alone will not provide a complete picture of a fund's behavior. Beta can be calculated using the performance figures for any time period. For example, a mutual fund might calculate the beta based on 36-months' returns. See **Volatility Measures**; see also **Correlation Measures, R^2, S&P 500 Index**.

Bill (Treasury or T-Bill)   A government security with a maturity of a year or less.

Blue-Chip Stocks   Stocks of well-established companies that have had a history of earnings and dividend payments, as well as a reputation for sound management and quality products and services. Also known as large-cap stocks.

Bond   An interest-bearing promise to pay a specified sum of money—the principal amount—due on a specific date.

Bond Funds   Registered investment companies whose assets are invested in diversified portfolios of bonds.

Broker   A person who gives advice and handles orders to buy or sell stocks, bonds, commodities, and options.

Brokerage Firm   Financial-services firm that provides the services of buying and selling securities. Brokerage firms fall into two main camps: full-service brokers and discount brokers. Discount brokers charge far lower commissions than do full-service brokers and a growing number of deep discounters charge especially low commissions. A discount broker gives little or no investment advice. A full-service broker helps pick investments and devise a financial plan.

Callable Bond   A bond that the issuer is permitted or required to redeem before the stated maturity date at a specified price, usually at or above par, by giving notice of redemption in a manner specified in the bond contract.

Call Feature   The terms of the bond contract giving the issuer the right or requiring the issuer to redeem or call all or a portion of an outstanding issue of bonds prior to their stated dates of maturity at a specified price, usually at or above par.

Call Protection   The aspects of the call provisions of an issue of callable securities that partially protect an investor against an issuer's call of the securities or act as a disincentive to the issuer's exercise of its call privileges. These features include restrictions on an issuer's right to call securities for a period of time after issuance (for example, an issue that cannot be called for 10 years after its issuance is said to have 10 years' call protection), or requirements that an issuer pay a premium redemption price for securities called within a certain period of time after issuance.

Capital Appreciation   As the value of the securities in a portfolio increases, a fund's share price increases, meaning that the value of the investment rises. If the shares are sold at a higher price than was paid for them, there is a profit or capital gain. If the shares are sold at a lower price than was paid for them, there is a capital loss. See also **Capital Gains; Dividends**.

Capital Gains   The difference between an asset's purchased price and selling price, when the difference is positive.

Capital Gain Distribution   Payment to mutual fund shareholders of gains realized during the year on securities that the fund has sold at a profit, minus any realized losses.

Capital Loss   A loss realized when an instrument or asset is sold at a price below its cost.

Capital Market   The market where capital funds—debt (bonds) and equity (stocks)—are traded.

Collateralized Mortgage Obligation (CMO)   A mortgage-backed bond that separates mortgage pools into different maturity classes called tranches. This is accomplished by applying income (payments of principal and interest) from mortgages in the pool in the order of the CMO's payout.

Common Stocks   Stocks represent a share in the ownership of a particular company. If the company does well, the value of each share generally goes up. Although common stocks have a history of long-term growth, their prices fluctuate based on changes in a company's financial condition and on overall market and economic conditions.

Compounding   If an investment makes 10 percent a year for five years, the return is not 50 percent but 61.1 percent. The reason is that as time goes on, an investment makes money not only on the original investment but also on the accumulated gains from earlier years.

Convertible Bond   A corporate bond, usually a junior subordinated debenture, that can be exchanged for shares of the issuer's common stock.

Correlation Measures   Measures that show the validity of a comparison to a benchmark index based on the historical relationship between portfolio returns and index returns. See R^2; see also **Volatility Measures**.

Coupon   Term used colloquially to refer to a security's interest rate.

Coupon Rate   The annual rate of interest payable on a debt security expressed as a percentage of the principal amount.

Coupon Yield   See **Nominal Yield**.

Cover Your Short   A term used of investors who have sold short: The act of buying an equivalent number of stock shares or bonds and instructing the broker to deliver these against the short position; thus, closing the open position. Also used in a similar fashion in a short against the box when the investor instructs the broker to deliver the box securities against the short position.

Credits   Loans, bonds, charge-account obligations, and open-account balances with commercial firms.

Cumulative Total Return   Cumulative total return reflects actual performance over a stated period of time.

Currency Risk   The risk that shifts in foreign exchange rates may undermine the dollar value of overseas investments.

Current Income   Monies paid during the period an investment is held. Examples include bond interest and stock dividends.

Current Market Value   The amount a willing buyer will pay for a bond today, which may be at a premium (above face value) or at a discount (below face value).

Current Yield   The ratio of interest to the actual market price of the bond stated as a percentage: annual interest = current yield.

CUSIP   An identification number assigned to each fund by the Committee on Uniform Security Identification Procedures.

Cyclicals   Stocks of companies whose business prospects are tied to economic cycles. For example, steel companies often do poorly in a recession, when consumers buy fewer large items such as cars and refrigerators.

DAX 100   The Deutscher Akteinindex (DAX) 100 is a market capitalization-weighted index of the 100 most heavily traded stocks in the German market.

Denomination   The face amount or par value of a security that the issuer promises to pay on the maturity date.

Depression   A severe downturn in an economy that is marked by falling prices, reduced purchasing power, and high unemployment.

Discount   The difference between a bond's current market price and its face or redemption value.

Diversification   Diversification is the concept of spreading investment dollars across different types of investments and/or issues to potentially moderate investment risk.

Dividends   Mutual fund dividends are paid out of income from the fund's investments. The tax on such dividends depends on whether the distributions resulted from interest income or dividends received by the fund.

Dollar-Cost Averaging   With dollar-cost averaging, a fixed amount is invested on a regular basis regardless of current market trends. The investor buys more shares when the price is low and fewer shares when the price is high; the overall cost is lower than it would be if a constant number of shares were bought at set intervals. Dollar-cost averaging does not assure a profit or protect against a loss in a declining market. Shares must be purchased both in up and down markets. The goal of dollar-cost averaging is to attain a lower average cost per share.

Dow Jones Industrial Average (DJIA)   The Dow Jones Industrial Average is an unmanaged index of common stocks comprised of major industrial companies and assumes reinvestment of dividends.

Duration   Duration estimates how much a bond's price fluctuates with changes in comparable interest rates. If rates rise 1 percent, for example, a fund with a five-year duration is likely to lose about 5 percent of its value. Other factors also can influence a bond fund's performance and share price. A bond fund's actual performance may differ.

Efficient Market Theory (EMT)   Security prices depend on future cash flows, for example, interest or dividend payments. If new information suggests that these flows will be altered, the market rapidly adjusts the security's price. Thus, an efficient financial market implies that a security's current price embodies all the known information concerning the potential return and risk associated with the particular security.

Exchange-Traded Funds (ETFs)   ETFs are baskets of stocks, grouped so that they can be traded like shares of common stock. ETFs provide dividends as does ordinary stock. And, like stock, ETFs can be held for either the short or long term. How a particular ETF tracks the market is determined by its composition, the percentage weight of each component, and the method of calculating the index.

Expense Ratio   The percentage of the fund's average net assets spent for the operation and management of the fund, includes the management fee. See **Management Fee**.

Federal Home Loan Mortgage Corporation (FHLMC or Freddie Mac)   A federally created corporation established to facilitate the financing of single-family residential housing by creating and maintaining an active secondary market for conventional home mortgages.

Federal National Mortgage Association (FNMA or Fannie Mae)   A government-sponsored private corporation authorized to purchase and sell mortgages and to otherwise facilitate the orderly operation of a secondary market for home mortgages.

FT-All Shares   The FT-All Shares Index is a market capitalization-weighted index of 750 stocks traded in the U.K. market.

Fundamental Analysis   Analysis technique that looks at a company's financial condition, management, and place in its industry to predict a company's stock price movement.

General Obligation Bond (GO)   A municipal bond that is backed by the full faith and credit (taxing and borrowing power) of a municipality.

Government National Mortgage Association (GNMA or Ginnie Mae) An agency of the federal Department of Housing and Urban Development empowered to provide special assistance in financing home mortgages that is responsible for management and liquidation of federally owned mortgage portfolios. GNMA guarantees, with the full faith and credit of the U.S. government, full and timely payment on mortgage-backed securities.

Graduated-Payment Mortgage (GPM)   Mortgage featuring lower monthly payments at first, which steadily rise until they level off after a few years. GPMs, also known as "jeeps," are designed for young couples whose income is expected to grow as their careers advance. A graduated-payment mortgage allows such a family to buy a house that would be unaffordable if mortgage payments started out at a high rate. Persons planning to take on such a mortgage must be confident that their income will be able to keep pace with the rising payments.

Great Depression   The worldwide economic hard times generally regarded as having begun with the stock market collapse of October 28–29, 1929 and continuing through most of the 1930s.

Growth and Income Funds   Growth and income funds are designed to pursue long-term growth as well as regular dividend income. Some growth and income funds are weighted more heavily toward growth, others toward income.

Growth Funds   Growth funds are designed to pursue capital appreciation over the long term. Some growth funds are broad-based, meaning that they have a wide range of stocks and industries in which they can invest. Others have a narrower focus, for example, they may invest in a particular type of stock, such as small-cap or cyclical stocks, or use a specialized approach to stock selection, such as investing only in stocks that are currently underpriced. Growth funds are more volatile than more conservative income or money market funds and generally reflect changes in market conditions and other company, political, and economic news.

Growth Stocks   Stocks of companies that have shown or are expected to show rapid earnings and revenue growth. Growth stocks are riskier investments than most other stocks and usually make little or no dividend payments to shareholders.

Hang Seng Index   The Hang Seng Index is a market capitalization-weighted index of the stocks of the 33 largest companies in the Hong Kong market.

Income Distributions   For tax purposes, a mutual fund generally passes along dividends and interest it receives from securities it owns. A fund also passes along an investor's share of the profits it makes when it sells securities for a higher price than it paid for them. The investor may choose to have these distributions sent to him or her or he or she may want to reinvest them. Distributions are subject to federal tax, and may also be subject to state and/or local taxes. Distributions are taxable when they are paid, whether the investor takes them in cash or reinvests them.

Index   An unmanaged group of securities whose overall performance is used as a standard to measure investment performance.

Index Funds   A passively managed, limited-expense (advisor fee no higher than 0.50%) fund designed to replicate the performance of an unmanaged stock index on a reinvested basis.

Inflation Risk   The chance that the value of assets or income will be diminished as inflation shrinks the value of a currency.

Interest   The amount paid by a borrower as compensation for the use of borrowed money. This amount is generally expressed as an annual percentage of the principal amount.

Interest Rate   The annual rate expressed as a percentage of principal, payable for use of borrowed money.

International Funds   These funds invest in securities of countries outside the United States. International funds can be global in scope or limited to a particular country or region, with the narrower-focused funds subject to increased volatility. Foreign investments, especially those in emerging markets, involve greater risk than do those of U.S. investments.

International Monetary Fund (IMF)   An organization set up by the Bretton Woods Agreement in 1944. Unlike the World Bank, whose focus is on foreign exchange reserves and the balance of trade, the IMF focus is on lowering trade barriers and stabilizing currencies. While helping developing nations pay their debts, the IMF usually imposes tough guidelines aimed at lowering inflation, cutting imports, and raising exports. IMF funds come mostly from the treasuries of industrialized nations.

Interpolate   A mathematical term to estimate a value between two known values.

Investment Grade   The broad credit designation given bonds that have a high probability of being paid and minor, if any, speculative features. Bonds rated Baa and higher by Moody's Investors Service or BBB and higher by Standard & Poor's are deemed by those agencies to be investment grade.

Investment Grade Bonds   Corporate and municipal bonds given one of the top four ratings by independent agencies. Issues rated BBB to AAA are considered investment grade.

Investment Objective   The identification of attributes associated with an investment or investment strategy designed to isolate and compare risks, define acceptable levels of risk, and match investments with personal goals.

Issue Date   The date on which a security is deemed to be issued or originated.

Issuer   A state, political subdivision, agency, or authority that borrows money through the sale of bonds or notes.

J.P. Morgan Emerging Markets Bond Index Plus   The J.P. Morgan Emerging Markets Bond Index Plus is a market capitalization-weighted total return index of U.S. dollar and other external currency denominated Brady bonds, loans, Eurobonds, and local market debt instruments traded in emerging markets.

J.P. Morgan Global Bond Index   The J.P. Morgan Global Bond Index is a total return index that tracks the traded sovereign issues of 13 international markets. Each market is weighted according to its traded market capitalization in U.S. dollar terms and all issues included in the index are liquid with remaining maturity of greater than 13 months.

Junk Bond   A bond rated lower than Baa/BBB also called a high-yield bond. Junk bonds are speculative compared with investment grade bonds.

Lehman Brothers Aggregate Bond Index   The Lehman Brothers Aggregate Bond Index is a market value-weighted performance benchmark for investment-grade, fixed-rate debt issues, including government, corporate, asset-backed, and mortgage-backed securities, with maturities of at least one year.

Lehman Brothers Intermediate Government/Corporate Bond Index   The Lehman Brothers Intermediate Government/Corporate Bond Index is a market value-weighted performance benchmark for government and corporate fixed-rate debt issues with maturities between 1 and 10 years.

Lehman Brothers Municipal Bond Index   The Lehman Brothers Municipal Bond Index is a total return performance benchmark for investment-grade municipal bonds with maturities of at least one year.

Lehman Brothers 1–3-Year Government/Corporate Bond Index   The Lehman Brothers 1–3 Year Government/Corporate Bond Index is a market value-weighted performance benchmark for government and corporate fixed-rate debt issues with maturities between one and three years.

Lipper Funds Averages   Lipper Analytical Services, Inc., is a nationally recognized organization that reports on mutual funds' total return performance and calculates their rankings. Peer group averages are based on universes of funds with the same investment objective. Peer group averages include reinvested dividends and capital gains, if any, and exclude sales charges.

Lipper Ranking   Fund ranking calculated quarterly or annually by Lipper Analytical Services of New York. Each fund is ranked within a universe of funds similar in investment objective. Lipper Analytical Services, Inc. is a nationally recognized organization that reports on mutual fund total return performance and calculates fund rankings.

Liquidity   The ability to buy or sell an asset quickly or the ability to convert to cash quickly.

Load   A sales charge added to the price of the fund. Mutual funds that have no sales charges are called no-load funds.

Load Funds   Mutual funds that charge a sales commission, as opposed to no-load funds that do not levy a fee when bought or sold. Some fund groups that sell directly to the public offer low-load funds, which charge an upfront fee of 2 percent or 3 percent, but most load funds are sold by brokers. To compensate brokers, load funds usually charge either a front-end sales commission when an investor buys the fund or a back-end sales commission when he or she sells. In addition, many broker-sold funds charge an annual 12b-1 fee, which is also used to compensate brokers. The 12b-1 fee is included in the fund's expense ratio.

Long Bond   The 30-year bond is the longest maturity issued by the U.S. Treasury. It is also the most widely traded bond, not only in the United States but worldwide. Because it is such a key security, the most recently issued 30-year Treasury bond, known as the long bond, is viewed as the benchmark against which all other bonds are measured.

Management Fee   Fee paid by a mutual fund to its investment manager or adviser for overseeing the portfolio. A management fee is usually between 0.5 percent and 1 percent of the fund's net asset value.

Marketability   The ease or difficulty with which securities can be sold in the market.

Market Capitalization   The total market value of a company or stock. Market capitalization is calculated by multiplying the number of shares by the current market price of the shares.

Market-Neutral Position   Selectively hedging an investment position. Generally used to reduce taxes. Using a short-against-the-box strategy or selecting a proxy security that has a high correlation factor to the security to be hedged.

Market Risk   The risk that the price of a security will rise or fall due to changing economic, political, or market conditions, or due to a company's individual situation.

Market Timing   Shifting money in and out of investment markets in an effort to take advantage of rising prices and avoid being stung by downturns.

Mathematical Symbols   The * is the symbol for multiplication, the ÷ is the symbol for division, the + is the symbol for addition, and the – is the symbol for subtraction.

Maturity or Maturity Date   The date on which the principal of a security becomes due and payable to the security holder.

Maturity Value   The amount (other than periodic interest payment) that will be received at the time a security is redeemed at its maturity. On most securities the maturity value equals the par value.

Merrill Lynch High Yield Master Index   The Merrill Lynch High Yield Master Index is a market capitalization-weighted index of all domestic and Yankee high-yield bonds. Issues included in the index have maturities of at least one year and have a credit rating lower than BBB-Baa3, but are not in default.

Mid-Cap Stocks   An investment categorization based on the market capitalization of a company.

Mortgage-Backed Securities (MBS)   Securities backed by mortgages. The Federal Home Loan Mortgage Corporation and The Federal National Mortgage Association issue such certificates. The Government National Mortgage Association guarantees others. Investors receive payments out of the interest and principle on the underlying mortgages. Sometimes banks issue certificates backed by conventional mortgages, selling them to large institutional investors. The growth of mortgage-backed certificates and the secondary mortgage market in which they are traded has helped keep mortgage money available for home financing.

Moving Averages   The average price of a mutual fund calculated periodically over some designated period of time. For example, to calculate a 39-week moving average, total the weekly closing prices for 39 weeks and divide by 39. The average price is plotted on a chart against actual prices. The effect of a moving average is to minimize short-term price fluctuations and highlight long-term price fluctuations.

MSCI EAFE Index   The Morgan Stanley Capital International Europe, Australia, Far East Index is an unmanaged index of over 1,000 foreign stocks. The index may be compiled in two ways: a market capitalization-weighted (cap-weighted) version and a gross domestic product-weighted (GDP-weighted) version.

MSCI Emerging Markets Free Index. The Morgan Stanley Capital International Emerging Markets Free Index is a market capitalization-weighted index of over 850 stocks traded in 22 world markets.

MSCI Emerging Markets Free-Latin America Index   The Morgan Stanley Capital International Emerging Markets Free-Latin America index is a market capitalization-weighted index of approximately 170 stocks traded in seven Latin American markets.

MSCI Europe Index   The Morgan Stanley Capital International Europe Index is a market capitalization-weighted index of over 550 stocks traded in 14 European markets.

MSCI Far East ex-Japan Free Index   The Morgan Stanley Capital International Combined Far East ex Japan Free Index is a market capitalization-weighted index of over 450 stocks traded in eight Asian markets, excluding Japan.

MSCI France Index   The Morgan Stanley Capital International France Index is an unmanaged index of over 75 foreign stock prices, and reflects the common stock prices of the index companies translated into U.S. dollars, assuming reinvestment of all dividends paid by the index stocks net of any applicable foreign taxes.

MSCI Germany Index   The Morgan Stanley Capital International Germany Index is an unmanaged index of over 75 foreign stock prices, and reflects the common stock prices of the index companies translated into U.S. dollars, assuming reinvestment of all dividends paid by the index stocks net of any applicable foreign taxes.

MSCI Hong Kong Index   The Morgan Stanley Capital International Hong Kong Index is an unmanaged index of over 38 foreign stock prices, and reflects the common stock prices of the index companies translated into U.S. dollars, assuming reinvestment of all dividends paid by the index stocks net of any applicable foreign taxes.

MSCI Japan Index   The Morgan Stanley Capital International Japan Index is an unmanaged index of over 317 foreign stock prices, and reflects the common stock prices of the index companies translated into U.S. dollars, assuming reinvestment of all dividends paid by the index stocks net of any applicable foreign taxes.

MSCI Nordic Countries Free Index   The Morgan Stanley Capital International Nordic Countries Index is an unmanaged index of over 95 foreign stock prices, and reflects the common stock prices of the index companies translated into U.S. dollars, assuming reinvestment of all dividends paid by the index stocks net of any applicable foreign taxes.

MSCI Pacific Index   The Morgan Stanley Capital International Pacific Index is a market capitalization-weighted index of over 400 stocks traded in six Pacific-region markets.

MSCI United Kingdom Index   The Morgan Stanley Capital International United Kingdom Index is an unmanaged index of over 143 foreign stock prices, and reflects the common stock prices of the index companies translated into U.S. dollars, assuming reinvestment of all dividends paid by the index stocks net of any applicable foreign taxes.

MSCI World Index   The Morgan Stanley Capital International World Index is a market capitalization-weighted equity index of over 1,500 stocks traded in 22 world markets.

Municipal Securities   A general term referring to securities issued by local government subdivisions such as counties, cities, towns, villages, or special districts, as well as securities issued by states and political subdivisions or agencies of states. A prime feature of these securities is that interest on them is generally exempt from federal income taxes and, in some cases, state and local taxes too.

Mutual Fund   An investment that pools shareholders' money and invests it toward a specified goal. A professional investment manager invests the group's money.

NASDAQ Composite Index   An unmanaged index of over-the-counter stock prices that does not assume the reinvestment of dividends.

NASDAQ 100 Index   Represents 100 of the largest nonfinancial U.S. and non-U.S. companies listed on the NASDAQ stock market. This index is a modified capitalization-weighted index, which is designed to limit domination of the index by a few large stocks while generally retaining the capitalization ranking of companies.

NAV Change   The difference between today's closing net asset value (NAV) and the previous day's closing net asset value (NAV).

NAV Change %   The percentage change between today's closing net asset value (NAV) and the previous day's closing net asset value (NAV).

Net Asset Value (NAV)   The dollar value of one share of a fund determined by taking the total assets of a fund, subtracting the total liabilities, and dividing by the total number of shares outstanding.

Net Yield   Rate of return on a security net of out-of-pocket costs associated with its purchase, such as commissions or markups.

Nikkei Stock Average   An index of 225 leading stocks traded on the Tokyo stock exchange.

Nominal Yield (Coupon Yield)   The stated interest rate paid on a bond, computed by dividing the amount of annual income by the bond's par value.

Note   A debt obligation similar to a bond, but with a maturity date less than five years from date of issue.

Offer Price   The lowest price that a seller is willing to accept from a prospective buyer. In the case of a mutual fund with a sales charge, this price is the net asset value (NAV) plus the sales charge. In the case of no-load funds, it is the NAV.

Offering Date   The date on which a distribution of stocks or bonds will first be available to the public.

Opportunity Risk   The risk that a better opportunity may present itself after an investor has already committed his or her money elsewhere.

Paper   Any short-term debt security.

Par   The nominal or face value of a security as given on the certificate or instrument. The par value is the amount on which interest payments are calculated.

Portfolio   A collection of securities held by an investor.

Portfolio Diversification   Holding a variety of securities so that a portfolio's return is not reduced by the poor performance of a single security or industry.

Premium   The amount by which a bond sells above its par (face) value.

Present Value   The value at the current time of a cash payment that is expected to be received in the future, discounted to reflect the fact that an amount received today could be invested to earn interest for the period to the future date.

Price/Earnings (P/E) Ratio   Also called a P/E ratio or multiple. A ratio to evaluate a stock's worth. It is calculated by dividing the stock's price by its earnings-per-share figure. For example, if a stock is selling for $20, with earnings of $2 per share, that stock has a P/E of 10. If the P/E is calculated using the past year's earnings, it is called the "trailing P/E."

If the P/E is calculated using an analyst's forecast for the next year's earnings, it is called a "looking forward P/E."

Primary Market (New Issue Market)   The market on which newly issued securities are sold, including government security auctions and underwriting purchases of blocks of new issues, which are then resold.

Principal   The amount of money that the investor puts into an investment.

Quant   Slang reference to an analyst who uses quantitative research techniques.

Quantitative Funds   Mutual funds whose portfolio management decisions are based on quantitative analysis, which is usually developed using computerized statistical models of market behavior.

R^2   A measurement of how close the portfolio's performance correlates with the performance of a benchmark index, such as the S&P 500. R^2 is a proportion, which ranges between 0.00 and 1.0. An R^2 of 1.00 indicates perfect correlation to the benchmark index, that is, all of the portfolio's fluctuations are explained by performance fluctuations of the index, whereas an R^2 of 0.00 indicates no correlation. Therefore, the lower the R^2, the more the fund's performance is affected by factors other than the market as measured by that benchmark index. See **Correlation Measures**; see also **Beta, Volatility Measures, S&P 500 Index**.

Ratings   Designations used by investors' services to give relative indications of credit quality.

Redemption   The paying off or buying back of a bond by the issuer.

Redemption Fee   A fee you pay when you redeem, or sell, your shares. Not all funds charge redemption fees.

Refunding   The replacement of a bond issue by a new bond issue at conditions generally more favorable to the issuer.

Relative Strength   The price movement of a stock compared with the movement of an index, market, or industry sector.

Relative Volatility   A ratio of a portfolio's standard deviation to the standard deviation of a benchmark index. See **Volatility Measures**.

Return per Unit of Risk   A ratio that compares the average annual total return of a fund to the average standard deviation of those returns over a historical 36-month period. Return Per Unit of Risk (RUR) attempts to show the relationship between the fund's historical return and the amount of risk associated with the generation of that return. For example, an RUR of 1.00 means that for every percentage point of volatility (annualized standard deviation) there has been one percentage point of return. See **Volatility Measures**.

Revenue Bond   A municipal bond payable solely from net or gross non-tax revenues derived from tolls, charges, or rents paid by users of the facility constructed with the proceeds of the bond issue.

Risk   Anything that causes an investment to behave differently from what the investor expects. The Y-Process risk is determined by the percent of the time an investor is in the market and not in the money market on an annual basis.

Russell 1000® Index   The Russell 1000® Index consists of the largest 1,000 companies in the Russell 3000® Index. This index represents the universe of large capitalization stocks from which most active money managers typically select. The index was developed with a base value of 130.00 as of December 31, 1986.

Russell 2000® Index   The Russell 2000® Index is an unmanaged index of 2,000 small capitalization stocks.

Sales Charge   Fee on the purchase of new shares of stock, indexes, or a mutual fund. A sales charge is similar to paying a premium for a security. The customer must pay a higher offering price. Sometimes called a load.

Salomon Brothers GNMA Index   The Salomon Brothers GNMA Index is a market capitalization-weighted index of 15- and 30-year fixed-rate securities backed by mortgage pools of the Government National Mortgage Association (GNMA).

Salomon Brothers Mortgage Index   The Salomon Brothers Mortgage Index is a market capitalization-weighted index of 15- and 30-year fixed-rate securities backed by mortgage pools of the Government Na-tional Mortgage Association (GNMA), Federal National Mortgage As-sociation (FNMA), and Federal Home Loan Mortgage Corporation (FHLMC), and FNMA and FHLMC balloon mortgages with fixed-rate coupons.

Salomon Brothers 3-Month T-Bill Index   Represents the average of T-bill rates for each of the prior three months, adjusted to a bond equiva-lent basis.

Salomon Brothers Treasury/Agency Index   The Salomon Brothers Treasury/Agency Index is a market capitalization-weighted index of U.S. Treasury and U.S. government agency securities with fixed-rate coupons and weighted average lives of at least one year.

Salomon Brothers World Government Bond Index, Unhedged   The Salomon Brothers World Government Bond Index, Unhedged is a market capitalization-weighted index of debt issues traded in 14 world government bond markets. Issues included in the index have fixed-rate coupons and maturities of at least one year.

SBF 250   The Societe des Bourses Francaises (SBF) 250 is a market cap-italization-weighted index of the stocks of the 250 largest companies in the French market.

Secondary Market   The market for securities previously offered or sold.

Sector Funds   Sector funds invest in the stocks of one specific sector of the economy, such as health care, chemicals, or retailing. These funds tend to be more volatile than funds holding a diversified portfolio of stocks in many industries.

Security   Generally, an instrument evidencing debt of or equity in a common enterprise in which a person invests on the expectation of fi-nancial gain. The term includes notes, stocks, bonds, debentures, or other forms of negotiable and non-negotiable evidences of indebtedness or ownership.

Share Price   The value of one share in the fund. With most funds, the share price is calculated every day, because the value of a fund's securi-ties changes every day in response to the movements of the stock, bond, and money markets. For some funds, share price is calculated on an hourly basis.

Shareholder   The owner of one or more shares of stock in a corporation or one or more shares or units of a mutual fund. Shareholder rights can vary according to the articles of incorporation or the bylaws of a particular company.

Short   A transaction in an investor's security account that causes both a credit and an obligation of future performance. For example, an investor sells borrowed stock security from a broker. The investor is short because there is a credit of proceeds on the sale of the security and the investor is obligated to return the borrowed security. The term is not used if there is a credit but no future obligation.

Short Against the Box   Descriptive term for offsetting a long and short position in the same security in an investor's account. For example, "The investor is long 500 shares of NASDAQ 100 and short 500 shares." This technique establishes a perfect hedge whereby the investor can neither gain nor lose from that point onward. The technique can be used to transfer the tax consequences of a long position to a future tax year.

Short the Market   A term often used when an investor shorts one of the market indexes. Primarily, DIA (Dow Jones Industrial Average), SPY (Standard and Poor's 500 Index), MDY (Standard and Poor's 400 Index).

Small-Cap Stocks   An investment categorization based on the market capitalization of a company.

Standard & Poor's Mid Cap 400 Index (S&P 400)®   The Standard & Poor's Mid Cap 400 Index is a widely recognized, unmanaged index of 400 medium-capitalization stocks.

Standard & Poor's 500 Index (S&P 500)®   The S&P 500 is a widely recognized, unmanaged index of large-cap common stocks of 500 of the largest corporations headquartered in the United States.

Standard Deviation   A statistical measure of the historic volatility of a portfolio. Standard deviation measures the dispersion of a fund's periodic returns (often based on 36 months of returns). The wider the dispersions, the larger the standard deviation. This is an independent measure of volatility; it is not relative to an index.

Taxable Equivalent Yield   The interest rate that must be received on a taxable security to provide the holder the same after-tax return as that earned on a tax-exempt security.

Technicals   Short-term trends that technical analysts can sometimes identify as significant in the price movement of a security or a commodity. Such trends may be in the demand and supply for securities, options, mutual funds, and commodities based on trading volume and price studies. Technical analysis is generally not concerned with the financial position of a company.

Term   The time during which interest payments will be made on a bond or certificate of deposit.

Thirty-Day Average Yield   See **Average Yield, 30-Day**.

TOPIX   The Tokyo Stock Exchange Index (TOPIX) is a market capitalization-weighted index of over 1,100 stocks traded in the Japanese market.

Total Return   Return on an investment, taking into account capital appreciation, dividends or interest, and individual tax considerations adjusted for present value and expressed on an annual basis.

Trading Symbol   An abbreviation for fund names for use with Fidelity's automated brokerage trading and quote services. Can also be used by Quotron and other electronic information systems for access to fund performance data.

TSE 300   The Toronto Stock Exchange (TSE) 300 is a market capitalization-weighted index of 300 stocks traded in the Canadian market.

Turnover Rate   A measure of the fund's trading activity calculated by dividing total purchases or sales of portfolio securities (whichever is lower) by the fund's net assets.

Underwrite   To purchase bond or note issues from the issuing body to resell them to the general public.

Unit Investment Trust (UIT)   A Securities and Exchange Commission-registered investment company that invests in a portfolio of securities on behalf of investors who share a common objective. Investors receive periodic interest and, on maturity, redemption values. The UIT is not actively managed.

Value Stocks   Stocks that are considered to be undervalued, either according to their book value or their current or projected earnings. Such stocks can be those of smaller, less well-known companies and may be more volatile than those of larger companies.

Volatility Measures   Volatility measures seek to compare a portfolio's relative share price fluctuations or total returns to those of a relevant market, represented by the benchmark index. Measures of volatility are based on historical performance; they are not calculated for funds that are less than three years old. See **Beta, Relative Volatility, Return per Unit of Risk**; see also **Correlation Measures**.

Whipsawed   (1) Subjected to a double market loss through trying inopportunely to recoup a loss by a subsequent short sale of the same security; (2) Slang for the financial effect of a rapid upward price movement followed by a rapid decrease if a person is exposed to financial risk on both the up and down sides; (3) Usually used as a past participle: whipsawed. In using the Y-Process trading strategy, being whipsawed is a buy signal followed quickly by a sell signal (within a week) or vice versa.

Wilshire 5000 Stock Index   Broadest index covering NASDAQ stocks and all stocks traded on the New York Stock Exchange and American Stock Exchange. It is a market value-weighted index.

Yankee Bonds (Yankee Credits)   Dollar-denominated bonds issued in the United States by foreign banks and corporations.

Yield   The percentage of return an investor receives based on the amount invested or on the current market value of holdings.

Yield Curve   The relationship at a given point in time between yields on a group of fixed-income securities with varying maturities, commonly, Treasury bills, notes, and bonds. The curve typically slopes upward since longer maturities normally have higher yields, although it can be flat or even inverted.

Yield to Call　Yield on a bond assuming the bond will be redeemed by the issuer at the first call date specified.

Yield to Maturity　Used to determine the rate of return an investor will receive if a long-term, interest-bearing investment, such as a bond, is held to its maturity date. Yield to maturity takes into account purchase price, redemption value, time to maturity, coupon yield, and the time between interest payments.

Y-Process　A stock market-timing model founded on two concepts: (1) the law of supply and demand, and (2) that stock prices tend to move in trends. The model uses an exponential moving average with a smoothing constant of 0.1177. See Chapter 9 for the Y-Process derivation.

YTD　Stands for Year to Date. Used in mutual fund tables to indicate the rate of return of the fund from the beginning of the year to the present date.

Zero-Coupon Bond　A bond where no periodic interest payments are made. The investor purchases the bond at a discounted price and receives one payment at maturity. The maturity value an investor receives is equal to the principal invested plus interest earned compounded semiannually at the original rate to maturity. Interest income from zero-coupon bonds is subject to taxes annually even though no payments are made.

About the Author

Edward M. Yanis is the chairman and CEO of Yanis Financial Services, Inc. which provides a weekly investment letter containing market commentary as well as buy, hold, and sell recommendations on 25 major market indexes. Mr. Yanis is the developer of the Y-Process, a revolutionary stock market-timing model that forecasts crucial market turns before most professional money managers recognize that these turns have occurred, thus, enabling the investor to reduce risks and enhance returns.

Formerly, Mr. Yanis was the General Electric Company's systems engineering manager involved in the design, testing, and production of the AEGIS Combat System for the U.S. Navy AEGIS Cruisers, "Ticonderoga" class warships. He held that position for more than 20 years.

Prior to joining General Electric, Mr. Yanis taught applied electronics at the U.S. Army Signal School for two years and after-hours courses in systems engineering and operations analysis at the U.S. Department of Agriculture. He also took graduate electrical engineering courses for a Ph.D. in engineering at the American University and University of Pennsylvania.

Mr. Yanis holds a Bachelor of Electrical Engineering and a Master of Electrical Engineering from the Polytechnic University of New York. He also holds a Master of Business Administration in finance from Southern Illinois University. He is a member of the National Scholastic Honorary Society, Beta Gamma Sigma; the society for AACSB-accredited business programs. He is also a registered Professional Engineer in both New Jersey and Virginia in addition to being a member of the American Society of Naval Engineers. Mr. Yanis is a past vice chairman of the Institute of Electrical and Electronic Engineers committee on Reliability.

In 1970, Mr. Yanis invented the "Functional Flow Diagram and Descriptions" (F^2D^2) technique, an operations analysis methodology that defines, designs, and verifies large-scale complex computer systems prior to implementation in hardware and software, thus providing large cost savings. The U.S. government still uses this methodology and continues to teach system engineering courses based on the F^2D^2 approach.

Using his expertise in both finance and systems engineering, Mr. Yanis solved the long-standing, number one concern facing warship designers of the U.S. Navy—*affordability*. Mr. Yanis used a revolutionary approach to develop a unique balance between system affordability and fighting capability for U.S. Navy warships. His mathematical model proved that properly networked computer systems would extend the useful fighting life of a U.S. Navy frigate at only 17 percent of the cost of building a new frigate. He presented a technical paper on this subject to the Royal Institute of Naval Architects conference in London, England, at their request, representing the General Electric Company. This paper was also submitted to the U. S. Navy for introduction into the fleet.

Mr. Yanis's technical career required extensive travel, for example, to Spain, Japan, Taiwan, and Israel to support the naval computer system designs for which he was in charge as a contractor officially representing the U.S. Navy.

His office is located in historic Cherry Hill, New Jersey, where he resides with his wife, Judith, who is cofounder of Yanis Financial Services, Inc.

Index

Get 13 Free Weeks of the
Y-PROCESS® INVESTMENT LETTER

USE THE Y-PROCESS® TO BUILD AND MANAGE YOUR OWN PORTFOLIO.

PROTECT YOUR EQUITY FROM STOCK MARKET DOWNTURNS. KNOW WHEN TO GET IN & OUT OF THE MARKET.

SUBSCRIBE TO THE Y-PROCESS® INVESTMENT LETTER TODAY.

Please fill out the form on the reverse side, cut, and mail or fax to: 1-856-424-1975.

Cut Here

Place
Stamp
Here

Y-PROCESS® INVESTMENT NEWSLETTER
YANIS FINANCIAL SERVICES, INC.
35 Cooper Run Drive
Cherry Hill, NJ 08003-2244

Y-PROCESS® INVESTMENT LETTER

FREE 13-WEEK subscription to the Y-Process® Investment Letter, with the buy, sell, and hold numbers of key stock market indexes, mutual funds, and stocks. Build your own equity portfolio the easy way: Use the Y-Process model described in *Riding the Bull, Beating the Bear: Market Timing for the Long-Term Investor*, the best stock market-timing book available today. Get on track and create extraordinary wealth the Y-Process way. Learn how to obtain stock market security by visiting our website www.yprocess.com. In addition, you will receive our weekly Executive Summary via email.

At the end of the 13-week trial, you will be notified about the 3, 6, or 12 month renewal, for as low as $3.00/week.

If you do not have internet access, you can receive the 13-week newsletter free via U.S. Mail* or fax.

*Newsletters sent by U.S. Mail are subject to the speed of the U.S. Mail delivery service.

Cut Here

....

Y-PROCESS® INVESTMENT LETTER

☐ **YES,** sign me up for my free 13 weekly issues (for new clients only) of the Y-Process® Investment Letter and trial membership to the www.yprocess.com website (a $49.40 value).

Mr/Ms/Mrs: _____

Address: _____

City/State/Zip: _____

Email: _____ Fax: _____

Tele.#: Day ( ) _____ Eve.: ( ) _____

I will receive via email my password & ID # for my personal website access.

☐ I do not have Internet access.
I would like my subscription ☐ mailed or ☐ faxed to me.

Y-Process® is a Registered Trademark of the Yanis Financial Services, Inc.